EDWINA

ALSO BY RICHARD HOUGH

Mountbatten: Hero of our Time
Louis & Victoria: The First Mountbattens
(ed.) *Advice to a Grand-daughter: Letters from Queen Victoria to Princess Victoria of Hesse*

AND AMONG OTHERS:
The Fleet that had to Die
Admirals in Collision
The Potemkin Mutiny
The Hunting of Force Z
First Sea Lord
Captain Bligh & Mr Christian
One Boy's War (autobiography)
The Murder of Captain James Cook

EDWINA

Countess Mountbatten of Burma

RICHARD HOUGH

WILLIAM MORROW AND COMPANY, INC. NEW YORK 1984

For Judy

First published in 1983 in Great Britain
by George Weidenfeld & Nicolson Ltd

Library of Congress Catalog Card Number: 83-62979

ISBN: 0-688-03766-6

Printed in the United States of America

First U.S. Edition

1 2 3 4 5 6 7 8 9 10

Contents

Illustrations

Picture research by Lynda Poley

A condensed family tree of Edwina, Countess Mountbatten of Burma

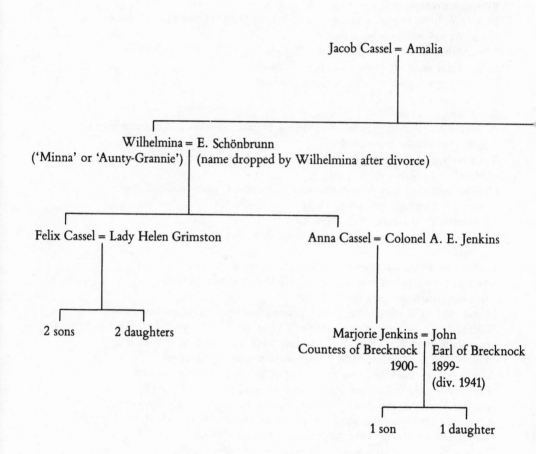

- Jacob Cassel = Amalia
  - Wilhelmina = E. Schönbrunn
    ('Minna' or 'Aunty-Grannie') (name dropped by Wilhelmina after divorce)
    - Felix Cassel = Lady Helen Grimston
      - 2 sons
      - 2 daughters
    - Anna Cassel = Colonel A. E. Jenkins
      - Marjorie Jenkins = John
        Countess of Brecknock 1900- | Earl of Brecknock 1899- (div. 1941)
        - 1 son
        - 1 daughter

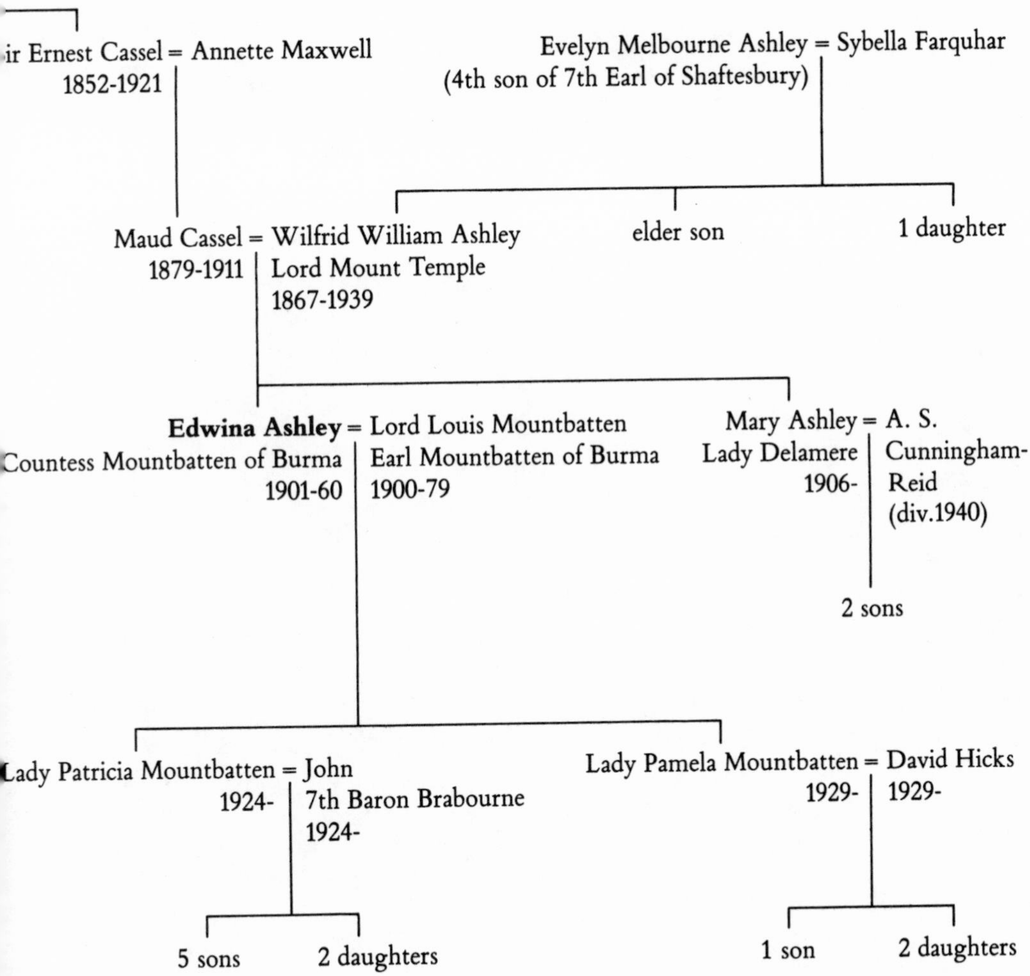

ir Ernest Cassel = Annette Maxwell
1852-1921
Evelyn Melbourne Ashley = Sybella Farquhar
(4th son of 7th Earl of Shaftesbury)
Maud Cassel = Wilfrid William Ashley
1879-1911
Lord Mount Temple
1867-1939
elder son
1 daughter
Edwina Ashley = Lord Louis Mountbatten
Countess Mountbatten of Burma
1901-60
Earl Mountbatten of Burma
1900-79
Mary Ashley = A. S.
Lady Delamere
1906-
Cunningham-
Reid
(div.1940)
2 sons
Lady Patricia Mountbatten = John
1924-
7th Baron Brabourne
1924-
Lady Pamela Mountbatten = David Hicks
1929-
1929-
5 sons
2 daughters
1 son
2 daughters

Foreword

I had known Lord Mountbatten for many years at the time of his tragic death in 1979. We had worked together on the family history I wrote in the early 1970s and on a number of other projects related to his family and his own life. After his death, and while working on my biography of him, I became even more interested in his wife and the part she had played in his career as well as in her domestic and social life; her world-wide travels for her own enjoyment before the Second World War; and in the course of her remarkable and sustained work for the charities of which she was chief – both during the war, in the cruel and tumultuous aftermath of victory in Europe and the Far East, and in the years until her death in 1960.

I therefore determined to round off my biographical work on the Mountbatten family by making a closer study of Lady Mountbatten, born Edwina Cynthia Annette Ashley, the second half of the duo whose contribution towards the winning of the war and the peace that followed was so significant, and about whom an element of mystery, misunderstanding and illusion still endures.

To write a responsible biography of Edwina was clearly only possible with the knowledge and support of many of those who knew her, from early childhood until her death. This co-operation has been readily given by a wide range of people who have written to me, talked to me and sent me papers and photographs. I am grateful to them all.

I wish to single out for special thanks Mary, Lady Delamere, who recounted so many reminiscences, remembered names, facts and incidents and anecdotes about her sister, and was kind and hospitable throughout. Miss Marie Seton, the biographer, was at school with Lady Delamere (when she was the Hon. Mary Ashley), knew Edwina in the 1930s and was living in the Nehru household in Delhi when Edwina stayed there for the last time. She, too, has been immensely helpful. Noel Turner helped me on the first and last chapters, allowed me to draw on his unpublished memoirs, and guided me on a number of points. Sir Charles Baring, Bt, knew Edwina in the critical period in her life between school and marriage, and again as a young married woman. Robert Everett recalled in remarkable and often moving detail his boyhood at Broadlands with Edwina and Mary in the ten years or so before they were married.

My special thanks are also due to Maître Suzanne Blum and Michael Bloch for permission to draw on and quote from the Duke of Windsor's Archives. Judy Coombs was generous enough to allow me to quote from the unpublished memoirs of Miss Stella J. Underhill. In India Mrs Indira Gandhi and Mrs Ranjit S. Pandit especially were most generous in the time they gave me to recall Edwina in India from 1947 until her death.

Besides a number of contributors who expressed a preference for remaining anonymous and are therefore not named here or in the text, the following people were also good enough to recall their memories of Lady Mountbatten at various times and on various occasions during her life: Sir John Biggs-Davison MP, Brian Connell, Captain G.T. Cooper OBE, RN (rtd), Captain P.J. Cowell DSC, RN (rtd), Brigadier Paul Crook CBE, DSO, MA, R.C. Dagge, Major A.W.M. Dickie, Mrs Eileen Douglas-Pennant, David Holloway, Miss Judy Hutchinson, Ralph Kitson, Captain G.T. Lambert RN (rtd) and Mrs Lambert, J.M.K.P. McAllister, Captain P.B. Marriott DSO, DSC, RN (rtd), Mrs Yehudi Menuhin, C.H. Ormerod, Mrs Molly Passmore, Mrs Margery Price, Mrs Jane K. Sartin, Mrs Peggie Scott-Elliot, Oliver Sebag-Montefiore, C.G. Taylor, H.S. Taylor-Young, Sir Woodrow Wyatt MP, Mrs Joan L. Wynne-Thomas FSA.

Finally, my thanks go to my ever-patient, ever conscientious typist, Jackie Gumpert, and to Marina Majdalany for diligent and understanding research.

1
Borneo Catastrophe

The temperature in the cabin of the poorly ventilated Viscount aircraft was high in the nineties and the passengers and cabin crew were all feeling the discomfort and strain of the long flight from Singapore to North Borneo. They had already landed at Kuching, the capital of Sarawak, and then at low altitude continued up the north-western coast of Sarawak, Brunei and North Borneo, touching down to disembark or embark passengers and freight at three more points. In a direct line from Singapore to Jesselton, the capital of North Borneo, the distance is less than 1,000 miles. But these diversions extended the route and added to the fatigue.

Among the passengers on the flight on 18 February 1960 was Edwina, Countess Mountbatten of Burma. She was on one of her tightly scheduled and ferociously demanding tours of inspection on behalf of the St John Ambulance Brigade, of which she was Superintendent-in-Chief, the Red Cross and the Save the Children Fund. She was dressed in the tropical uniform of the St John Ambulance, a lightweight white cotton short-sleeve jacket and skirt. The jacket had brass buttons, and above the left breast pocket were five rows of medal ribbons, including those of the Imperial Order of the Crown of India, Dame Grand Cross of the Order of the British Empire, Dame Commander of the Royal Victorian Order, the American Red Cross Silver Medal and the Brilliant Star of China. The range of colours and patterns reflected in miniature the marvellously accomplished and full life this woman had lived.

Lady Mountbatten - always 'Lady Louis' professionally - was fifty-eight years old. The beauty of her bone structure, the brightness of her light blue eyes, the set of her head and her long, graceful neck recalled with instant pleasure the debutante heiress who had first come East at the age of nineteen. And now, as through all her life, she was a guest of those in command. On this occasion her host was to remark on her beauty and grace, while others noted her 'thin, almost desiccated bony arms' and the stiffness in her cheek which spoilt the symmetry of her mouth when she smiled and talked.

Edwina Mountbatten's tour had begun with her departure from London on 17 January 1960. It was, as always for her, a relief to get away. The spring of restlessness that began to wind tighter day by day when she was at home, and led her to seek release in travel, was as powerful as ever. Edwina always liked to leave on a high note when she embarked on one of her journeys. This time domestic satisfaction provided it. Her younger daughter Pamela, with whom Edwina was especially close, had married on 13 January – 'a fairy-tale wedding with snowflakes falling', as Edwina's husband, the Earl Mountbatten of Burma, had romantically called it. The bridegroom was neither royal nor aristocratic. David Nightingale Hicks was an interior designer, the son of a stockbroker, but the family liked him and Pammy was clearly very much in love. Prince Philip was present at Romsey Abbey, Princess Anne was a bridesmaid. The Queen would certainly have been there, too, but she was expecting her third child; after the wedding Edwina went to Sandringham, wished her well in her confinement and said good-bye.

There was added cause for satisfaction in the family because it was now known that Princess Margaret was shortly to be engaged. The Queen's sister and Edwina's younger daughter were contemporaries and close friends. So, by the time she returned, Edwina knew that there would be another royal child (Prince Andrew), the engagement would have been officially announced, and Pammy and David would have returned from their honeymoon in the sun.

Edwina's plane flew direct to Cyprus, the first destination in her ten-week tour. There the taxing, familiar routine began from the moment she stepped onto the tarmac: receptions, inspections, listening to reports from the charities' officers, listening to enquiries about funds and conditions elsewhere, listening to wave after wave of small talk and, intermittently, important talk crucial to future plans and operations. Edwina charmed everyone, and they also felt the respect with which they regarded her renewed and their own importance and the importance of their work enhanced by her visit and the recognition it offered – not least the prospects of a decoration, an MBE or perhaps an OBE.

A long-drawn-out dinner with long-drawn-out speeches, a hundred more faces, a hundred more voices, including her own as she made her crisp contribution. The firm correction of some maladministration, a few words of reproof when called for, and many more words of praise. The ceremonial farewell, relaxation at last with the jet rumbling out for take-off, alone for a few hours.

Then Delhi, where she was met at the airport and whisked straight to the house of Pandit Jawaharlal Nehru, Prime Minister of India ever since those stirring, eventful days when, as the last Vicereine, Edwina had played such a significant part in the transfer of power from Britain to the people of the great sub-continent. At seventy, Nehru still looked wonderfully fit and bronzed. Edwina's pleasure at being with him again was undiminished, as all could see. 'And how is Dickie?' And 'dear Pammy's wedding' had to be minutely described.

Time and again, sometimes several times in one year, Edwina had contrived to return to this land and the home of the Indian leader with whom she had been so close since 1945 – a period of anguish and turmoil in Singapore after the surrender when Edwina and her husband had broken British officialdom's attempt to humiliate Nehru. That had been the real beginning of this remarkable and massively influential relationship.

This time Edwina had arranged her programme to coincide with the Republic Day Parade in Delhi along the Vista of Rajpath, from the great Secretariat building to the India Gate. An added reason was the presence of the Soviet President, Marshal Voroshilov. The opportunity of talking with these two world leaders was not to be missed.

On the day of the Parade, 26 January, Edwina watched once again the dynamic effect of the Prime Minister's arrival, the cheers and hand-clapping as loud and long as she and her husband had received on their last day as Viceroy and Vicereine in 1947.

The Parade was as impressive as any the Russian President had witnessed in Red Square, though with much less military emphasis. Then the private reception in the Moghul Garden, presided over by Nehru, like a miniature Buckingham Palace tea party. At first a formal introduction, partly through an interpreter, with Nehru saying in his familiar refined English, 'Edwina, I would like you to meet the Russian President, Marshal Voroshilov, who is our guest. Mr President, the Countess Mountbatten of Burma.' Smiles, slight tilts of the head. But for neither of them – the woman whose uncle by marriage had been the last Tsar of all the Russias, and the man who had presided over Russia for nearly seven years – was there any use for small talk. At once the President was in deep conversation with Edwina, who was known to be a socialist and republican in her own country yet was related by marriage to almost every crowned head in Europe.

They sat down on white wickerwork chairs on the lawn, joined briefly by Nehru's daughter, Indira Gandhi. For a while the Marshal and Countess remained talking. Then, with characteristic suddenness, Edwina arose, detached herself from the hierarchy and began to walk among the guests, confident not only of recognition but also of admiration from them all. 'As she talked she revealed the charm of her independent spirit,' one observer noted. 'The Bright Young Thing of the twenties had made something of herself which had nothing to do with status, but a great deal to do with vitality.'

For Edwina there followed two days of intensive work for the St John Ambulance and her other charities, inspecting and consulting and presiding at meetings, but still reserving time in the evenings for Nehru. On the afternoon of 29 January she acted as additional hostess at the Beating the Retreat ceremony, with massed military bands playing stirring marches, and the spectacular Camel Corps among the military marching and wheeling about with their colours. Then there was dancing and tea on the Prime Minister's lawn – Punjabi Bangra dancers and dancers from Manipur; and, to the cheers of the crowd, Nehru himself appeared, wearing a garland, spirited in his dancing and still moving easily, enjoying the attention and the happiness about him.

Edwina appeared as if from nowhere, 'the most vivid spot of colour in an ocean of colour', wearing a dashing pink and red suit with matching sandals. She joined Indira and Marie Seton, another old family friend of Nehru, and sat on the grass with them to watch some spectacular Naga dancers. They wore little more than feathers and seemed to possess demoniacal energy.

'Don't they have beautiful bottoms,' Edwina remarked lightly.

'Very beautiful,' Miss Seton agreed.

Indira wanted to know if there was any tea left. The dancing finished and Edwina disappeared again into the crowds. And not long after, she left Nehru's house, and the India she loved, for the last time.

Malaya next, then Singapore, the scene of so much sickness and suffering when she had arrived shortly after the surrender, another historic act presided over by her husband. The pressure was beginning to tell when she had taken off from Singapore with three intensive days ahead of her before returning to Singapore and then on to Hong Kong and Korea. But she would 'rise above it' – one of her favourite rallying phrases in times of pressure or difficulty – and be better for the work and its satisfactory accomplishment. Yes, rise above it. Work, as always, was the cure, the panacea.

The Viscount landed late in the morning in Brunei, the last stop but one. It would have been regarded as a slight if she had not paid her respects to the Sultan, and that entailed transferring to a car and driving to the palace. More ranks of Malays to be greeted, more hand-shaking in the mid-day heat. Back to the airport, a last halt at Labuan. At 2 p.m. they were flying low over the sea on a north-easterly course parallel with the coast of North Borneo, the lower slopes of the mountain range dark green forested, the heights obscured by rolling mists and cloud.

Edwina had been here, too, in October 1945 when it had been a land of misery, sickness and starvation, the internment camps packed with men, women and children, many of them dying on the bare floors of the huts. It had been a sight to which she was already accustomed but not hardened. As in Malaya, Singapore, Batavia, Vietnam and Sumatra, she had extinguished her anguish and anger with a hurricane of work and organization. Now, from her seat in the Viscount, everything below looked in good order, with figures busy in the paddy fields and walking or cycling or riding behind bullock carts on the dirt roads. The shattered, gutted villages had been rebuilt and the ruin of Jesselton, the capital, which she now saw coming into sight ahead, had been transformed into a neat, tight collection of white buildings and busy roads along the waterfront.

There was an island just north of Jesselton, and the Viscount banked round it, approaching the airport from the north. There was a passing view of intense green of the island's forests, the deep blue of the sea and the sky, and then the plane was on its final approach. It was 2.15 p.m. on Thursday, 18 February 1960. The collection of figures and the assembly of cars by the terminal buildings told the usual story of the reception awaiting her.

The man responsible for this reception, for the organization of the North Borneo tour, and for the hospitality as Edwina's host, was Robert Noel Turner CMG, forty-seven years old, a senior officer of the Colonial Service and Acting Governor. Noel Turner was a veteran of the Far East, having served first in the Malayan Civil Service back in 1935. He had been the Assistant Resident in Brunei when the Japanese invaded and locked him up in his own jail. He had been interned for nearly four years, suffering the full rigours of undernourishment and his captors' cruelty. This experience had prejudiced him against Japan, but not the East, where, after a period in the West Indies, he continued to serve. He had been Chief Secretary of North Borneo since 1956.

Turner had married in 1946, and his attractive wife Evelyn was beside him, together with Peter Hewitt, Turner's private secretary, and Miss Checkley, a St John headquarters' officer. 'Evelyn and I were keenly looking forward to meeting a lady who, by common consent, was one of the most remarkable personalities of the century,' Turner wrote. In this quiet backwater of a surviving remnant of the British Empire, all the hierarchy and especially the European and local officers of the Red Cross and St John Ambulance had been keyed up expectantly for the visit.

Edwina turned to thank the cabin staff and descended the Viscount's steps. Turner and his wife were the first to greet her. Her appearance was familiar to many of those present, some forty in all including a St John Ambulance and Red Cross guard of honour. As always, the vivacity and emanation of charm surprised everyone, and in the eyes of her host and hostess she showed no evidence of the gruelling journey she had already undergone that day.

Edwina accepted the bouquet, smiled at the introductions, and shook the hand of every one of the guard of honour, pausing at several of the members for a further word. As Edwina was an almost-royal, she had almost as much experience of inspecting parades as members of the Royal Family.

Turner guided her to his big Austin Princess limousine, and they drove away together, his wife, Miss Checkley and his secretary following in a smaller car. It was a mile and a half to the Turners' house which was on a hill outside Jesselton. Turner explained that it was one of the few to survive the war. 'As you see, we have fine views. That is the island you flew over just now – it is called Gaya.' Turner, standing on the terrace, pointed inland. 'Lost in the cloud there, Lady Mountbatten, is Mount Kinabalu, 13,500 feet high and by far the highest in North Borneo. It is also spectacularly beautiful but is covered by cloud like this for most of the day at this time of the year. Sometimes early in the morning the cloud and mist clear for a few minutes, and if she may, my wife will wake you up if the summit is clear tomorrow morning because it is a sight that shouldn't be missed.'

Edwina laughed and said she would like that very much. The others had now arrived, and Evelyn at once took Edwina to her room. The Turners' house had three bedrooms, each with a bathroom *en suite*, the two largest on the first floor and facing one another. The third bedroom led off a landing half way up the stairs, and the Turners had decided that Edwina should have this one because its air-conditioning was the most efficient, while Miss Checkley had the larger bedroom opposite their own.

Evelyn left Edwina to rest, suggesting that she should come down to tea when she wished. She did so, dressed now in a light-coloured cotton print dress, cut to the length of some four inches below the knee fashionable at that time. She remarked again on the beauty of the views from the house. Miss Checkley joined them and they had tea on the terrace before undertaking the first event in her timetable.

Noel Turner had already noted with relief what an easy guest Edwina was, animated, full of curiosity and enthusiasm for everything. There was certainly none of the *grande dame* about her, and both he and his wife by the end of tea felt that she might have been an old friend or relation who had come to stay. Turner now drove with Edwina down towards Jesselton some three miles distant. This was a circuitous route to the St John headquarters where Edwina was due to pay a preliminary visit. 'I thought you might like to see our little town on the way,' said Turner, explaining how the Allied air raids of 1945, during the closing weeks of the war, had reduced the town to a few skeletons rising from rubble. Edwina recalled her own first visit to North Borneo later in that year, and remarked on the fine new government offices of the Secretariat – 'the gin palace', quipped Turner as they drove down the hill to the town. He explained that the majority of Jesselton's citizens were Chinese while outside in the country most of the people were Brunei Malays, Bajaus and Suluks with about twenty-five per cent Dusuns, themselves divided into several groups.

'In some of the more inaccessible parts of the interior there are primitive Muruts, still practising shifting cultivation and using spears and blowpipes for hunting,' Turner said. 'And as for religions, Christianity is represented by Anglican and Roman Catholic missions, and in a few rural areas there are Borneo Evangelicals and Seventh Day Adventists as well.' But he emphasized what a contented population North Borneo had. 'I'm glad to say that there are absolutely no racial tensions here.'

Turner left Edwina at the St John building, where she was greeted by the hierarchy with many curtseys to which Edwina was not strictly entitled but which she had given up trying to suppress. And why should she do so? she had reasoned long ago in her work. It gave them pleasure and did no harm.

Later in the evening, Turner and his wife wondered again at Edwina's apparent tirelessness. They had put on a small dinner party in her honour, just sixteen people in all. 'She was animated and full of vivacity throughout,' Turner later reported. Nobody could have appeared better able to continue the rigorous programme she had laid down for the rest of her Far East tour, especially after the following day, which had been called not altogether accurately 'a day of rest'.

Mount Kinabalu, to Turner's disappointment, was shrouded in heavy cloud early the next morning. But a few minutes after 7 o'clock, the clouds suddenly parted, and Evelyn hurried to Edwina's room. Edwina came out at once in a silk dressing-gown, and they stood on the balcony gazing up at the saw-tooth summit of the towering peak which at once seemed to reduce the foothills, the rolling countryside and the sea itself to diminished proportions. 'It's venerated by the Dusuns who live on the lower slopes,' Turner remarked. 'They believe it is the resting place of the souls of the dead.' A few minutes later the curtain of drifting clouds swiftly closed about the mountain, obscuring it for the remainder of the day.

It was still only 8 a.m. when they all left on an expedition up the coast which was to fill most of this 'day of rest'. The plan was to drive some fifty miles north to a township called Kota Belud, where the British Army was preparing a new training area and a Gurkha detachment was building a causeway across the river. The travelling was arranged as before, with Turner and Edwina in the big Austin, Evelyn, Miss Checkley and Peter Hewitt in the car behind. 'There was never any difficulty in finding something to talk about with Lady Mountbatten,' said Noel Turner. 'She was in excellent spirits and we talked almost the whole time, covering a wide range of topics from the Federation in the West Indies, and President Voroshilov of Russia, to matters of local concern.'

On a rise outside Kota Belud, the cars stopped for a look at the view. Edwina picked some flowers and two large toadstools which were placed on the floor of the car as 'trophies', as she called them. Three Europeans were nearby taking photographs of them from a distance, and when they began to drift away Edwina said, 'Do call them back. Let's talk to them.'

They were soldiers in 'civvies' on their way to Jesselton, and Edwina spoke to them, asking their names and where they came from. Then she suggested that they should all be photographed together, and Peter Hewitt carried out this duty, to the delight of the soldiers.

Edwina, after twenty years in prominent public life, had attended numberless receptions, some of them – especially in India – spectacular and gaudy. At Kota Belud the posse that met her made a fine sight: fifty Bajaus and Dusuns on ponies, who divided into two as vanguard and rear to take them into the town. Prince Philip had recently visited Jesselton and they had entertained him, too, in this way. Their repeated choruses of whoops was broken by the jingle of bells on the ponies' bridles.

At the Rest House, a heavy drizzle was falling, but brushing aside protests and umbrella alike, Edwina insisted on 'inspecting' her escort, shaking hands with every rider and offering a pat on the nose to every pony. She was quite wet when she at last came inside for a cup of coffee, but was soon off again, this time in a Land-Rover to visit the causeway. The Camp Commandant, and Major Radford, the CO of the 68th Field Squadron, Gurkha Engineers, were there to greet her, and she was driven by Major Radford down onto the causeway and across the river, which flowed swiftly between the vehicle's wheels. For the return trip, the Army showed off their new powered pontoon.

There were numbers of natives about, their relaxed manner and laughter contrasting with the formal style of the Gurkha soldiers. To help everyone feel relaxed, Edwina characteristically took off her shoes and began paddling in the river towards the soldiers to talk to them. There was much laughter.

It was the same story on the way back to the village. Shy children nearby needed coaxing by Edwina from their hiding-places. The touch was almost magical. The children, and everyone else, soon fell under her charm, and the laughter was much less strained when she was offered and drank heartily from a coconut. Then she watched some natives working and weaving, waved them all good-bye and was taken off to the house of the District Officer on the summit of a hill overlooking the Kota Belud plain. His wife was a bride of only a few weeks, and there were twenty more guests. Again, Edwina eased the rather tense, anxious atmosphere without appearing to do so, and by the time they all sat down to a curry lunch it seemed more like an ordinary social evening in the township than the semi-royal visit which had been so expectantly awaited.

The first sign of Edwina's distress did not become evident until that evening, back at the Turners' house. She had asked for the use of a secretary from Government House so that she could dictate some letters. Only five had been dealt with when she said that the rest could wait until the next day. To Miss Checkley she said that she was feeling tired and not very well, and that she would go and lie down. A strenuous evening still lay ahead, a dinner for over one hundred guests at the Jesselton Hotel given by the St John people. Before leaving the house, Miss Checkley asked Edwina if she could call a doctor, but, according to Miss Checkley, 'she pooh-poohed the idea', saying that she would be seeing the Commissioner of the Brigade, Dr R.H. Blaauw, at the dinner and would speak to him about her state of health. For Edwina to contemplate discussing her health at a social occasion with someone she hardly knew suggested that she was feeling quite seriously ill, and worried.

The meal was Chinese, an eight-course one. Edwina toyed with her food as course followed course. She was flanked by Dr Blaauw and Noel Turner. The Commissioner arose and made a short speech of welcome.

When Edwina stood up to reply, she appeared as animated as she had been earlier in the day, as if her pain and weariness had disappeared. She spoke for ten minutes without notes, telling the guests how impressed she was by the countryside 'and the happy atmosphere I have found everywhere I have been'.

Back at the Turners' house later that evening, she was helped out of the limousine, and began to walk between her host and hostess up the incline leading to the steps. Suddenly she appeared to stagger and reached out for the rail. Evelyn caught her other arm and helped her into the house.

'I do have rather a headache,' Edwina confessed when they were indoors. 'But thank you both for a most enjoyable day.' She declined the offer of an aspirin and went to her room. It was already late, but an hour later, Evelyn Turner, very concerned about her guest, noticed that the light in Edwina's room was still on. She knocked gently on the door and asked if she was all right. 'Yes, fine,' came the reply.

Saturday, 20 February, was to be a busy working day, starting with the Red Cross after breakfast. Noel Turner was up first and found a message received from the local radio station reporting that the Queen had given birth to a prince. He scribbled a note to Edwina and left for his office at Government House, confident that the news would please her. Miss Checkley later took in the note and Edwina said how delighted she was that Charles and Anne had a baby brother. But she also confessed that her headache was no better, and Miss Checkley telephoned to Dr Blaauw who came at once. His examination took some fifteen minutes. He was unable to make a satisfactory diagnosis but thought that the patient might have 'flu or perhaps the early stages of malaria. Edwina insisted on keeping to her programme, first at the Red Cross and then at the Queen Elizabeth Hospital. Evelyn Turner accompanied her, and at the hospital managed to warn the medical officer on duty that Edwina was unwell and that it might be advisable to curtail her programme.

After the hospital visit there was to be a coffee party. Meanwhile Turner had been telephoned by the hospital and informed that Edwina was looking poorly. The Acting Governor telephoned to warn his wife, who was feeling equally anxious but was unable to cancel the coffee party at such short notice. Evelyn Turner did, however, persuade Edwina to retire to her room after chatting to some of the guests, and Turner succeeded in cancelling her attendance at the lunch engagement which followed. When she heard, Edwina commented that this was 'rather drastic' but seemed reconciled to remaining on her bed until well into the afternoon, drinking only a little egg-flip for lunch.

At 4.15 p.m. Edwina Mountbatten was on parade as if nothing had happened, and it was just one more engagement in half a lifetime of duties to be performed, on time and with one hundred per cent efficiency and dedication. She was in her white uniform again, this time with her full row of medals, brushing aside enquiries about her health but indicating that all was still not well by asking to be excused from attending the tea party afterwards.

Noel Turner took Edwina off to the Secretariat. There were some sixty members of the St John for inspection, and in the background there was music from the police band. Turner took the salute, and then Edwina carried out the inspection, shaking hands with everybody and exchanging words with many of them. Then she made a short speech, presented some certificates and watched a first aid demonstration - oh, how many of these she had witnessed in the past twenty years!

That was not all for the day. At 7.15 p.m. 120 guests were due at the house for a reception in Edwina's honour. Meanwhile Miss Checkley had again telephoned Dr Blaauw, who came at once and gave Edwina a more thorough examination. Again he could find no cause for concern. Yes, she would be able to continue her tour, leaving on Sunday for Singapore. And, yes, he quite understood how anxious she was to keep to her programme. But Edwina was clearly relieved by the suggestion that she should not greet her guests, but should come down to talk informally to them for the last half hour.

Edwina descended to the murmur of conversation soon after 8 p.m. She was, by all accounts, looking pale, her deeply lined face drawn with pain. Hers was a performance to match Bernhardt's in *Daniel*, as professionally effective as if in the full flood of strength and health. Evelyn Turner took her to a sofa and discreetly summoned in turn a selection of her guests to sit beside her. All told later of her charm, the way she put them at their ease, the impression she gave that they were more important to the work than she was.

After twenty minutes, Evelyn suggested that it was time for Edwina to retire and led her away. Noel Turner met them at the bottom of the stairs, suggesting that she should cancel her reservation on the morning flight to Singapore. 'There is a Viscount on Monday instead of a Dakota,' he said, 'and that will be much more comfortable.'

Edwina smiled. 'I'll see in the morning,' she said. 'And thank you so much for all you have done.'

The guests began to leave, talking quietly amongst themselves; the lights of the last car traced the Turners' drive and faded away towards Jesselton.

At 7.30 the next morning, Miss Checkley knocked on the door of Edwina's room, and when there was no response, more urgently, knowing what a stickler she was for keeping to timetables. She entered, suddenly anxious, hearing the steady murmur of the air-conditioning and noting that the curtains had been drawn back, letting in the early morning sun. At first Miss Checkley thought that Edwina might be heavily drugged, but that was for only an instant. Her training and experience, and a touch on the cold cheek, told her that Edwina was dead.

2
The Roots of Wealth

No woman could have had more mixed and remarkable antecedents and ancestors than Edwina Mountbatten. On her father's side she was descended from a long line of aristocratic, adventurous and sometimes eccentric politicians and benefactors – 'an amazing bunch', Lord Mountbatten once called them. On her mother's side she could trace her ancestry back to Jewish Central European bankers and moneylenders of relatively unexceptional personality and monetary success until the line reached her talented and successful grandfather, Ernest Cassel, one of the richest men in the world and the closest intimate of King Edward VII, after whom Edwina was named.

Edwina's father was Wilfrid William Ashley, later Lord Mount Temple, who died in 1939, leaving her (amongst much else) Broadlands House in Hampshire and Classiebawn Castle in Ireland, where Lord Mountbatten was murdered in 1979. Wilfrid Ashley was the only son of Evelyn Ashley (1836–1907), the fourth son of Anthony Ashley Cooper, seventh Earl of Shaftesbury.

The Ashley family tree is many-branched and rises so high that its topmost branches fade into the grey stratosphere of genealogical history. It is still clearly traceable long before Queen Elizabeth I, whose War Secretary at one time was Sir Anthony Ashley, who sailed with Drake and raided Cadiz. He had a daughter who married into the Cooper family of nearby Rockbourne Manor. Their son, born in 1621, inherited vast properties from both sides of the family and assumed the name Ashley Cooper.

Anthony Ashley Cooper was created first Earl of Shaftesbury on 23 April 1672, just 275 years before Edwina's husband was created first Earl Mountbatten and she became the first Countess. This first Earl was quite as remarkable a figure as Mountbatten, and quite as enthusiastic a royalist, turning all his considerable powers and wealth towards the restoration of the monarchy after Cromwell's death. As Lord High Chancellor he was responsible for the introduction of the Act of Habeas Corpus. Dryden wrote of his discerning eyes and clean hands, 'unbribed, unbought, the wretched to redress, swift of despatch, and easy of access'.

Anthony Ashley Cooper had interests in the slave trade and plantations in Barbados (then respectable), and in 1663 was given a grant of Carolina. Six years later John Locke drew up its constitution, which was notable for its liberal and tolerant qualities. The Ashley and Cooper rivers which meet at Charleston were named after this remarkable man.

The Shaftesbury motto is 'Love and Serve'. Edwina was much attached to that motto, was loyal to it all her life, and was always interested in that great charity, 'Shaftesbury Homes'. The seventh Earl probably interpreted the word 'Love' more narrowly and severely than his great-granddaughter, but his record of charitable works forms an astonishing roll of benevolence throughout the greater part of the nineteenth century. It has been said that Shaftesbury was a major influence in reducing the likelihood of revolution during his lifetime, 'softening the bitter spirit between rich and poor'.[1] Among those who benefited most were the mentally retarded, those working in mills and factories, the thousands of chimney 'climbing boys' (whose sufferings were so graphically made public by Charles Kingsley in *The Water Babies*) and tens of thousands of illiterate urchins who were saved from the worst effects of slum life by the 'Ragged Schools'. Shaftesbury fought in Parliament to get through the Lodging House Act, described by Charles Dickens as the best piece of legislation ever to be enacted. Besides being 'the impersonation of the philanthropic spirit of the nineteenth century',[2] Shaftesbury was always prepared to face hostile crowds, and did so at great peril to his life in 1848 when the mobs seemed likely to get out of hand in London.

Edwina was to inherit many of Shaftesbury's strengths and qualities. She, too, never flinched from facing mobs; and the portrait of Shaftesbury at Broadlands showing him as a handsome man with fine regular features bears a certain likeness, which Edwina always enjoyed, to her own head.

Of all this seventh Earl's children, his favourite and the one who gave him least trouble was his fourth son Evelyn, born in 1836. Even he gave his parents some concern while at school, and we find his mother writing to him at Harrow: 'I am sorry to say that again your Monthly Character mentions that you are rather giddy and fond of trifling and want method and perseverance in keeping your good resolutions. Try, darling, to overcome this tendency.' Then the Countess cited the fate of a young friend, 'taken by brain fever in the midst of folly and vanity without time for anything but regret, if even that. These things are meant as Warnings.'

Edwina's grandfather evidently heeded these warnings, and he grew up a steady but by no means dull and unadventurous young man. He emulated his father and more distant relations by turning to politics. His grandmother was Lord Melbourne's sister, who married for the second time Lord Palmerston when Evelyn was three years old. Evelyn became Palmerston's Private Secretary when he was Prime Minister in 1858 and from that time learned politics fast and from the inside.

Evelyn's family tradition, instincts and beliefs steered him towards the liberal element in politics, and he was prepared to risk his life (and cause something of a sensation) by joining Garibaldi in camp in Italy in 1860 to follow his campaign of liberation. Three years later he was arrested in Russia on suspicion of supporting Polish insurgents. In literature he wrote the official life of Melbourne; in law he became a barrister in 1863; in politics a Liberal Member of Parliament for Poole in Dorset and, later, the Isle of Wight, always supporting the cause of the underdog. In 1888 he inherited the great properties which would one day be his granddaughter's.

Edwina's paternal grandmother, Evelyn's first wife, was Sybella ('Sissy') Farquhar, daughter of Sir Walter and Lady Mary Farquhar. A close look at the Farquhar family tree reveals similar American connections to her husband's. Just before Christmas 1606, the future explorer John Smith was one of a party of colonists heading for Virginia on board three ships. A year later, after proving his enterprise and leadership qualities, he was captured by Indians led by King Powhatan. It has been recounted how the comely King's daughter, Princess Pocohontas, prevailed upon her father to release the Englishman. Six years later, Pocohontas herself was captured and kept as hostage for some English prisoners. In James Town she 'renounced publicly her country's Idolatry' and married a colonist called John Rolfe. The young couple sailed to England, where they were greatly fêted and received at Court, and the well-known portrait of Pocohontas was engraved by Simon de Passe. She died before she could return home, leaving one son, who in due time married Jane Pybus. Their son, Anthony, was a direct ancestor of Sissy Farquhar.

Evelyn Ashley and Sissy married in 1866, and in 1867 Sissy gave birth to Wilfrid William Ashley. The boy was a chip off the old block only in appearance. At Harrow and at Magdalen College, Oxford, he grew into a tall and magnificently handsome young man – 'lofty and fine drawn' as one of his acquaintances wrote; 'Handsome Wilfrid' as he was later known in the House of Commons; '*par excellence* the county squire and country gentleman'. He also had a very good opinion of himself, and was renowned for his meanness: 'He always had his pockets sewn up,' his second daughter recalls. Flouting family tradition, he developed a deep blue conservative view of politics. Wilfrid also joined the army, served ten years in the Grenadier Guards and rose to the rank of colonel. From that time, until he was raised to the peerage as Baron Mount Temple of Lee, he was always known as 'the Colonel' by his staff and tenants.

Staff and tenants had become much more numerous when he was fortunate enough to inherit the Shaftesbury estates from his great-grandmother Lady Palmerston and set up home at Broadlands and Classiebawn Castle. He entered Parliament in 1906, and from that time the stately, patrician figure of the millionaire landowner, Justice of the Peace and Alderman for the county of Hampshire, became a familiar figure of the extreme right in the palace of Westminster, a Conservative Whip from 1911 to 1913.

Although one of the most eligible young men in England, Ashley remained unmarried until he was thirty-three, when by chance he met at a country house a pretty, wistful young girl, Maud Cassel, the only child of a highly successful German-born banker, Ernest Cassel. They fell in love and became engaged. The year was 1900.

The family tree on Edwina's mother's side is like a single stem by contrast with the Shaftesbury-Palmerston forest, including its roots in the West Indies and the ancient colony of Virginia. But this stem is a stout one, and from it can be recognized a power that did much to shape the personality and found the achievements of Edwina Cynthia Annette Ashley. By the time Edwina was born on 28 November 1901, her maternal grandfather was one of the richest and most powerful men in the world. It was also a world Lord Melbourne would not have understood.

Edwina's grandfather, Ernest Cassel, was born in Cologne on 3 March 1852, the last child of Amalia and Jacob Cassel. They were a typically urban, middle-class Jewish family concerned with business and the arts in about equal measure. Jacob's business was not unusual either, being that of banker and moneylender in a small but successful way. In the evenings the family played chess and music. Ernest became a talented chess player and enjoyed his violin, too. He was, it seems, a pale, plain boy, but his brain had an exceptional edge to it, as sharp as his resolution and ambition were granite hard.

While Evelyn Ashley, Ernest Cassel's senior by sixteen years, was practising law in England and contemplating entering politics, Cassel left school in Germany at fourteen (not penniless but with little to spare) to work at a local bank. It was the first step in a career which in less than three decades would net a fortune beside which the wealth of the Shaftesburys, based on centuries of exploitation in the West Indies and America and thousands of acres of rich farmland at home, would seem puny by comparison.

Just as British industrial world leadership was already being challenged by the new furnaces and machines of Germany, France and the United States, and the rigid social and political leadership in Britain could see the coming era of the common man, so a new breed of wizard fortune-maker, brash, ruthless, entrepreneurial, had come into being. He had been born because, as always in the world of capitalism, his conception was the product of need.

This new child, represented by the fourteen-year-old Ernest Cassel making his way on foot across Cologne to Eltzbachers every morning, was not in the business of landlordism, whether in the tea plantations of India, the new goldfields of southern Africa or the sugar fields of the West Indies; nor was he in the business of building railways across the American Midwest or the pampas of Argentina. He was certainly not in the business of actually manufacturing steel or ships or guns, and did not relish the complications and responsibility of tenant farming 10,000 acres.

Ernest Cassel, as his father Jacob had done before him, was entering the world of finance itself, the money that made all the other businesses and industries possible, and could be lent and moved and manipulated with a minimum of fuss and the very smallest of payrolls. Jacob Cassel had made a reasonable living as a financier. For his son Ernest, a generation later, the times were infinitely riper, the potential of fortune-making infinitely richer. Moreover, he had all the qualities this new activity demanded: a mind like a modern camera that can focus on tiny objects with a micro lens and on the world at large with a wide-angle lens; a character that was at once courageous and aggressive; a flawless judgement; and an instinct that was as accurate as it was discriminating. Above all, he was a gambler.

Cassel's first job taught him how limited the business future was in Cologne. In little more than a year he asked his parents if he could take up the offer of employment in England. Permission granted, young Ernest set off with a small bag and his violin. The job was with a grain merchant and netted him £2 a week. Next he went to Paris to gain experience at the Anglo-Egyptian Bank. Unfortunately, the Franco-Prussian War broke out almost at once, and not for the last time he found himself on hostile soil and was obliged to return to London. There he learned that the financial house of Bischoffsheim and Goldschmidt were seeking a confidential clerk. There were, it seems, countless applications, many full of self-adulation. Cassel's letter, he remembered in later years, ran austerely:

Dear Sir,

I apply for the position in your office and refer to my former chiefs, Messrs. Eltzbacher, Cologne.

Yours sincerely,

Ernest Cassel

The impression he made on these shrewd men was favourable enough to get him the job, at £200 a year. Within twelve months Cassel had become Bischoffsheim's trouble-shooter. His first assignment was in Constantinople where a firm in which the company had invested heavily was in severe financial embarrassment. Cassel was at his most brilliant when charged with converting financial catastrophe to success. Instead of taking a year, Cassel was back home in three months. His firm's interests were saved, and with the commission he earned he was able to lay the first stone of the giant edifice his fortune was to become.

Cassel was as quick to recognize his own value as that of a promising business enterprise. When Bischoffsheim offered Cassel the post of manager and £500 a year, Cassel (as he recounted later) quickly replied, 'You mean £5,000.' 'Yes, yes, of course, £5,000.'

From this time Cassel worked on an ever higher level, taking increasing responsibility upon himself with the blessing of his employers. The second Industrial Revolution, a hundred times larger than the first, was leaving its mark all over the world: mines to be exploited, mills, factories and docks to be built, ships and engines of war and peace of all kinds to be manufactured, railways and roads to be built – in Siam and Chile, all over Africa and Asia. Between 1870 and 1914 the world required finance as never before nor since, and this was the precise span of time when Cassel's genius flowered most vividly.

Cassel had become a hard bargainer, manipulator, sponsor, promoter, speculator, and venturer of the very highest calibre with the priceless gift of instinctive guidance and feel, sniffing out merit and demerit with equal delicacy. Moreover he got on well with those whom it was important to get on well with. International bankers were his first and closest associates, in Amsterdam and Hamburg, Paris, London and Rome. Cassel's biographer has written:

They maintained between them an incredibly accurate network of economic, political and financial intelligence at the highest level. They could withdraw support here, provide additional funds there, move immense sums of money with lightning rapidity and secrecy from one corner to another of their financial empires, and influence the political decisions of a score of countries.[3]

One of Cassel's closest liaisons was with a fellow German Jew who had chosen the United States instead of Britain as his base. He was Jacob Schiff of the New York commercial banking firm of Kühn, Loeb and Co., for whom Cassel acted as London agent to his enormous profit for many years. Theirs was much more than a banking relationship, and they even took holidays together. Great bankers seem to have a special kinship with great mountains, and Schiff and Cassel would holiday together in Switzerland on the rare occasions when they took time off from their work. Once on a family climbing expedition on Mont Blanc Schiff's daughter slipped and fell hundreds of feet down a steep slope before being held by a shrub, badly hurt. Cassel unhesitatingly descended and held her until rescue could be organized. From that time a special and unbreakable bond was forged between the two men.

A generation earlier, Cassel might never have established himself in Society in England as he was comfortably able to do in the 1890s when there was much more social flexibility. The severe puritan tone established by Queen Victoria and her Prince Consort was fast fading and was being overwhelmed by the brash chorus led by 'the Marlborough Set'. When the Prince of Wales wanted a West End club over which he had control of the membership, he established one in Pall Mall opposite Marlborough House and filled it with his 'fast' cronies, men with plenty of money and style. They and their wives and mistresses represented a section of Society that was more likely to be found at the baccarat table than a Buckingham Palace soirée, in the paddock at Ascot than a box at Covent Garden. They were an urbane crowd; a cynical wit, a talent to amuse and willingness to take high risks being admired qualities. They drank and ate and fornicated a great deal, and were as far distant from the hushed darkness of the Court at Windsor as from the slums of Tyneside.

The Prince of Wales, denied State responsibility by his disapproving mother, settled instead for reintroducing the free licence of the earlier Hanoverians. Prejudice against Jews in the Prince of Wales's circle was as unthinkable as prejudice against actresses. Both were plentifully numbered among his friends. But the Prince's friendship with Ernest Cassel was of a special nature. They first met, suitably enough, on the racecourse. On the face of it, they had little in common except their looks, the cut of their beards and their German origins. On early acquaintance Cassel was cold, remote and secretive, with a repartee that was sharp rather than waggish. At first they were drawn to one another by mutual need, Cassel for respectability and recognition, the Prince for the sound financial advice his extravagant lifestyle required.

Cassel took the future King-Emperor's investments in hand and did wonders for them, with his customary impenetrable discretion. The Prince of Wales liked to be entertained by his rich friends, who invariably lavished the very best upon him. Cassel acted the part of host with great gusto and style. His tastes were over-ornate by contemporary standards and ridiculous by present-day standards. But so were the Prince's. And the Prince came increasingly to value Cassel for the worldly judgement of his cool, clever, objective mind on far wider issues than money.

In 1906, with his old friend now firmly on the throne, Cassel acquired Brook House in Park Lane, the summation of vulgar opulence amongst his many properties in Britain and abroad. Most new house owners redecorate and even carry out some structural alterations to suit their taste. Cassel stripped this great mansion, imported some 800 tons of marble from the Michelangelo quarries in Italy and proceeded to line most of the rooms, including the six kitchens, with it. The dining room, seating a hundred, was spared this treatment and was panelled in oak, the library in cherry wood. A surviving member of the staff who lived there later wrote:

> The walls of the entrance lobby were panelled with lapis lazuli and green-veined cream-coloured marble used alternately. The double doors leading into the main hall were of looking glass, and there was a large mirror over the hall table. The main hall, the grand staircase and the gallery were of white marble. On the first floor there was a suite of reception rooms, each one having connecting doors of looking glass which could be pushed back into slots in the wall, and the four rooms could be made into one large room for receptions and balls. The floors were parqueted and the ceilings painted, and the windows which had balconies looked out over Hyde Park.
>
> The three rooms on the ground floor each had double doors with handles in the middle. If anyone of importance was announced, the footman could open both these doors at the same time as one knob opened the door on the right and the other released the bolts at the top and bottom of the other door.
>
> There were many beautiful pictures in Brook House all of which came to Lady Louis. In the dining room were four large Van Dycks – Charles I, Henrietta Maria, Madame Vinck, and the famous one of Lords John and Bernard Stuart. There were Reynolds and Raeburns, several Hoppners, Nattier and Zorn, and a good Franz Hals. Sir Ernest used to get Sir Joseph Duveen to

advise him on his purchases, and Sir Joseph often came to see him when he was in England.

The depression engendered by all this marble and dark wood and general vulgar opulence was lifted partly by these paintings and the flowers everywhere. Cassel loved flowers and grew them in abundance on his country estates. Carnations were his favourite flower. 'It was not at all uncommon to have twelve to eighteen dozen malmaisons up during one week if there were to be any dinner parties.'

Dinner parties and luncheon parties were Cassel's lifeblood; and it was in this setting of Brook House that he would entertain with unlimited extravagance King Edward VII, his mistress Mrs Keppel, and the leading politicians, bankers and industrialists.

No one knew quite how much Sir Ernest Cassel (as he had now become) was worth. The estimates were usually between five and ten millions - say £150 to £250 million in present-day money. Cassel had achieved as much material success as he could ever have dreamed of. But riches had brought him little happiness, and in his private life he was a sad and lonely figure.

Back in 1877, Cassel had met the daughter of Robert Thompson Maxwell, a Catholic landowner who lived in Yorkshire near Darlington. Her name was Annette. Something in this pale, intense young German Jew appealed to her sensitive nature. Three years earlier Cassel had experienced his first domestic tragedy with the death of his mother. A year later his father and elder brother both died. An orphaned and lonely expatriate, Cassel felt deeply the loss of his family. He sought consolation in his work, the pressure of which was intensified. His meeting with this young English girl brought a breath of sweetness and a new awareness of a gentler side to life which he had lost in early boyhood.

They married the next year, and the young couple seemed set for a reasonably prosperous middle-class life on the £150,000 Cassel had by then accumulated as capital. A child was born to Annette a year later, a daughter, Amalia Mary Maud. Cassel, for the first time in his life, enjoyed spiritual and domestic contentment. He had never been so happy, and was never to be so happy again. Within a few months of Maudie's birth, Annette contracted tuberculosis. She rapidly declined. Beside himself with grief, Cassel sought the best medical help. Annette, knowing that she did not have long to live, begged her husband to enter the Catholic Church so that she could console herself that they would meet again in the after-life.

A broad-minded priest who was attending Annette baptized Cassel without more ado on condition that he studied the faith. Annette died; Cassel met his obligations, smothering his new grief in Catholic theology, but finding this new conversion, in contrast to his English naturalization on his marriage, more difficult to accept. His Jewish blood and the Jewish faith of his childhood and his forefathers were too strong, and though he remained nominally a Catholic, the dogma was too alien. Instead, his mind turned back more strongly than ever to his work and the accumulation of wealth. There was a new edge to his ambition now, a new impulse. Ernest Cassel intended to make his beloved daughter the richest woman in the world. For her, he believed, money would 'answereth all things'. It was the only way he knew of ensuring her happiness.

Maudie grew up wanting for nothing, her every wish at once fulfilled, while her father won for Britain the contract for building great dams in Egypt, reorganized the Swedish, Mexican and numerous other railway systems, amalgamated and doubled the efficiency of some of Britain's greatest armament and shipbuilding companies - Barrow, Vickers, Maxim and Nordenfelt - helped the Bank of England when the Argentine economy collapsed, and established national banks in many foreign countries. It was a one-man show which had never been equalled and never could be matched in the future, if only because the conditions could never occur again.

Cassel had already dispensed substantial gifts to a number of charities when, at the very end of 1900, the *British Medical Journal* announced that an anonymous donor had placed at the disposal of the Prince of Wales the biggest single donation to charity ever made, no less than £200,000. 'This money,' ran the statement, 'by the Prince of Wales's direction, is to be devoted to the erection of a sanatorium for tuberculosis patients in England.' It did not require much speculation before it became generally known who this donor could be: the richest man in the land, whose wife had died so young of tuberculosis. It was also known that Cassel had already contributed generously to the Prince of Wales's Hospital Fund for London. The general view was that this was Cassel's celebration of the new century on 1 January. But it was nothing of the kind. It was a celebration of the fact that the Prince of Wales had approved of the forthcoming marriage of his rich friend's daughter, and had agreed to come to the wedding.

Maudie had grown up in the care of nursemaids and teachers who were as closely observed by Cassel as the fluctuations of his Consols. She was aware of her uniquely privileged upbringing, and of the care, love and wealth lavished upon her. But she had inherited the good sense and judgement as well as the sensitivity of her mother and remained remarkably unspoilt through her girlhood. She loved music, loved to paint, and her conversation was precociously intelligent. 'She was a delightful companion,' wrote a friend, 'with a great sense of humour and *joie de vivre*.... She had the most exquisite complexion I have ever seen, clear hazel eyes and very pretty hands and feet.'[4] It was also impossible to ignore the fact that she tired easily and was forced to rest after any physical or social strain.

Maudie, like almost all girls of her class, was taught mainly at home, by the best teachers of course, first at 2 Orme Square in Bayswater, and then, when Maudie was ten, at the great Mayfair mansion Cassel bought prior to Brook House, 48 Grosvenor Square. Here she 'came out' in 1899 when she was nineteen years old, and threw herself into the debutante's round of social events with all the gusto her rather frail constitution allowed.

When Cassel learned of Maudie's meeting with the ultra respectable Wilfrid Ashley, and later of their wish to marry, he was quick to recognize that this was a match that reached the sky-high standard he had always planned for his daughter. In the handsome Wilfrid Ashley he saw a blend of ample material wealth (it would never have done for the heiress to the Cassel fortunes to marry a man of only modest means) and the respectability of being a scion of one of the oldest and most esteemed families in his adopted country.

To Cassel all the auguries seemed to be favourable, and the liberal Ashley Cooper families accepted without a qualm the half-Jewish blood in the bride's veins. The Melbourne side of the family as well as Ashley's father, now sixty-three, and living at Broadlands, were gratified to see the only child – and such a beautiful talented heiress – entering the family.

Because of the Queen's frailty and failing health, the Prince of Wales's official duties had multiplied, and in the aftermath of Christmas and the New Year it was not possible to find a Saturday when he was free to attend a purely social event. On the first Saturday of the new century, 5 January, he was due to go to Sandringham; on the Thursday he had to take part in the royal welcome being given in London to Field-Marshal Lord Roberts VC, fresh from his popular triumphs in the South African War. Friday was the only day he was free.

In the last part of the nineteenth century a strong superstition had formed about Friday weddings bringing ill-luck. Maudie characteristically pooh-poohed this nonsense. She and Ashley would get married on Friday 4 January, 'An unbroken record of blank Fridays, lasting over twenty-five years,' reported the *Daily Chronicle*, 'is being ended at St George's Hanover Square.'

Lord Roberts was duly welcomed on the day before the wedding when the Prince and Princess, accompanied by the Duke and Duchess of York (the future George V and Queen Mary), the Princess of Wales, the Duke of Connaught and his son Prince Arthur, the Duke of Cambridge and the Duke and Duchess of Teck and more of the grandest in the land, met the Field-Marshal at Paddington Station. The gaily decorated streets were lined with sightseers (including the bride and groom of the morrow with their families in privileged seats) 'who greeted the hero of the day as he passed with continuous cheering'.

The wedding day of Edwina's parents dawned 'dark, gloomy and foggy', and so it remained. The sight of the wedding presents laid out at 48 Grosvenor Square served to offset the weather outside – a sparkling mass of more than 400 of them: exquisite cut-glass from Venice, the finest solid silver cutlery from France and England, jewellery in great quantities, suitably topped by 'an all-round diamond crown of great beauty and value' from Cassel for his Maudie.

By 2.45 p.m. the church was packed. The guests included the Queen's fourth daughter HRH Princess Louise, the Duchess of Argyll, with the Duke, the Duchess of Wellington, the Marquis of Blandford, the Prince of Wales's mistress, the stunningly beautiful Mrs George Keppel, the American ambassador and his wife, a number of Ashleys, the artist Alma Tadema and his wife, Lord and Lady Raglan and almost as many more titled personages as could be contained in *Burke's Peerage*.

The Prince of Wales entered discreetly and last by the vestry door, accompanied by his equerry, Captain John Fortescue, another hero recently returned from the South African War. 'The church was handsomely decorated and the service was fully choral,' reporters told their readers. Maudie with six bridesmaids and two pages entered on the arm of her father. She wore the exquisite white dress once worn by her mother. She appeared small beside the tall figure of Wilfrid with his best man, the Hon. George Hamilton Gordon (family motto 'Not Unmindful'), who had celebrated his thirtieth birthday the previous day and felt less thirsty than many of the guests for the reception champagne.

The ceremony was conducted by the Rev. W. Page Roberts, Canon of Canterbury, assisted by the sub-dean of the Chapel Royal and the church's rector. The choir sang beautifully, the Prince of Wales added his signature in the book, and by 4 p.m. Wilfrid and Maud were proceeding down the aisle to the 'Wedding March', the bells sounding out across Hanover Square where a large crowd of sightseers had gathered in the dusk. Then carriages took the guests across Mayfair to champagne, cake-cutting speeches and present-admiring at the Cassel house. At last Wilfrid and Maudie were able to leave, the bride in warm tweed (part of the £5,000 trousseau her father had given her), taking the Ashley carriage to Waterloo Station, thence by train and carriage to Wilfrid's brother's estate, Milburn near Esher in Surrey, which had been lent to them for the first part of their honeymoon. Meanwhile the Prince of Wales returned to Marlborough House, glad to have seen his friend so proud of his daughter. The day had been a busy one, but the best part lay ahead. That night he was taking a bevy of his grandchildren to the pantomime *Sleeping Beauty and the Beast* at the Drury Lane Theatre. Dan Leno, Herbert Campbell, Madge Lessing and Fred Emney were all in the huge cast. The evening was a roaring success.

Before travelling south across Europe to the relative warmth of the Mediterranean, the Ashleys rested at Broadlands, establishing a practice which was to be followed by their elder daughter on her honeymoon, their daughter's cousin by marriage, Princess Elizabeth, after her marriage to Prince Philip of Greece in 1947, and in 1981 by the Prince and Princess of Wales.

Maudie Ashley had stayed in this lovely house as a guest of her future father-in-law when she was engaged and had admired it for its beauty and comfort and the simplicity of its style and decor by contrast with the extravagant ornateness of her own father's houses. Broadlands is situated a mile and a half south of the pretty little market town of Romsey and seven miles north of Southampton. The River Test, swift-flowing and sparkling with trout, passes through the garden 100 yards below the house. Broadlands is pleasing to the eye more by virtue of its modest size and fine balance than for any spectacular qualities. The size of the rooms as well as the Palladian exterior are comfortable to embrace and call forth no exclamations, but produce a sense of satisfaction. The drive on the east side winds to the gates and sweeps before the front doors as easily as the river cuts through on the west side on its way to the sea. The rooms are finely proportioned, and below there are cellars and kitchens, a real 'downstairs'.

Another King Edward, the son of Alfred the Great, had been on the throne when his daughter founded a Benedictine nunnery in 907 which became the Abbey of Romsey and embraced the estate of Brodelandes. The Abbey, rebuilt in Norman times, and the Manor were surrendered to King Henry VIII in 1539 who separated the Abbey from the house, which found itself in due course in the possession of the St Barbe family. John St Barbe, who set a record by being made a baronet at the age of eight, lived in the house for over sixty years. He was visited in the 1690s by his relation, the adventurous traveller and chronicler, Celia Fiennes.

Much of what Celia Fiennes recorded about Broadlands in her *Journeys* is recognizable today, from the moment when she rides on her horse between 'the rows of trees in the avenues ... to the front of the house' where 'you enter a Court that's wall'd in and blew iron gates, the Court has a round in the middle rail'd in, designed for a Bowling Green, and the Coaches drive round it to come to the Entrance which is severall stone stepps to a broad space that is railed with balls and bannisters'.

Celia Fiennes later describes the room occupied by the honeymoon couple, in which Edwina was doubtless conceived a little over 200 years later. 'On the left hand is a very large bed chamber which indeed is the best good tapistry hangings, here is design'd a velvet bed, its painted white, there are very good Pictures.'

John St Barbe made numerous improvements to the original manor house before he died in 1723. Unfortunately his cousin who inherited the estate was forced to sell it to pay off the mortgages brought about by speculations in the South Sea Bubble. When the first Lord Palmerston bought it for £26,500 thirteen years later it had deteriorated badly. He and his successors were responsible for bringing it to the state of beauty which can be seen today, rendering the house 'suitable for a gentleman to live in', as he defined it.

Over the following years builders pulled down part of the house, removed the farm, altered the coach houses and stables. Palmerston's son did even more for the place. Henry, second Viscount Palmerston, was a cultivated young man who had travelled widely in Europe. He employed the contemporary Duveen, Gavin Hamilton, as adviser on pictures, and Capability Brown and Robert Adam contributed their talents to laying out and planting the estate and gardens as they are today. For the interior, Palmerston took the advice of Henry Holland, Angelica Kauffmann and Josiah Wedgwood himself, who produced the decoration of the book room. Hervé tables were brought from France, exquisite marble from Italy. Sir William Hamilton, Ambassador at Naples and husband of Horatio

Nelson's mistress Emma, advised on Italian statuary and the best way of bringing it to England.

The famed statesman Harry, third Lord Palmerston, inherited the estate from his father when he was seventeen, and the complex weaving of the families of Melbourne, Palmerston and Shaftesbury, which was to lead to Broadlands' ownership by Edwina in 1939, began with the late marriage of Lord Palmerston to Lady Cowper, the widowed sister of the Prime Minister (Lord Melbourne), in 1840, following the Cowper-Ashley marriage ten years earlier. Palmerston was then the young Queen's admired Foreign Secretary, and she was both puzzled and disapproving of the elderly match. According to Elizabeth Longford, Palmerston 'had much better manners than Melbourne, an equally good but more robust temper and a jolly taste in waistcoats and women'. The Queen never really reconciled herself to the marriage. It 'soon seemed to the Queen to have affected his chivalrous manner towards herself. She told Lord M. that somehow she didn't like him as much as she used to.'[5]

Broadlands, little changed after the onslaught by the second and third Lord Palmerstons, passed to Lady Palmerston after the death of her husband, and then to her second son William Cowper, and thence to Evelyn Ashley in 1888, who bequeathed the estate to his only son Wilfrid.

When Wilfrid and Maudie returned from the long second part of their honeymoon abroad in the late summer of 1901, Maudie was expecting a child. Because of her frail constitution her husband (and her father) ensured that she had the best medical advice. She went into labour in their London house on Wednesday 27 November and, as had been feared, she had a difficult time, attended by two of the best gynaecologists in the country, hastily summoned from Harley Street. She at last gave birth soon after noon the next day. She knew that her father and husband had both hoped for a boy, but it was a girl and she was not in the least disappointed, only relieved to be at the end of her ordeal. Ernest Cassel had already filled the house with flowers to celebrate the event. The Cassel line was intact, if only through a female.

It seemed to Cassel at this time that perhaps his luck was on the turn and that the tide of fortune which he had brought about by his own talents and industry would be matched by improved family fortunes, unscarred by further tragedies. The Friday wedding superstition was as dead as the old Queen, whom they had buried almost a year ago now. This was to be a new century blessed by happiness and affluence. The King agreed to stand as godfather to the infant girl. He gave her an inscribed silver mug, her father gave her a pearl necklace, the two gifts together forming the modest foundation for a great fortune.

3
The Growth of Promise

In his early, lonely years in England, Cassel had invited over from Germany his sister Wilhelmina Schönbrunn as a companion and hostess. She had married in Germany, given birth to two children, and been divorced. Her brother was therefore now taking on the responsibility of a family. Wilhelmina ('Minna' and to Edwina always 'Aunty-Grannie') assumed the name Schönbrunn-Cassel, soon found this a grave handicap and, at her brother Ernest's suggestion, dropped her married name altogether, becoming simply Mrs Cassel, which, when they lived under the same roof, confused people greatly. Minna's son Felix married Lady Helen Grimston in 1908 and became a famous advocate. Minna's daughter Anna married Colonel Atherton Edward ('Tiresome Teddy') Jenkins of the Rifle Brigade, the officers of which always referred to her as 'Black Maria' for her dark Jewish looks. As a wedding present from Cassel they acquired Wherwell Priory near Andover, up the River Test valley from Broadlands. Their daughter Marjorie, born twenty months before Edwina, became her closest and life-long friend.

The Cassel side of the family figured more often and more importantly in Edwina's early life than the Shaftesburys. She remembered her childhood as one spent always on the move, a restless and nomadic existence, which was greatly to influence her adult life. Rich people are mostly tireless travellers as if in search of something money and privilege cannot buy. In Edwina's age of plans and preparations, packing and unpacking of endless trunks, and arrangements with servants, of journeys by train and steamer, of greetings and farewells, new rooms with new views, of seasonal hospitality, of new games, pastimes, sports and dalliances in new places with friends and relations – even in this world where nothing remained the same for long except the abiding need to occupy time pleasurably, Edwina led an unusually peripatetic life. During her years of infancy a panorama of faces constantly paraded before her – friends and relatives.

friends of friends and relatives of relatives – as she was taken, overwrapped like all children of her generation, from Dorset to Wiltshire, to Hampshire, to Sussex, to Norfolk, to Yorkshire, and back to 13 Cadogan Square or 32 Bruton Street, London, or to Broadlands.

Among these faces, several developed a reassuring constancy: her nursemaid first of all, and next her grandfather, all beard and nose, and Aunt Anna Jenkins. Only these three possessed a degree of serenity that every young child finds reassuring. The nursemaid was Scottish, gentle and soft-spoken. Grandpapa Ernest's appearances were less frequent than the impression he made suggested – his deep, guttural, strangely attractive voice, and the all-pervading smell of cigars.

Other faces that marked themselves on Edwina's infant consciousness were Aunty-Grannie, herself as guttural-voiced as Grandpapa Ernest, associated with visits to her home Lilliput House (near Bournemouth) bought by Cassel for her; the Shaftesburys, Anthony and Constance at St Giles House in Dorset, and their son Anthony, a year older than Edwina; less frequently the Earl's sisters, Margaret, Evelyn, Mildred, Susan and Ethel, married to army and navy officers, barons and earls, and scattered about England and Scotland; a whole tribe of Pakenhams when they were in Ireland. Then there was another sea of faces, associated always with Grandpapa Ernest, men like Herbert Asquith, Winston Churchill and Lloyd George, who gave her affectionate if perfunctory attention, men full of talk and restlessness, their wives all big hats and never-ending cups of tea on the lawns of Cassel's racing or shooting estates near Newmarket.

And someone Edwina often confused with Grandpapa Ernest, the same big body criss-crossed with gold chains, the same heavy beard and big cigar, the same deep guttural voice speaking kindly. But Edwina, sensitive to atmosphere and the 'feel' of an occasion, was early aware of the special aura surrounding the arrival of this semi-Grandpapa, and of the people accompanying him, too: the faintly mysterious figure of Mrs Keppel; the dashingly handsome equerry Captain John Fortescue always at his side. Soon she called him Kingy.

And what of her father and mother, Wilfrid and Maudie? Neither figured much in her infancy and early childhood, a deprivation that was to have a strong part in shaping Edwina's strength and character. Her father, remote and cool, she rarely saw, and then only as an answer to some duty call, as if he were reluctantly voting for a Commons motion because the Whips decreed it. Edwina loved him, but it was an unrequited love. Wilfrid Ashley, 'a very pompous, rum fellow', as one of his acquaintances described him, did not care for children, and certainly not girls, and that was that. There were always excuses for being in Whitehall or shooting big game in Africa. Although he had loved and married a half-Jewish young woman he found Cassel company hard to bear, with its strong elements of Central Europe, harsh accents and attitudes towards money and liberal virtues which were quite alien to his own reactionary views. Wilfrid Ashley and his set (Clubs: Brooks's, Carlton) judged it to be bad form to discuss money and possessions, and held the Liberal Party to be traitorous, no less. With the decline in his wife's health, Wilfrid Ashley saw less of her, too, and was always relieved when her father took her abroad.

Maudie Ashley was not lacking in mother love. 'I remember a large children's party we went to,' recalls a contemporary of Edwina's. 'I was a child in a sailor suit. I remember Maud sitting by the fireplace. She looked beautiful, with reddish-golden hair.' She adored her first born who so closely resembled the paintings of her own mother. But Maudie was also incorrigibly sociable, seeking new friends and new diversions at a rate her frail health was unable to support. She became furious with her constitution for its inability to keep up with her demands, and treated it mercilessly. One of the few people who wrote of her during her brief life as a married woman was the Italian-born Vittoria Colonna, Princess di Teano, 'the reigning beauty of Rome' and a great favourite of King Edward VII when she was in England.

Vittoria was always welcome at Broadlands (which she loved) and the Ashleys' London house, and threw herself with relish into Maudie's social life. She was the first to record Maudie's 'keen intellect', and also her beautiful looks. Maudie was, according to her friend,

> very popular wherever she went and frankly enjoyed society, though her health was so delicate that she got terribly over tired. I think she enjoyed a good game of bridge, and now and then some poker, as much as anything, and, for those days, played rather high stakes. It was very bitter that she who had so much in life to make her happy should have been denied the one essential – good health.[1]

Maudie conceived a second child at the end of 1905. She was staying at the large house her father had given her, The Grove, Stanmore, just north of London, towards the end of July 1906, when she felt the baby coming on two months premature. 'My mother just walked up the road to her aunt's house and informed her that she was about to give birth,' Lady Delamere recounts today. It was a difficult, long-drawn-out labour, and when the baby was born on 22 July her life was despaired of. The doctor sent urgently to London for an incubator, one of the first to be used in England, and the baby's life was saved. She was christened Ruth Mary Clarice Ashley.

Wilfrid Ashley was away at the time. When he returned he was not pleased. 'My father was livid with me because after a big gap I was another girl. I was a seven-month baby who could be said to have virtually killed her mother. Add to the indignity of that, I was a girl. So I wasn't prime favourite for an Edwardian father who wanted a son to fuss over.'

Baby Mary was the favourite of servants and nursemaids for her easiness, charm and anxiety to please. Her occasional outbursts of temper were treated tolerantly by everyone in the house. 'I can remember lying on the nursery floor, screaming and banging my heels on the floor because I didn't get my way,' she remembers. Edwina, even when exasperated almost beyond bearing, did not lose her temper. She simply concealed and tucked away her resentments.

These resentments grew with the passing years and the decline in her mother's health, which kept mother and daughters more and more apart. As if in compensation, pets slipped into Edwina's life before she could walk. Edwina's store of young affection, which she held cautiously in check for the people in her life, flowed in abundance for animals and was to continue to do so all her life. At The Grove, Broadlands and St Giles, there were dogs and goats, pet lambs and donkeys. At Moulton Paddocks, his racing stables and stud farm near Newmarket, Grandpapa Ernest gave her her first pony. In London there were the cats. Until the Second World War, when the nature and frequency of her travelling made it quite impossible, Edwina was rarely without pets at her side – dogs which sprang up whenever she entered a room, cats curled up on her lap, a horse groomed and saddled up at the door whenever she called for it. Edwina and animals seemed indivisible, and later in life when on safari she would terrify her companions with her fearlessness and unguarded friendliness with wild animals.

But in Edwina's life of frequent moves, there was much unhappy parting with pets. At Broadlands, because no one in the house was interested, Edwina and Mary had to leave their pets in the charge of the land agent's family. The Everetts were of great importance in Edwina and Mary's childhood. Douglas Everett had been appointed steward to Evelyn Ashley in 1892, a post of great responsibility and one which brought with it a closer social intimacy with his employer than any of the servants. Everett married, and he and his wife Blanche had two boys, Henry and Robert, of about the same age as Edwina and Mary. They lived in a house on the estate a short distance from Broadlands. As was usual in these relationships, everything that went on at the big house was known to the land agent's family.

Robert Everett today recalls how his family acted as guardians to Edwina and Mary's pets when they were away, and how Cassel, in his anxiety to keep his granddaughters happy, would often send exotic and sometimes inconvenient additional pets. There was the Chinese cat he sent Edwina, which she had to pass on to Robert because no one would feed it in her absence.

> He also gave her a lovely Arab horse, but again there was only old Worsfold [the coachman] to look after it so it was passed on to us. Another time he gave them some golden pheasants which had to be confined to a loose box in the stables. The consequence was that Edwina and Mary loved to come to us and enjoy our animals. Susan, a ginger pig that we rode, was a great attraction – so were the ponies, dogs, goats, rabbits, dormice, not to mention the lizards, newts and jackdaws – and of course Mary's white rat which she loved.

Edwina and Mary's relationship with the Everett boys was close, affectionate and completely down-to-earth. Robert used to ride round the estate with his father most afternoons, and so knew every detail of every wood, field and stream. 'We loved to show Edwina and Mary the places we knew about,' Robert recalls. 'Nightingale Wood for primroses, Yew Tree Copse for daffodils, and cowslips by the river – birds-nesting and mushrooming. They lived a perfectly natural life but nobody took much trouble to look after them.'

During the pheasant season the shots rattled like intermittent machine-gun fire. Robert remembers:

> Wilfred Ashley was a very keen shooting man. My father arranged these enormous shoots. I remember hundreds of pheasants flying over the garden. There was a lot of poaching at that time, and terrible trouble when it was discovered that Buckingham, the head keeper, had been selling pheasants to various pubs. He is the only man I remember being sacked. We knew all the people on the estate, and what a wonderful lot they were, all individualists and real craftsmen. Mr Worsfold and Mr Thirlby the head gardener and the rest were all kind characters who must have influenced Edwina. There was also a great bond of sympathy between my mother and Edwina. Edwina would always confide in her and keep her informed about all she was doing.
>
> Whenever they were at Broadlands we either went there or they came to us at Park House. We usually used the back door at Broadlands and went in past the servants' quarters. The enormous kitchen always attracted us. Mrs Turner the housekeeper was diminutive in black with a high-neck collar and hundreds (or so it seemed) of keys attached to her waist. She usually had something good

to eat for us. Mr Davis the butler was also a great friend. The Colonel told my father that we could come and go when and where we liked, and the only thing we could not do was shoot his pheasants or catch his salmon.

My father got on well with him and ran the estate more or less as he wished. My father quite often went up to Broadlands to discuss matters during the evening when the children came downstairs. Edwina often came to these sessions and had quite a lot to say. One evening my father returned somewhat depressed as Lloyd George had just imposed a tax which Colonel Ashley thought would be the end of the large estates.

Later, Cassel asked Douglas Everett whether he would also look after the estate he had given to the Jenkins's. He agreed to take on this additional responsibility, and enjoyed going over to Wherwell Priory where he would ride round with 'the Colonel' and his daughter Marjorie, who was an outstanding rider from early childhood.

There was a lot of to-ing and fro-ing between Wherwell and Broadlands. 'Marjorie was Edwina's best friend,' Robert Everett states, 'and I remember her telling me she was going to marry her and nothing would stop her.' Edwina evidently changed her mind in due course, for Robert also remembers being visited by Mary when he was in bed with shingles. 'Mary shut the door and said she and Edwina had been talking about who they would marry. She said she had decided to marry me. So I said, "What about Edwina? Is she going to marry my brother Henry?" She said, "No, Edwina's decided to marry someone important." '

Governesses came and went. Robert Everett remembers 'a German woman who was not too popular. Then Miss Atwood who was obviously kind and liked by Edwina and Mary. But I think Miss Laura Devéria was their favourite.'

Laura Devéria found Edwina wilful and difficult but, when she felt inclined, unusually quick and intelligent. Miss Devéria found Mary easier, 'my favourite', as she frequently told her next charges. Mary adored her in return. 'She was a charming nursery governess, delightful, sweet and kind.'

There was no molly-coddling of Edwina and Mary. The regime was quite strict. They lived on the top floor, which is not much more than an attic, cold in winter, hot in summer. Food was plain. Bread and butter one day for tea, bread and jam the next. Broadlands peaches were famous and much in demand. 'They used to sell for as much as eight shillings in London,' Mary recalls. 'A fortune in those days. Needless to say, we never saw one.'

Christmas was a great occasion at Broadlands, and there were food treats, too. 'Marjorie Jenkins, Lavender and Diana Sloane Stanley and Joan and Dermot Pakenham were the most frequent visitors. Christmas Eve was great fun. Tea in the Head Room, so named for all the animal head trophies on the walls, a Christmas Tree lit up in the hall where all the house party used to assemble and watch the children enjoy themselves. We played Brandy Snap.' This was an elaborate and messy game requiring great skill, with sixpenny pieces as a reward. 'I remember Edwina being *covered* in flour!'

In the summer of 1908, when Edwina was six, her travelling became wider. Grandpapa Ernest took her for the first time to his Swiss house. Cassel's love of Switzerland had easily survived that long-ago accident; he returned year after year to the clean thin air and the mountains, and he bought a house on the Riederfurka high above the Aletsch Glacier and south of the Jungfrau in the most spectacular part of the Alps. As soon as they neared this eyrie, which was accessible only by a rough track on foot or on mule-back, Edwina could see her grandfather relax and forget the professional pressures and even some of the domestic sadness and worry about the health of her mother. Cassel climbed well for a stout man in his mid-fifties, and conquered the Finsteraarhorn, while Edwina played for hours with his great mountain dog which lived with the village priest for the rest of the year.

Maudie's health improved on the Riederfurka. She coughed less and seemed in better strength and spirits. For Edwina it was all a marvellous adventure; for Grandpapa and the rest of the family sometimes too much of an adventure when she would wander off for hours on her own, until the law had to be laid down firmly about never venturing any distance without an adult escort.

Every summer Classiebawn became their home for the month of August. The first Lord Palmerston had inherited this estate of some 10,000 acres in County Sligo on the west coast of Ireland, and in the early years of the nineteenth century had taken steps to improve it and the dreadful conditions of his tenants. He built a school and roads, renovated the parish church and created the little harbour from which Lord Mountbatten sailed to his violent end in 1979. The 'castle', high on a headland, might have been built as a direct provocation to the republican movement by an absentee landlord, a symbol of English occupation. It was not intended to be. On the contrary, Palmerston was deeply concerned to improve Anglo-Irish relations. But this monument to an outdated regime, all mock-Gothic turrets, castellations and windows, is also a hideous blot on the wild and beautiful Atlantic shoreline.

During Edwina's childhood, the Ashley invasion of County Sligo began towards the end of July when housekeeper, maids, the kitchen staff, butler, governesses and nannies, a doctor and nurse for Maudie, all moved in. There was fishing, shooting, brisk walks and cool bathing, games and recreations of all kinds on the private beach, and endless bicycling for Edwina and Marjorie.

There were other, more exotic trips with Grandpapa. To Ernest Cassel a cruise always meant chartering his own ship, and that is how the family cruised early one summer up the Norwegian coast to North Cape and thence to Spitzbergen in the midnight sun. There was another, longer cruise up the Nile to the Assouan dam, which Cassel had financed, and then back through Palestine.

When Edwina was eight, breathtakingly sweet with her perfect rose-tinted complexion, light brown locks over her shoulders, Cassel took her in his private railway carriage to Biarritz to stay with the King. This was a repeat of a holiday in 1907 with her mother as well as her grandfather. Then there had been long games of croquet with Winston Churchill, Mrs George Keppel and the King, which the King always had to win. Edwina had been only five and remembered little of the people or places.

This second holiday for Edwina was to be the King's last visit to his favourite resort. He was already in poor health, catching a severe chill *en route* in Paris, and almost constantly wheezing and coughing, but bright and interested in everything in between. There was a steady flow of visitors to the Hôtel du Palais where the King stayed with Mrs Keppel, his secretary and equerries, and – in a separate suite – Cassel and his party, including Edwina. By 21 March the King insisted on going out, though the weather remained appalling. He chatted and played with Edwina, dressed in white muslin and lace, on the lawn in a rare spell of sunshine, and the two ageing, bearded, fat old friends, respectively the richest and most powerful men in the world, smiled at the camera and joked with the little girl before she went off to play with the dog – 'I am Caesar, the King's dog' inscribed on his collar. But there was no risk of his getting lost when he was with Edwina. Soon the King was taken indoors again in a wheelchair.

On 25 April Edwina watched the most elaborate fireworks display she had ever seen. Biarritz was saying good-bye – in the event, for the last time – to King Edward, who had been their winter friend for so many years. From her hotel bedroom she looked out at the marching soldiers and sailors and heard the town band playing far into the night. The year was 1910, and this royal accolade and grand ceremonial was the first of many she was to participate in or witness over the next half century.

* * *

There was something else of which Edwina was all too conscious in this year of epochal change, when English parliamentary government was to be put to the challenge by Herbert Asquith and his Liberals struggling towards a welfare state; naval competition with Germany was to take the Empire closer to war with Germany; and the republicans in Ireland were to bring the country to the brink of civil war. Death had been in the damp air of Biarritz, and Edwina felt it, too, at Broadlands when Grandpapa brought her home and she went to visit her mother, who had never really recovered from the shock of Mary's premature birth. For both Maud Ashley and the King were dying, and Grandpapa was distraught with anxiety and grief. For Edwina this meant sadness and change. For Cassel it meant the end of his world.

News of the King, when Cassel reached London, was desperate. Bronchitis once again held him in its grip, and this time it was to be fatal. On the morning of 6 May 1910 Cassel sat alone amongst the marble and statues and old masters of Brook House. He was waiting to see his old friend at 11 o'clock. Shortly before he was to leave for Buckingham Palace a message arrived to tell him that, with regret, the visit was cancelled. For a short time Cassel thought he would never again see his sovereign who had done so much for him, and for whom he had done so much. Then came a second message, summoning him urgently to the Palace.

Cassel saw first the King's physician, Sir Francis Laking, then Queen Alexandra, who had hurried back from Corfu. 'Please try to stop him from talking too much,' the Queen begged. 'And don't stay too long.'

In spite of his weak condition, the King had insisted on getting out of bed and dressing for his old friend. He was sitting in his chair, fully dressed, Caesar beside him, and he dragged himself to his feet when Cassel entered. Cassel noted the oxygen cylinder nearby, and the pain and difficulty with which the King spoke.

Some years were to pass before Cassel told Edwina about this last visit before the King died late that evening. To Maudie he immediately wrote this letter:

Brook House,
Park Lane,
6/5/10

Own and dearest,

At 11 o'clock this morning Davidson called me to the telephone to say that the King was too unwell to receive me. Half an hour later there was a message from Lord Knollys that I should come up to the Palace at once. Laking saw me

> first and asked me to let the King speak as little as possible. Then I was taken up to the Queen first who enquired most fully after you, and also exhorted me to stay a few moments. Then came Princess Victoria with the same enquiry about you. Forgot to mention that on the stairs I met the Prince of Wales who asked me to go into details about your illness and the return journey. I had to be short, but you see from all this that the Royal Family take a great interest in your progress.
>
> At last I was asked to go into the King's room, but then evidently the order came out that an Equerry was to bring me and it took some doing to find me. Finally, I was ushered in and found the King dressed as usual, in his sitting room, rising from his chair to shake hands with me. He looked as if he had suffered great pain, and spoke indistinctly. His kindly smile came out as he congratulated me on having you brought home so much improved in health. He said, 'I am very seedy, but I wanted to see you. Tell your daughter how glad I am that she has safely got home and I hope she will be careful and patient so as to recover complete health.' He then talked about other matters and I had to ask his leave to go, as I felt it was not good for him to go on speaking....

Cassel's life, once so full and eventful, was shrinking under the chill touch of death. He had little interest in the new King. Their style and interests were incompatible and Cassel withdrew from royal circles of his own accord, concentrating his time and resources on preserving for as long as possible the life of his daughter.

But the improvement was brief. Maudie Ashley spent the last months of her life at Broadlands, an unfavourable place for a consumptive. Celia Fiennes had written correctly of 'its no very good aire'. But Broadlands was Maudie's favourite place, and she longed for the murmur of the Test, the Hampshire sky, the trees and the gardens. 'My father supervised the construction of a chalet in the garden near the orangery,' Robert Everett recalls, 'where she could be treated in the open air. All her milk was pasteurized and the nondescript herd of cattle was disposed of and a new herd of Friesians was imported.'

Cassel called in every specialist, who tried every known cure, and like some disciple desperate to placate the wrath of the gods, showered her with gifts of furs and jewels and even great sums of money. The Princess di Teano visited her several times during these last months, deeply moved by what she saw.

> Maudie, with her unfailing sense of humour, would show me feebly her father's gifts. 'And all I need now are a few nightgowns,' she would murmur. He even gave her a valuable Pekinese, Fo, who rather bored her, and who – according

> to her own account – disliked her so much that he had to be chained to the bedpost during Papa's visit, not to hurt his feelings.[2]

Later, Fo became inseparable from Cassel, following him everywhere, sitting in front of him at his desk as he wrote, a constant reminder of Maudie, whom Cassel thought had been devoted to the animal.

In a last desperate effort to preserve her life Cassel took Maudie away to Egypt again, where on her previous visit she seemed to benefit from the warm, dry air. To insulate her from any disturbance he also engaged the floors above and below their own suites in the hotel. When they steamed along the length of the Mediterranean in their chartered liner, she seemed a little better.

All through that last winter of 1910–11 Wilfrid Ashley made frequent visits to his wife from London, often bringing the two girls at Maudie's request. She died at last in the winter of 1911. This second blow was almost too much for Cassel, who never fully recovered his spirits and old zest.

For Edwina the blow appeared to be less severe. In her calm, seemingly cool way she gave the appearance of someone who had long since anticipated the state of motherlessness; and it seemed so long since she had been able to draw anything but an enfeebled affection from the dying woman, that the loss might not be so severely felt. But the fact that she never spoke of this time and never referred to her mother's fatal illness even to her younger sister suggests only too clearly the damage she sustained from this loss. 'Edwina was being forced to grow up too fast,' said one of her contemporaries. 'She appeared tightly buttoned up and only became a young girl when she was with her cousin Marjorie or her dog or pony.'

Even to her sister Edwina appeared almost as a grown-up. Lady Delamere recalls:

> I looked on her as a mother, and I worshipped the ground she trod on. She would look after me and comfort me and be firm when I had my tantrums. I loved her as a child and I loved her all her life. During holidays she would write out a prayer from her prayer book for me every night. I have them still and can remember them, like 'Jesu tender shepherd hear me/bless thou little lamb tonight/through the darkness be thou near me/keep me safe till morning light....' And then it would end 'For Mary from Edwina' and the date. If Edwina was away for a few days when she came home she would say, 'Darling – did you say the little prayer?'

The love between the sisters was deepened by the death of their mother but Edwina remained very much the elder sister who lived on a different plane, with different friends and activities, showing briskness as well as tenderness towards Mary. Lady Delamere tells of summer holidays in the country, herself playing her own private games, and Edwina and her cousin Marjorie 'bicycling about all over the place. When they came back they would leave their bicycles at the front door – strictly forbidden – and Edwina would call out, "Maria – put those away!"'

Edwina was eleven and staying with Aunty-Grannie at Lilliput House when she met for the first time a woman who was later to play an important role in her life and provide a steadying influence in some of the more difficult years that lay ahead. Stella Underhill was a sensible, intelligent, reliable and well-organized woman of forty-two, one of nine children. Her father was the founder of Oxford High School and Stella had been taught logic there by Charles Dodgson ('Lewis Carroll'). Like all her sisters she was a proper young bluestocking. Stella became a schoolmistress and then governess-tutor to the Orr Ewing family. In 1913 Cassel had felt the need for a social secretary and had learned through mutual friends that Stella might suit him. She went for an interview at Brook House and afterwards was asked to go and see his sister down at Bournemouth, Cassel having complete faith in her judgement in these matters.

'I therefore went down to Bournemouth,' wrote Stella Underhill, 'and stayed the night at the Branksome Towers Hotel where Mrs Cassel had engaged a room for me. I arrived in the afternoon at Lilliput House and had a talk with Mrs Cassel and then tea, at which the two great-nieces, Edwina and Mary Ashley were present.' Some years passed before Edwina met her again.

Edwina's lessons continued as before. She showed great enthusiasm for geography. Maps fascinated her, talk of distant lands gripped her attention, and she would read travel books voraciously. Even before she was in her teens she was longing to break loose and get out into the world, roaming freely at her own whim. She was on holiday at Broadstairs in the summer of 1914 when the first rumours of war began crossing the Channel in which she and Mary paddled or swam every day. Their father took fright and brought them back to London and then sent them on to Aunty-Grannie at Bournemouth. The most miserable years in Edwina's life were about to begin.

For a long time Cassel had been using all his influence to prevent war breaking out between the country of his birth and his adopted Britain. He had many friends at the highest level in financial circles in Germany, including the powerful Albert Ballin, who was almost as close to the Kaiser as Cassel had been to Edward VII. With the King's death, Cassel temporarily retired from the informal diplomatic-financial negotiations he had been carrying on. With the arrival of Cassel's friend (and bridge partner), Winston Churchill, at the Admiralty in 1911, he was asked by the new First Lord to proceed to Germany for unofficial conversations about a reduction in the pace of naval shipbuilding, which was becoming out of hand and must eventually lead to war. Cassel achieved considerable success for a while, but everything broke down with the Kaiser's determination to negotiate further only when he was assured that the *Entente Cordiale* would be broken up.

Even when the Austrian–Serbian crisis reached its peak towards the end of July 1914, Cassel could not believe that Europe would commit the folly of war. His contacts in Germany confirmed his hopes. On the evening before he was due to make his annual pilgrimage to Switzerland he was playing bridge at Brook House, partnering Winston Churchill. Churchill did not share his host's optimism. Cassel departed the next day none the less, and regretted his rare misjudgement when, with the declaration of war, he was obliged to make his way home again. The journey took the best part of two days, and there was not a seat on the train for the multi-millionaire the whole way.

An uncomfortable journey was nothing compared with the ordeal he was soon to face at home. Amid the anti-German hysteria which seized Britain during the winter of 1914–15, when shops with German names and dachshunds alike were stoned and anyone born in Germany publicly vilified, Cassel became a target of the Anti-German League which was blind to the enormous patriotic contributions and charitable bequests of the financier over the past twenty-five years.

Aghast at this persecution, Cassel wrote a letter to *The Times* in an effort to defend himself.

> Nearly half a century of my life has been spent in England and all my interests – family, business and social – are centred here. All my male relatives of military age are serving with the King's forces. My unfailing loyalty and devotion to this country have never varied or been questioned, and while affirming this I desire also to express my deep sense of horror at the manner in which the war is being conducted by the German government.

The cause of prejudice and bigotry could not be halted by a single protest in print. There was a strong measure of anti-semitism behind the campaign, too, which led to the League entering a process in the High Court of Justice calling on Sir Ernest 'to show why he should not be removed from his membership of the Privy Council'. The ordeal lasted for months with counsel arguing legal niceties, and it was not until

December 1915 that the Lord Chief Justice announced the court's decision that the relators' contentions had failed. By this time Cassel had retired into his marble shell on Park Lane and was rarely seen in public. He would sometimes speak to his family of the one-time friends who had been glad to accept his hospitality and his racing tips in the old days and who now openly treated him as a pariah. His family remained his only comfort, and most of all his two granddaughters, who loved him in return. 'I had a great affinity with him,' Lady Delamere remembers. 'He filled a great gap in my life. I wasn't frightened of him at all. I think a lot of people round him were frightened of him but I never was. Gale, his valet, was permitted great liberties but even he became frightened if things went wrong. You didn't trifle with Sir Ernest, I can tell you!'

Shortly after Maudie's death, Wilfrid Ashley began seeing more frequently an old friend, the Hon. Muriel 'Molly' Forbes-Sempill, the daughter of a Herefordshire countryman, Walter Spencer. She had married into the Sempill family of Chippenham in Wiltshire, which had roots almost as deep and as obscure as the Shaftesburys. At the age of thirty-three, she had divorced her husband, Commander the Hon. Arthur Lionel Ochoncar Forbes-Sempill RN, whom she had married in Sydney, Australia, in 1903. The infidelities on both sides had been numerous. The prospect of Broadlands and Classiebawn with their accompanying land wealth was irresistible and she accepted Wilfrid's proposal, no doubt with great alacrity. When the decree absolute was granted they were married on 28 August 1914 at the Savoy Chapel in London.

All that Edwina had read in books of fairy tales about wicked stepmothers appeared to be manifest in this ambitious, handsome, busy, unfeeling woman, and the conflict was 'awful to witness' to those who were present. A friend of Edwina described her stepmother as 'most unkind. She was a great pusher, politically and socially.' When Mountbatten later met her, he described her as 'a wicked woman, a real bitch'.

Incompatibility between stepmother and stepdaughters was complete and final. Edwina studiously avoided her at Broadlands and sought solace, as always, in the pets at the Everetts. Life became intolerable for everyone except Wilfrid and Molly. The worst thing the new Mrs Ashley did was to send away Laura Devéria, which had a catastrophic effect on Mary, now eight years old. 'It was a terrible blow,' Lady Delamere recounts today with tears in her eyes. 'I adored her. But when my stepmother arrived she saw this very good-looking and charming governess who possibly might take some of the attention from herself, and sacked her. That really upset me very much. At that time I hated my stepmother and continued to hate her at intervals afterwards.'

Miss Devéria was replaced by a governess, carefully chosen by Molly Ashley. 'Her name was Miss Slater, a prim Victorian lady, very tall and dressed entirely in black,' a subsequent charge described her. Edwina hated her.

Except, one presumes, for Wilfrid Ashley, no one loved Molly. Robert Everett remembers the last visit to Broadlands of Harry, the son of Evelyn Ashley's second wife, Lady Alice. Harry was devoted to Edwina and might well have married her. But he was badly wounded in the war and confined to a wheelchair. On one occasion he managed to push himself along to the Dutch garden. 'A wheel slipped and cut the edge of the turf. This made Molly Ashley lose her temper, and she ordered him off. I don't think he came back to Broadlands after that. Anyway, he was desperately ill and died shortly after.'

Douglas Everett, all-perceptive and all-knowledgeable about Broadlands affairs, scented trouble the first time he set eyes on Molly. Cassel's attendance at the wedding was unexpected. Robert recounts that he

> always felt that he gave his blessing because he thought it would be easier to get Edwina to live with him in the future. On one occasion Molly took my mother round the garden accompanied by Mr Thirlby. Molly asked for a peach and he picked a very poor specimen, and then presented my mother with a perfect peach. Molly was not pleased. This attitude of any employee was quite typical.

As a future distinguished gynaecologist, Robert Everett was fascinated to learn that a doctor one day visited Broadlands 'to try to artificially inseminate Molly, with Wilfrid Ashley as donor'. But this last, desperate effort to have a male heir, who would eventually inherit Broadlands, Classiebawn and much else, failed – to the benefit of the future Mountbattens.

War had been raging for more than a year. Molly, 'doing her bit', began to fill Broadlands with convalescent Army officers. Wilfrid had left for the Western Front with his battalion of the King's Liverpool Regiment. It was Anna Jenkins who came to Edwina and Mary's rescue. She recognized their plight and misery and suggested that they should go away to school in the autumn of 1916. With considerable relief, Molly Ashley agreed. A school was carefully selected, The Links School, Eastbourne, Sussex, which was very exclusive and had been started by Princess Alice's ex-governess, Jane Potts.

At first all went well, and Edwina was writing to Mrs Everett at Broadlands to say how much they both enjoyed it. But Edwina's welcome by the girls was in fact a mixed one. They all knew that this was her first boarding-school, that she was joint heiress with her sister to a great fortune, that her grandfather was a German-born Jew and was being publicly vilified for this misfortune. Mary, aged ten, was young enough to avoid Edwina's difficulties.

The money problem, which was to haunt Edwina all her life, became strongly evident here for the first time. Whatever she said about her prospective money and her home lifestyle could be, and usually was, maliciously misinterpreted. 'It was sheer hell,' Edwina recounted later. 'They all thought I ought to fill the offertory plate with sovereigns on Sundays. But if I gave too much they thought I was showing off, and if I gave the ordinary amount they said I was being mean. In fact I had no more pocket money than the rest of them and a good deal less than some. I was always kept on a very tight string.' 'No, she didn't like The Links at all,' Mary remembers, 'though I did. I was blissfully happy. Edwina was very mature in her teens, and her sights were fixed on anything but school.'

Edwina came to hate the heartiness and the strict routine, the early morning cold showers, the games on muddy fields exposed to the fury of the wind whipping off the Channel, the food which became increasingly sparse and austere as the war continued. Her letters to Grandpapa became unashamedly piteous. 'Please take me away, dear Grandpapa, if you love me at all.' It was a delicate situation for Cassel, who had no formal responsibility for Edwina and disliked what he had seen of Molly Ashley as much as Edwina had. He put the problem to his sister and his niece, who worked on it, eventually with favourable results. Edwina and Mary were taken away from The Links, Mary continuing her education at Heathfield.

As one of her contemporaries put it, 'For poor Edwina, when she left school it was out of the frying pan into the fire.' The kitchen analogy is appropriate. For her stepmother had decided that, if Edwina was ineducable, she could at least be taught how to run a house and kitchen, and become a polished hostess. It was December 1918, the Great War had been over for barely a month, and many mothers felt uneasy about sending their daughters to the fashionable finishing schools on the Continent. This provided an incentive to send them to institutions like Alde House, Aldeburgh, on the draughty east coast of Suffolk.

Alde House had been established for some years as a small senior wing to Belstead Girls' School, owned and run by Mrs Hervey, a stately widow.

Alde House was dedicated to turning young ladies into efficient housekeepers as well as teaching them comportment, etiquette and nice manners. It was not expected that any of the pupils, when married, would seriously engage themselves in the laundry room, make and mend dresses, or cook and wash up at the sink. But it was thought suitable that they should know how to in order to supervise their staff when they were married.

A pupil, Peggie Scott-Elliot, *née* DuBuisson, recalls that this domestic wing was run by Miss Agnes Higham who

> was very strict but quite fair, and we had become accustomed to discipline at our boarding-schools. We liked Edwina very much. We shared dormitories between two or three of us, and there were about twenty of us in all at any one time. Alde House had a nice sitting room. But it was rather cold when we got up at 7.30 in the morning in winter.

The course, which lasted a year, was divided into four subjects, and the girls did sequences of one week of each - cooking, laundry, dressmaking and housework. 'We worked in the mornings and played games with the main school in the afternoons, and we had concerts and plays. And we could get out into the town sometimes so we didn't feel too confined. For lacrosse we wore gym tunics with a braid belt round our hips, tied with a knot at the side.'

Mrs Scott-Elliot also remembers their working dress of long green overalls and white mob caps. 'They were quite becoming and they made us all look the same.'

Edwina arrived at Alde House in January 1919, at the same time as Peggie DuBuisson and Syssyllt Franklin, who became her two closest friends. 'We were all slightly miffed at having to go back to school.' They knew that her grandfather was a millionaire but that really didn't make any difference at that time, her fellow pupils felt. 'She was quite unassuming and never flaunted her background. She wasn't exactly shy but withdrawn and unobtrusive. She was very quiet but friendly.'

During her adult life Edwina was known as a fast-mover, always in a hurry. It is, perhaps, a reflection of her state of mind at this time that she is remembered as being 'a non-rusher'. 'I don't think she much liked games, wasn't very good and didn't move very quickly.' Another pupil and friend, Eileen Douglas-Pennant, recalls, 'I often had to do Edwina's jobs for her as she "hadn't a clue"!' Nevertheless, when she decided that she wanted to get into the first tennis team, which should have been beyond her ability, she saw to it that she did so. 'Typical Edwina!' as one of her contemporaries remarked.

At a time when food in the country was still scarce, and at girls' boarding-schools was never varied or appetizing, Edwina is also remembered for her hampers. 'A doting grandfather,' Peggie Scott-Elliot recalls, 'used to send her hampers of delicacies, which led to us being taught how to pluck and draw pheasants and gut and skin rabbits. I can remember the two of us standing over the kitchen sink struggling with the latter.'

Edwina left Alde House in July 1919. She had not completed the full duration of the course. In adult life she agreed that Alde House had given her a rudimentary knowledge of cooking at a time when women got married without being able to boil an egg, and of some of the art of being a hostess which might otherwise have taken her longer to learn at home. Above all, she now knew what life must be like 'downstairs', and always in the future, wherever she lived, regularly checked on the working conditions of the servants.

After the austerities and confinement of the kitchen, Edwina felt the need to spread her wings. She told Grandpapa that she would like to travel. Cassel suggested that she should go to Italy and view the galleries and the architecture. Molly Ashley agreed, and with the war only recently over, Edwina took the train from Victoria with Marjorie and a chaperone at her elbow and an assortment of leather cases in the van, for Florence and Rome, Venice and Siena. In every city, the authorities, the diplomatic and consular staff, and influential friends were alerted. The result was that this seventeen-year-old, beautiful, fair-complexioned and coolly sophisticated English girl was given the best guides and protection, and was suitably entertained in the evenings. This was the treatment to which Edwina became accustomed, and even expected, on her travels all her life. But it was the first and last time that she travelled under such stiff and formal conditions with the arts as her main preoccupation. It was a tame and unexciting business in her eyes, which were already set on more distant and exotic places. Travel to Edwina spelt adventure, and there was none of it on this minor Grand Tour.

Edwina's quick mind and retentive memory derived a good deal of benefit from this Italian trip. But the arts in isolation never meant a great deal to her. She loved to be surrounded by beautiful and especially by beautiful *valuable* objects. But the Romneys and other old masters at Broadlands she saw as part of the general tone and proprietorial quality of the place, and not in isolation. She thought the paintings in the Accademia in Venice were marvellous in themselves, and the whole city breathtakingly beautiful. But she felt no personal or emotional attachment to the place, felt no urge to remain for more than a day or two before striking out for the next destination.

A friend once explained that Edwina derived her aesthetic satisfaction from discovery mixed with danger and adventure. 'Edwina was never happier than when digging up some old carving on a remote and beautiful archaeological site miles from anywhere. Ideally food should be running short, the natives unfriendly and the light aircraft she had borrowed difficult to start. Oh yes, and she has just befriended a brown hyena cub.'

There was no more excitement for Edwina when she returned to Broadlands, only a cool welcome and a look of 'whatever-are-we-going-to-do-with-you-now?' in the eyes of her father (working his way back into politics and Parliament) and stepmother, who was working full time on the restoration and improvement of Broadlands, which had become an obsession with her. Rebellion was near the surface. Edwina knew that she could not tolerate the restrictions which would be imposed on her at home or the censorious attitude of Molly Ashley.

She did not at once learn that her grandfather, like some ageing gallant knight, had already taken steps to rescue his princess and fulfil his long-felt wish. He had divined how unhappy and intolerable her own home would be on her return and had approached the Ashleys with the proposition that Edwina should come to live in Brook House as his hostess. With the end of the war he was beginning to return to his former lifestyle with dinner parties and other forms of entertainment. It would be invaluable experience for her. She would meet the great people of the land and learn how to please them. The experience would polish her socially (though that was scarcely necessary), and on her own engagements outside she would be chaperoned everywhere. She would not be permitted to wear make-up (that was unnecessary, too, with her fine complexion), and would have to live on an allowance of £300 a year, buying all her own clothes.

Robert Everett recalls Edwina, a young woman now, inviting him to her bedroom at Broadlands. 'She showed me a photo of her grandfather and said he had asked her to go and live at Brook House, and she thought Daddy would agree.' Wilfrid and Molly Ashley did indeed tell Cassel that, as far as they were concerned, it was a satisfactory arrangement, but Edwina herself must decide. Edwina did so, with lightning speed and firm decisiveness. Saying good-bye to all her pets and the horses, and taking with her only her dog, Edwina was escorted to London by her parents and, in short time, and with minimum fuss and demonstrations of affection, deposited at Brook House.

* * *

One of the first people Edwina met at Brook House was Stella Underhill, who had now been working for Cassel for six years. 'At first I was afraid of Sir Ernest,' Miss Underhill later recalled. 'I was so anxious not to make mistakes over my work, but after a short time I was able to overcome this.'

Miss Underhill found very few people incompatible, and she not only managed to get onto comfortable terms with this seventeen-year-old girl and work in harness with her, but clearly came to love and admire her, and also to be sorry for her.

> I think Sir Ernest hoped she would be a companion for him, but the difference in age was too great for any real companionship. I remember that middle-aged or quite old people were invited to these dinner parties which I thought made it very dull for Edwina though I daresay it was good experience for her. She used to come to my office to look at the dinner table plan and to see who she was to take in, and often asked me if I could give her another partner but of course I could not do this.

Later Edwina was given charge of the table plan and was able to arrange placings to suit herself, although sometimes no alternative was very attractive.

Miss Underhill had been warned by her previous employer that she would not be treated as one of the family in Cassel's house. Edwina was quick to discover, as Miss Underhill had discovered years before her, that Cassel showed no interest in his staff beyond their work for him, although he could be kind to those with family anxieties or sadnesses.

When Miss Underhill had begun work, with the house to run and the staff to supervise besides her social duties, there had been a valet, a butler with four footmen and an oddman under him, a housekeeper, her niece and six housemaids, the chef with five assistants in the kitchens, three chauffeurs, a house electrician and an odd-job man. The footmen always went into knee breeches and had powdered hair from 1 May until the end of July. These numbers had been somewhat reduced in the middle of the war, and there was rather less formality. Miss Underhill had also been responsible for the book-keeping, the paying of wages and the liaison with Cassel's office in nearby Green Street, which every day sent over a secretary for the more mundane task of taking down the letters.

During the war years social life at Brook House was very much reduced, but with the coming of peace Cassel intended to regain his old reputation for gregariousness. For this reason, Edwina's arrival was convenient all round, allowing Stella to pass over the entertaining to Edwina. Cassel's engagements were Edwina's first responsibility, and especially dinner parties. Dinner was served sharp at 8.30; Miss Underhill's duties had ended at this time and she would have dinner on her own in her office. Edwina's social duties, by contrast, began at 8.30 when she took her seat at the end of the table facing Cassel. The menu before her, the flowers on the table and, in the old lavish Brook House style, flowers all over the house as well, had all been Edwina's responsibility.

There now began a brief, curious, demanding and exciting period in Edwina's life when, with only the sketchiest of training, she took over the task of social secretary and of helping to run, with Stella Underhill, this enormous establishment. It was a severe test of her organizational powers, and entailed creating good relations with the servants - something which came to her easily - as well as the guests. There were several aspects of the job that came as a surprise to Edwina. Her grandfather was a stickler for punctuality. 'A minute late was too late.' And, although she had seen some evidence of this before, Edwina had not realized how unusually careful Grandpapa was about money. He had always spent lavishly, even extravagantly, on big things, and had proved his generosity time and again; but he practised economy in small ways, kept his sharp eyes open for discrepancies, and - for example - found it painful to tip at all, let alone adequately. The story has been told:

> On one occasion there were partridges for dinner, and after the meal one was left over. Next day Cassel sent for the butler and asked what had become of the partridge. The butler, knowing his employer's idiosyncrasies, was able to produce the bird. Edwina, young as she was, was a match for her grandfather, and when her eyes became diamond cold and her mouth obstinate, he rejoiced inwardly. . . .[3]

The small economies, some would call them petty meannesses, paraded as a virtue by Cassel, had a life-long influence on Edwina, and etched their mark on her later conduct and character. Some people thought her paltry tips, her eye for a bargain, funny, lovable or idiosyncratic. Others who witnessed this sharpness found it distasteful. It was all in the eye of the beholder. In any case, the impression was fleeting, and was swiftly swept aside by her vivacity and wit.

By this move to Brook House Edwina had not by any means gained her full freedom; she had gained only freedom from her father's coldness and her stepmother's antagonism and unkindness. Cassel gave her affection and guidance, but it was at first a severely regimented and restricted life for her. Both he and his sister were over-assiduous in their guardianship, examining her post, prohibiting any meetings outside the house without a chaperone. Brook House assumed the proportions of a castle from which golddigging suitors were driven off by the formidable defenders.

The same was true abroad. Cassel rented a luxury villa behind Nice for the winter of 1920–21. He had been suffering from heart trouble and his doctors advised him to leave the country during the cold weather. An ex-officer, Charles Baring, who had been seriously wounded in the war, was staying with friends nearby recovering in the sun of December 1920. He had met Edwina once before with her father, and Wilfrid Ashley had suggested that he should look her up, 'if you can get past the barriers'. He found the barriers formidable. Baring (now Sir Charles Baring, Bt) recalls:

> It was almost like a fortress, but Cassel regarded me as a 'safe' person, an 'also-ran' as a suitor in the racing parlance he enjoyed. She, I think, considered me as someone to whom she could talk without tiresome protestations of eternal love. Well, she did that. She was not on her guard with me, and I would often go round in the evenings and have a drink, and she talked very openly to me about life, and what she wanted from it. She knew nothing at that time, but she did know that she was going to play some significant part in the world. She really had a great sense of destiny but didn't know what it was.
>
> I did not find her at all happy though she loved her grandfather, and of course he adored her. She felt the restrictions badly. I remember saying to cheer her up, 'Soon you'll make a brilliant marriage, Edwina. You'll marry into the Royal Family or something like that.' 'Oh no – nonsense, nothing like that,' she replied.
>
> But I knew that Cassel had fixed his target for her at a very high level.

We have a clear picture of Edwina at this time, 1919–21, from those who knew her well and observed the unusual role she was playing. She was not yet twenty years old, utterly uncaring for her appearance, seemingly unconfident but with a half-hidden steely resolve that was missed on first acquaintance, the years of unhappiness and insecurity masking the real quality of her beauty. 'At that time she didn't know how to dress herself or anything of that sort,' one of her contemporaries remarked. 'Not at all *soignée* as I clearly remember. The fact that she had no mother to guide her was evident.'

Even her vivacity was subdued, by contrast with what it was to become; but not her intelligence. 'Her conversation was clever and she spoke quickly, often in the form of questions. She had this enormous curiosity about life and the world. And you could see she had this determination to succeed.'

Above left: Edwina's mother, Maud, only child of Sir Ernest Cassel, at the time of her marriage to Wilfrid Ashley, 9 January 1901

Above right: Edwina's father, Colonel Wilfrid William Ashley, grandson of the seventh Earl of Shaftesbury

Left: Edwina and her younger sister, Mary, photographed at Broadlands shortly before their mother's death

Above: Sargent's portrait of Edwina at the age of ten

Right: Edwina and Mary (mounted) at Broadlands, April 1910, with Robert Everett's younger brother Jack and the coachman, Worsfold

Below: Edwina and Mary's first school, The Links, Eastbourne

Edwina (standing left, aged sixteen) with members of the 1st Tennis Team at The Links, summer 1918. Also standing: Syssylt Franklin; sitting (l to r): Diana Sloane Stanley, Kathleen Cooper Abbs, Gwendoline Tritton; Esmé Whittall is on the rug.

Wilfrid Ashley with his younger daughter, Mary, at Broadlands

Sir Ernest Cassel's sister, Wilhelmina ('Minna' or 'Aunty-Grannie'), at Branksome

As eighteen-year-old hostess for her grandfather at Six Mile Bottom, *The Tatler*, 13 October 1920. In the party are Sir Ernest Cassel (extreme right), the Prince Albert (third from left) and Prince Henry (fifth from right).

Above: In India, February 1922, as a guest of the Viceroy, shortly before her engagement

Left: Admiral Prince Louis of Battenberg, now 1st Marquis of Milford Haven, with his two sons, Lord Louis Mountbatten (left) and Lord George

Edwina and Dickie engaged: an informal study

THE SKETCH

Registered as a Newspaper for Transmission in the United Kingdom and to Canada and Newfoundland by Magazine Post

No. 1538 — Vol. CXIX. WEDNESDAY, JULY 19, 1922. ONE SHILLING.

THE ROYAL BRIDEGROOM AND HIS BRIDE: LORD LOUIS MOUNTBATTEN AND MISS EDWINA ASHLEY.

The marriage of Lord Louis Mountbatten and Miss Edwina Ashley is the event which marks the close of this wonderful London season, which opened with the marriage of Princess Mary and Viscount Lascelles. Lord Louis, the handsome sailor brother of the Marquess of Milford Haven, is a cousin of the Royal Family, and Miss Edwina Ashley, his charming young bride, is one of the greatest heiresses in the country, as well as being a popular member of the younger set in London Society. The ceremony was fixed to take place yesterday, July 19, at St. Margaret's, Westminster, followed by a reception at Brook House. Photographs of the bridesmaids and coloured portraits of bride and bridegroom will be found in another part of this issue of "The Sketch." — *(Photograph by Keturah Collings and Humphrey Joel.)*

The royal wedding number of *The Sketch* celebrating the Mountbatten marriage

The ceremony in St Margaret's, Westminster, 18 July 1922. The best man, the Prince of Wales, stands at one side; George v is just discernible on the extreme right

With the sun beginning to break through, the newly married Mountbattens leave St Margaret's to the cheers of a vast crowd

THE WEDDING GROUP

Taken after the ceremony at St. Margaret's last Tuesday. The bridesmaids were: Miss Mary Ashley (the bride's only sister), Princess Margaret, Princess Theodora, Princess Cecile, and Princess Sophie (daughters of Prince and Princess Andrew of Greece and nieces of the bridegroom), Lady Mary Ashley-Cooper (eldest daughter of the Earl and Countess of Shaftesbury), and Miss Esther Pakenham (daughter of Captain Hercules and Mrs. Pakenham, first cousin of the bride)

LADY MARY CAMBRIDGE AND LADY HELENA GIBBS

PRINCESS MARY, THE PRINCE OF WALES, AND THE DUKE OF YORK

LADY BONHAM-CARTER AND MR. ASQUITH

globe of the world with the tracks of the Australian and Indian tours marked on it—as the bridegroom was on H.R.H.'s staff throughout both of them. The officers of "Renown" also gave a present that was entirely appropriate—a silver salver engraved with all their signatures. The first part of the honeymoon is being spent at Broadlands, Colonel Wilfrid Ashley's house at Romsey, and after that Lord and Lady Louis Mountbatten go on a motor tour through Spain and Central Europe.

The formal wedding photograph, and others, from *The Tatler*

Above: Greeting America for the first time from the deck of the *Majestic*
Right and below: USA honeymoon, 1922: Dickie shows off his fishing skill; Edwina her acting skill in a movie shot at the Fairbanks' home, with Charlie Chaplin directing

If Edwina was waif-like in 1920, she was a very lively waif; and she already possessed the charm which later became quite irresistible, as thousands of people were to attest. At Brook House dinner parties mothers with shrewd eyes watched her performance at the head of the table with admiration – enchanting a middle-aged banker on her right, a fashionable portrait painter on her left. 'My dear, she's still got to learn how to dress herself, but have you seen anything like that performance by a young gel?'

At Moulton Paddocks and Cassel's shooting estates the style of entertaining was more informal, with the partridge shooting and Newmarket Week the high points of the year. During the racing Edwina was expected to help entertain large numbers of guests, on the whole a rather more raffish crowd than in London, some for the day, others for the complete week. Edwina accepted racing as part of the social fabric of life without feeling special enthusiasm for the sport. She herself was a first-class rider, loved horses and became a good judge of horseflesh. She was also an extremely shrewd gambler and never allowed herself to be carried away. Cassel, who was not a successful gambler, admired and envied her prowess and encouraged her, but never persuaded her to go beyond the limits she set herself.

Edwina found the weaknesses of her grandfather as lovable as his qualities. It never ceased to amuse her that this brilliant financier who could judge the merits and demerits of a proposition, from an international loan of millions to a railway system in Venezuela, and was utterly modest about his achievements in this field, could remain so ignorant about horse racing while fancying himself as something of a genius. Edwina used to watch him after breakfast as he assembled a group of men, and one or two women whom he regarded as qualifying for the privilege, in order to go through the day's card. 'He believed he knew so much about racing that he thought he would revolutionize it,' one of his party observed many years later. 'None of us would ever question his judgement, but once I heard Edwina say, "Grandpapa, you know nothing about racing at all!" He was furious!'

Edwina's duties were not all that arduous, and the years 1920 and 1921 were marked by numerous parties, flirtations and celebrations, not least that of her own coming-out in May 1920. Never before had so many young people crowded into Brook House as for this ball. Park Lane was jammed with motors from 8 o'clock as if for a first night of a new H.M. Harwood play. The greatest and bloodiest war in history had ceased only eighteen months earlier, many of the young debutantes and their escorts had lost elder brothers or fathers. Now there was a general feeling that the time had come to end the mourning and celebrate the survival of those who had come through alive. A 'Negro jazz band' played in the drawing-room, cleared for dancing, and a traditional orchestra played in the ballroom proper. Considering that the country was supposed to be bankrupt, with vast loans from America to pay back, there seemed to be a great deal of money about, represented by 'diamonds the size of plovers' eggs' and massive strings of pearls. Edwina's dress of simple pale gold set her apart, bearing the unwritten label, which did not appear to bother her at all, of 'the richest heiress in England'.

Cassel recognized in Edwina all the recovered lost promise of his own wife – dead now for nearly forty years – and the daughter he had lost nearly ten years ago. She had so much of the beauty of Annette, the spontaneity and liveliness of Maudie. He was determined to supervise her social life carefully, and hoped that she would continue to enjoy herself unmarried for a few years yet, though she was certain to break many hearts and to receive many proposals.

Now that she was out, Edwina savoured every moment of this new life at Brook House, dancing the night away, in the fashionable phrase of the time. Cassel did not know that chaperoning was not what it had been in Victorian or even Edwardian times. Now it entailed escorting the charge, keeping an occasional eye upon her during the evening, and bringing her home at a decent hour. Edwina, basking in the attention she attracted, took the fullest advantage of this new freedom. Flirtations were not always public, she was quick to observe, and tactful provision for privacy was usually available. She became one of the recognized 'fast set' of debutantes, along with Thelma Cazalet, the Hon. Grisell Cochrane-Baillie, Audrey James and others. Barbara Cartland, a bright young deb herself, caught the abandoned mood in her first novel *Jigsaw*. This rapidly acquired racy reputation of Edwina's prejudiced few people against her.

Edwina had met several times the Americans Cornelius and Grace Vanderbilt, and liked them both. Their wealth, derived from his grandfather's fortune of some $100 million from shipping and railroads, was as great as Cassel's. They had a yacht, the *Atlantic*, and revelled in the English social round. In June 1921 they gave one of their famous balls at Claridge's Hotel. Edwina was invited, and there met for the first time a tall, remarkably handsome and lively young lieutenant RN. She had heard a good deal about Lord Louis ('Dickie') Mountbatten, his father who had been head of the Navy at the outbreak of war, and the royal connections which had led to the world cruise with the Prince of Wales from which he had recently returned. There was an undeniable and unusual aura of distinction about this officer, coloured by the strong rumour that he had been jilted by one of the most desirable debutantes of the previous year while he had been carrying out his royal duties at sea.

Grace Vanderbilt introduced the couple, and was not the only one to watch with unusual interest their dancing together a few minutes later.

4
An Indian Romance

A friend of Dickie Mountbatten once drew an interesting picture of his marriage to Edwina, which revealed the contrasts and parallels of their family backgrounds.

> They were both German really, and highly emotional and very talented. Think of it – Edwina's grandfather was a German Jew of relatively humble origins in Cologne who decided that he could best pursue his career in England, married an Englishwoman and reached the top. Mountbatten's father was a German minor princeling living 100 miles up the Rhine from Cologne. He was only a couple of years younger than Cassel, and he left Germany to pursue his career in England in the same year as Cassel, 1868. He married Queen Victoria's grand-daughter and reached the top. Curious, isn't it? Even more curious that they never met on the way, not until shortly before the generous-spirited great British public threw them both to the wolves in 1914.

Mountbatten and Edwina had plenty of German blood in their veins. Edwina was only one-quarter Jew, but her Jewish share was as evident as Mountbatten's German element, which dominated his style and manner, his reaction to setbacks, his defensive sensibility, his painstaking application and his certainty that he was right in everything. They were indeed an exceptionally intelligent couple, though her mind was even quicker than his and she took a much more commanding overall view of things than he did. 'She was worth three of him when it came to brains,' the same friend once remarked. This may be a trifle exaggerated, but not all that much, which gives some idea of how bright she was – 'So goddam bright it scares you,' a wartime American general remarked.

Mountbatten was born on 25 June 1900, seventeen months before Edwina, 'a beautiful large child' according to his godmother. (He was the last godchild of Queen Victoria, Edwina one of the first godchildren of the newly crowned King Edward VII.) He was a late child, a warmly welcomed 'mistake'. His eldest sister, destined herself to give birth to a late boy, Prince Philip, was fifteen, his younger sister twelve, his brother eight, when he was born. He was christened Albert Victor Nicholas Louis Francis, and at once asserted himself (as the oft-told story relates) by pushing the Queen's spectacles off her nose. The name Dick is said to have stemmed from intimate bedroom use by his middle-aged parents. He himself added the 'ie' and tended to be humorously scathing towards anyone with this name – like the present writer and one of Prince Philip's cousins – who did not do so.

Dickie's grandfather was Prince Alexander, brother of the Grand Duke Louis III of Hesse. Alexander nobly sustained the Hessian military traditions and then broke dynastic protocol by marrying a commoner. This lost him his title and his proud position in the *Almanach de Gotha*. Later he was forgiven and granted by his elder brother the title of His Serene Highness Prince Alexander of Battenberg, after the village close to the Rhine where they had a castle.

Their first-born was named Louis in honour of the Grand Duke who had recovered some sort of respectability for them. This boy conceived the ambition to be a sailor, which was considered highly eccentric for a prince of land-locked Hesse. A longing for the sea was instilled in him by one of Queen Victoria's sons, Prince Alfred, who had joined the Royal Navy. Louis began learning the rudiments of seamanship as a naval cadet just when his fellow expatriate Ernest Cassel was establishing himself as a student banker. Louis enjoyed all the benefits and suffered all the handicaps of royal patronage. The Prince of Wales was over-assiduous in offering the young ex-German privileges, and Louis's thick German accent, precise ways and rarely aroused sense of humour, did not endear him to his contemporaries. But Louis was also very determined and progressed against the tides of hostility. For all his life, he was better with women than men. Women were quickly charmed by him and readily slipped into bed with him. He had a particularly ardent affair with the Prince of Wales's favourite actress, Lillie Langtry, of whom her friend Oscar Wilde wrote romantically but not altogether accurately:

> . . . Lily of love, pure and inviolate!
> Tower of Ivory! Red rose of fire!

This affair led to the 'Jersey Lily' giving birth to a child. In spite of his own example of marrying a commoner, Louis's father would not countenance marriage, so swift and costly arrangements had to be made instead. Louis himself was hastily dispatched on a slow voyage round the world in a ship called *Inconstant*.

Louis Battenberg did, in fact, possess a strong sense of family pride and agreed with his father about the value of dynastic improvement. Soon after his return and while on leave in Germany he found himself in love again, this time more suitably, with the reigning Grand Duke's daughter, Victoria. The Grand Duke Louis IV had married Queen Victoria's second daughter Alice, cementing satisfactorily Hanoverian-Hessian ties. They had seven children, but haemophilia (of which Alice was a carrier) and diphtheria together took a terrible toll of this unfortunate family, leaving Victoria as the eldest and now motherless child to run the family with her bereaved and ineffectual father.

Queen Victoria, Princess Victoria's grandmother and now surrogate mother, thoroughly approved when she heard that the splendidly handsome Lieutenant Louis Battenberg RN had proposed to his cousin Victoria. The bonus, for the Queen, was that the Russian and German Courts might both disapprove, which indeed they did.

Princess Victoria of Hesse, the future Lord Mountbatten's mother, possessed an intellect and a love of the arts – especially of books – quite alien to her future husband. The Hessians had a strong tradition of intellectualism and egalitarianism, and Victoria had inherited both through her father. She liked to argue things through to the end and was an inexhaustible talker. She thrived on argument and when she was older would go to great lengths to provoke one. 'Pealing arguments would be worked up,' her grandson Prince Philip recalls. 'At meals these would be conducted in several languages considering who was there, but always it was her voice that dominated, whatever language was being spoken. The only thing that would stop her was her coughing.' From the age of fifteen, to the mixed horror and amusement of the Queen, Victoria smoked cigarettes, a vice she picked up from her cousin the future Kaiser Wilhelm II, and she coughed for the rest of her life, which was an exceedingly long and vigorous one.

Princess Victoria was not renowned for her beauty. But she possessed stateliness and handsomeness in full measure and she had what is sometimes called 'a fine face'. The courtship with Prince Louis was ardent and relatively brief, and Queen Victoria came all the way to Darmstadt for the wedding even though she hated Germany. They were married on 30 April 1884, and their first child, Alice, was born (unfortunately deaf) on 25 February 1885. She grew into a beautiful, highly emotional young girl. Another daughter, the future Queen of Sweden, was born four years later; a son, George, in 1892 – and finally the much loved little 'mistake' in the last year of the old century and in the last year of the old Queen's reign.

By contrast with Edwina's mainly unhappy and often lonely childhood, Dickie Mountbatten's early years were blissfully happy, surrounded by indulgent family, relatives and friends. Like Edwina, young Dickie spent much of his time on the move: from a rented house in London when his father worked at the Admiralty; to Sandringham or Windsor, great houses in the home counties; to Germany to stay with his mother's and father's families; out to Malta when his father was stationed there. In these early years of the century he experienced none of the tragedies or strains which Edwina endured. The Edwardian world seemed to smile at this pretty young prince with his fetching ways who strutted about as pleased with himself as everyone else seemed to be pleased with him. He loved to dress up and slipped naturally into the role of the actor he was to be all his life. Only when he was corrected or denied something he wished for was there any unpleasantness, and then he assumed the guise of a spoilt, sulky, uncontrite and obstinate boy.

Young Dickie's world was essentially a feminine one. His elder brother and his father were seldom at home, his mother and his sisters were rarely absent until Alice was married. There were also nursemaids about the house, and his mother's lady-in-waiting, Nona Kerr, who was never called lady-in-waiting by the egalitarian socialist Victoria – she was there, apparently, 'to assist us in the education of our children'. For a short time, Dickie went to a little boys' school in Eaton Square, but until he was twelve he was almost constantly in a feminine world. In later life, he denied vehemently that this had any effect on him. But it was a very powerful influence, none the less. It had much to do with the ease with which he got on with women and all the difficulties he had in striking a balanced relationship with men of his own age.

Dickie was unusually timid as a young child, and also accident-prone. The two may well have been related, and possibly connected with the slight imperfection in the control of his balance, which manifested itself more seriously in later life, unlike the timidity which soon disappeared under the pressures of competition. He experienced more grazed knees and cuts than most boys, and later when he was away from home his letters recounted details of frequent accidents and broken limbs. When he rode, he had many nasty falls, as he had accidents from misjudgements as a car driver.

His proneness to accidents is something else that he stoutly – even angrily – denied. But the record speaks for itself: a broken arm, a leg in plaster when he was taking his naval examinations, a collar bone twice. Some uncharitable people said that he was accident-prone with his ships, and certainly (as has been recounted) King George VI during the Second World War sighed with resignation when he heard that instead of a destroyer Dickie was to be given command of a giant aircraft carrier. 'Well, that's the end of the *Illustrious*.'

'The young Prince Louis', as Dickie was more formally referred to, went into the Navy almost as an act of automatic progression, like his elder brother before him. This was in May 1913. Already he was less of an innocent, less emotionally unscarred, as a result of more than two years at a boys' preparatory boarding-school, where he had been beaten and bullied. He made a vulnerable target with his feminine good looks, his title and connection with the Royal Family, and above all his German ancestry at a time of increasing national xenophobia. 'The Little Hun' was knocked down many times, and learned to defend himself and knock about boys bigger than himself – all of which he recounted with some pride to his mother in his letters.

Osborne Naval College on the Isle of Wight was tougher, and a great deal more austere and uncomfortable than the Eastbourne boarding-school to which Edwina was soon to be sent at the same age. Here the level of bullying was much worse, and it could seem sometimes that the cadets were really fighting for their lives with their fists. Black eyes and bloody noses abounded. Here Dickie learnt seriously the need for standing up for himself. 'Conditions were really tough in those days,' Mountbatten recalled later. 'They weren't much better for midshipmen, and it was not until David Beatty became First Sea Lord that conditions were improved.'

This harsh, bitter yet often immensely rewarding life at naval college contrasted sharply with holidays spent at the Hessian Court or stupendously grander Romanoff Courts in Russia, where Dickie's aunt was the Tsarina (then enjoying her strange and tragic relationship with Rasputin). In these royal family parties, all was laughter, games and loving kindliness, with caviar replacing tepid cod pie and rich Rhine wines the gritty evening cocoa of Osborne.

Dickie's father was, by the end of 1912, First Sea Lord, and professional head of the Navy that appeared hell-bent for war with Germany, with whom relations were already bad and rapidly worsening. Nobody, not even his civilian boss, Winston Churchill, appears to have warned Admiral Prince Louis that it might be injudicious to visit his German relations and German estates quite so frequently and for so long while he still owned no property in the land of his adoption. Dickie's father was building up an ammunition dump for his enemies of the future, and hardship and anguish for his younger son. While Ernest Cassel was working behind the scenes for peace at the behest of Churchill, Louis Battenberg was preparing the British Navy for war under Churchill and at the same time staying in Germany with his brother-in-law and the Kaiser's young brother, Grand-Admiral Prince Heinrich of Prussia. What is even more curious is that his son Dickie, when himself an Admiral of the Fleet sixty years later and defending his father's reputation, found it hard to see anything dangerous or even anomalous in this behaviour, and did not wish it referred to critically in his father's official biography.

Soon after Dickie's fourteenth birthday, the crisis that was to lead to European war began rapidly to develop. His father was busy with war plans and preparing, with Winston Churchill, to mobilize the reserve Fleet, a great undertaking involving hundreds of ships and thousands of civilian reservists. A number of wise people in high places, including Lloyd George, Chancellor of the Exchequer, feared the consequences of having a German-born admiral leading the Navy in war against Germany, not for any doubt that he was utterly loyal to his adopted country, but because the shrill voices of ignorance would soon force him from office.

Dickie was always proud of his father's achievement in 'standing the reserve Fleet fast' on his own initiative, as it was about to disperse after manoeuvres, when he recognized the inevitability of war. This resulted in the Royal Navy being ready for anything on 4 August. Dickie, in an early example of contriving to be at the centre of things in a crisis, was staying with his father at the Admiralty through all this drama. 'I was half excited and elated, half sorry for my father and very sorry that I was only fourteen,' Dickie later recalled. 'All the boys at Osborne knew that it was going to be a quick, crushing victory over Germany, and that there would be a huge battle in the North Sea which we would easily win.'[1] But, alas, it was to be nothing like that.

Victoria and her younger daughter Louise had chosen to go to Russia to stay with Victoria's sister at the Winter Palace. Here Dickie and his father had been due to join them for a summer holiday with the Tsar and Tsarina and their children. Dickie was already 'madly in love - goodness she was beautiful!' - with his cousin Grand Duchess Marie. The trip had been a fiasco. Two of the party succumbed to tonsillitis, the journey down the Volga in the imperial yacht had been hot and so dusty that they could not even see the river banks. Ekaterinburg, which was on their itinerary and was later to become the notorious scene of the murder of their host and hostess, indeed of the entire Russian imperial family including beautiful Marie, seemed ominously hostile. Here the party learned that war had begun and they therefore hastened home in great discomfort and some danger, feeling ill and having to bribe their way through Sweden and eventually find a berth on a ship from Norway. When many years later it was suggested to Mountbatten that this had been an 'ill-starred enterprise', he retorted sharply that it was, in fact, a highly successful cruise which had been much enjoyed. This was obviously arrant nonsense. But, as always, everything was a success when it came to family events.

The trouble about this form of inflated family pride is that it cannot always be sustained, even if, as Lord Mountbatten frequently claimed, he himself never made a mistake in all his life. When the family record is punctured the deflation is violent and the damage sustained almost irreparable. This is what happened to the Battenbergs in 1914.

Admiral Prince Louis, after his early success in having the vast British Fleet ready for war when it came, accomplished little else of value during the remainder of his term of office. The Royal Navy suffered a number of early setbacks. British ships were destroyed, enemy ships escaped destruction; and there was no sign of the expected second Battle of Trafalgar which, it had been hoped, would once again cover the Navy in glory. Churchill, who had by now accumulated a number of enemies, was partly blamed for these disappointments, but the finger of ignorance and prejudice pointed more steadily at Prince Louis. Why is a German running the war at sea? it was asked. Send him to the Tower!

The same shrill voices cried out at Osborne, taunting Dickie, to whom his father was like God: all-wise, all-good. When the Prime Minister, Asquith, and Churchill decided Prince Louis would have to go, and the Admiral sent in his resignation, it was, as Mountbatten later remarked, 'the worst body-blow I ever suffered in my life'. And he confirmed – 'yes, that's right – perfectly true' – the story that he was seen at attention on the parade ground at Osborne, alone beside the flagpole, the tears pouring down his cheeks.

As a single physical injury to a young man can give pain and disablement for life, this blow, this besmirching of family pride, affected Mountbatten until his death, sustaining the will to succeed and win, which up to then had been muted, adding passion and a steel edge to his manner and conduct. His goal was now set. It was the recovery of the Battenberg reputation so foully struck down by mean men. Dickie would win, there was no questioning that. He would do everything right in the struggle that lay ahead. His belief in his cause and its rightness remained like a Dreadnought's searchlight, bright, straight and true, guiding the twelve-inch shell to its target. This is why he could admit to no failure. Like the propaganda slogan in the Second World War, 'We are not interested in the possibilities of defeat – they do not exist', he did not consider anything but success.

Where the bigots had failed with Sir Ernest Cassel, they had won with Admiral Prince Louis. And soon, under further pressure occasioned by the popular hatred of anything German, the King had to ask his deposed First Sea Lord to change his name to something less compromising, just as the Royal Family now camouflaged its Hanoverian origins by calling itself The House of Windsor. So Battenberg became Mountbatten, and Dickie and his elder brother (who had fought in every major engagement at sea) lost their princely titles and became mere lords, the sons of a marquess.

Dickie joined the war at sea at the age of sixteen, a midshipman who, before his father's downfall, had not put on a brilliant performance. But he had completed his training with exceptional marks and merit in the newly acquired dynamic guise of world-beater. As a further pointer, he succeeded in getting himself appointed to the most admired and sought-after man-of-war, Admiral Beatty's *Lion*, flagship of the Battle Cruiser Fleet. Later he transferred to the Grand Fleet flagship, and at the ridiculously early age of eighteen (just) was appointed second-in-command of one of HM ships. It was only a small mass-produced patrol vessel designed to fight U-boats, and did not even boast a name. But to Dickie *P.31* had to be an exceptional man-of-war and the world had to know about it. He contrived to have it moored up the Thames at Westminster so that, at least inconvenience to the King and Queen Mary, they could come to inspect it. This had the required result of drawing reporters and photographers, at whom Dickie beamed proudly. 'Dickie is in agonies,' his mother recorded before this inspection. She need not have worried; her son could already put on a fine performance, and he loved every minute of it all.

Dickie Mountbatten's relationship with the Royal Family was like a moderate sea, undulant but never violent and never calm. By the same analogy, 'HMS Mountbatten' was a good sea boat, shipping little water, providing a steady gun platform and never at risk of sinking. The one-man crew made a good helmsman and a very good navigator.

The strength and weakness of Mountbatten was that he was neither English royal, English aristocrat nor English commoner. 'I am a semi-royal,' he used to define his rank, and claimed that his royal connections could be both helpful and unhelpful. He said that in his early years in the Royal Navy they were disadvantageous, but advantageous later on. The royal inspection of the *P.31* suggested that he intended to exploit every advantage from being a cousin to the sovereign, and on numerous subsequent occasions he made it clear for all to see that he was going to bind the relationship with the monarchy as tightly as he dared. There were setbacks, it is true, and on one very difficult occasion the good ship 'Mountbatten' almost turned turtle. The abdication of 1936 was indeed a sore trial for him, but somehow, as the great survivor, he weathered it all successfully.

Dickie's father had also succeeded in keeping relations with the reigning monarch warm. Queen Victoria adored him, saw that he was appointed to the Royal Yacht and made him her naval ADC. Relations with Edward VII were a little less close, but with George V – a near contemporary and a fellow sailor – very intimate. Louis suffered from one curious handicap which his younger son was to share: he had a socialist wife who did not really approve of monarchies. Victoria was always courteous with the Royal Family and, outside her family and friends, a paragon of discretion about her republican views. Personally she was very fond of the Royal Family, but of course they knew her views and reacted to them indulgently. When the family was forced to change its name and Prince Louis called it 'a terrible upheaval and break with one's past', his wife 'is splendid and is determined to give up her own title and rank'. 'I would prefer to be a "citoyenne" and beholden to nobody,' she told her lady-in-waiting. But one of the reasons she cited for making this choice instead of becoming a peeress was that she was 'unduly influenced by the recollection of brewers, lawyers, bankers Peers'. So she was not entirely without a feeling of repugnance towards lesser folk. Brewers indeed!

Dickie's strongest link with the Royal Family was the Prince of Wales. 'My friend David' at this time, according to his biographer, was 'young and loved above everything the pleasures of youth – dancing and night life, hunting and polo.'[2] When his close relationship with Mountbatten began in 1920 the Prince was twenty-six. They had met many times before, but the war and its aftermath had largely kept them apart. It was not until the second half of 1919, when Mountbatten was up at Cambridge doing a crash course in Ethnology and History of Geographical Studies, that they met at social events. At a Buckingham Palace dinner the Prince told Mountbatten about his experiences in Canada and the USA. It had been decided that, as a gesture of goodwill and gratitude for their contribution to the war effort, the Prince of Wales should make tours of some of the colonies and dominions. In 1920 he was to make a longer tour, to the West Indies, through the Panama Canal to a number of Pacific islands and to New Zealand and Australia. He suggested to Dickie that he should come as his ADC but later appeared to forget the offer until, after last-minute and near-desperate efforts by Dickie to see him again before he sailed, the offer was renewed.

The tour, in the battle cruiser *Renown*, from March until September 1920, was a success; for Mountbatten himself a great and important success. David had become a great friend and was a marvellous person, according to the letters he wrote home to his mother, and even the age difference had been no impediment. Next year it was to be India and the Far East, and it was a foregone conclusion that this 'vigorous and high-spirited young man' (as the Prince of Wales called Dickie) would accompany him.

For Mountbatten the sting in the tail of this tour was the discovery on his return that the girl he had intended to marry, against his mother's advice, had jilted him, as Edwina had learned. Even Dickie Mountbatten could not escape the sailor's occupational hazard. Audrey James had been one of the most beautiful debutantes of the 1919 season – *the* most beautiful, Mountbatten claimed, never enjoying the idea of second place, even for a false lover. They had become engaged in the autumn and planned to marry on Mountbatten's return. Meanwhile the young girl had met the immensely rich Major Dudley Coats and had agreed to marry him, preferring (as the current quip ran) the arms of Coats to the coats of arms.

It was one of Mountbatten's few rebuffs but he quickly rationalized the situation; in any case, he was so mercurial and so beset by the urge for pace in his life that he was soon in love again, and several times more, before the July ball at Claridge's when flirtations and passing fancies were briskly set aside to make room for 'the real and only love in my life, Edwina' as he referred to her in their thirty-eight-year-long marriage.

Cowes Regatta closely followed upon the Vanderbilt ball, a 9,000-strong Buckingham Palace garden party and Goodwood. It was a baking hot month and it was remarked censoriously that several gentlemen were seen carrying their morning coats. Cowes had been a great social as well as racing occasion for many years. Edwina was invited to stay at Nubia House, Cowes, the seat of Sir Godfrey and Lady (Eva) Baring. Their daughter Helen ('Poppy') was a contemporary and friend of Edwina's, an ex-girlfriend of Dickie's, and just as fond as Edwina was of the fast social life. A fellow guest was Margaret, Marchioness of Crewe, Lord Rosebery's daughter, a great yachting enthusiast and observed to be wearing 'the simplest of practical clothes'. She never missed a chance of being seen 'afloat in the *Sylvia*', the Barings' yacht, usually in company with Edwina.

The Barings had heard along the party grapevine of the special attention Lieutenant Lord Louis Mountbatten had paid to Edwina, and a number of invitations from hostesses for the sailing week were rearranged so that they could be observed together. It was not often that the name of such an eligible bachelor could be 'linked' (as gossip columnists put it) with such an eligible heiress. Veterans of the social season as discriminating and eagle-eyed as Lady Baring picked up the signals, judged them to be genuine and mentally registered the fact among her matchmaking memoranda.

The racing began on 1 August in high temperatures but sufficient wind to make it interesting. All eyes were on the King's *Britannia* which he helped to crew. The royal cutter was beaten by *White Heather* and *Moonbeam*, but to everyone's delight easily won the King's Cup on the second day. On the sloping lawns of Cowes Castle, the headquarters of the Royal Yacht Squadron, the titled and rich strolled about, gossiped, drank tea and champagne, applauded success and sympathized with failure. Eileen Sutherland invited Edwina to stay at Dunrobin Castle in a month's time, and then, independently, asked Dickie if he could come, too.

They spent a lot of time together at Nubia House, which was the social centre outside the Yacht Club. It had a tennis court, much used by those who wished to shake up their liver after too much sitting about watching the racing. They both played, Edwina rather well, Dickie very badly. One of the best was Prince Albert (Bertie), who used to play singles with Louis Greig, the Comptroller of his Household. Greig also attempted to control the Prince's language and temper ('Behave yourself, Sir!'). The Prince had proposed to 'Poppy' Baring and had been accepted, but the match was 'rejected very sharply by the Queen, and that was that', as one of the party recounted.

Nubia House, with its situation overlooking the Solent and its beautiful grounds, was the setting for several important days of courting for Edwina and Dickie that August 1921, and they danced, ate buffet suppers, drank champagne and walked in the gardens. Cornelius and Grace Vanderbilt had invited Dickie on a ten-day cruise along the Belgian and French coasts after the week was over. Edwina was now asked to join the party, too. The closed world of Society was now irresistibly bent on bringing about this match. It appeared as if they were already close to success when it became known that Dickie had invited Edwina to meet his parents, now the Marquess and Marchioness of Milford Haven. Louis was still only sixty-seven, but the shame of dismissal and the relatively unimportant life he had led for the past six and a half years had aged him. But he had been cheered by the recent courtesy promotion to Admiral of the Fleet, a second GCB from the King, and an invitation to join Dickie, who was serving in the battle cruiser *Repulse*, for a North Sea cruise. Victoria was as brisk and breezy as the last days of Cowes Regatta, smoking incessantly and throwing questions at the two of them.

Before the young couple left, Dickie's father took him aside. 'Edwina', he said, 'is the most remarkable and charming girl of this generation that I have met. She's got intelligence, character, everything. Now, you're very young, but if you do decide to marry her, you have my wholehearted approval. She'll make a wonderful wife for you.'

His mother liked her, too, though she was always less gushing and more cautious in her judgements. As Mountbatten recounted, 'this strongly influenced my decision to go ahead.' When he learned that Edwina would also be staying at Dunrobin, he planned to propose to her there, which would certainly have pleased the Sutherlands.

Events rapidly shaped that late summer of 1921 for Edwina and Dickie, although not as either of them had planned. Edwina took the train from King's Cross with a small party of guests and travelled north overnight, arriving the next day at noon at Dunrobin Castle's private railway station. The seat of the Dukes of Sutherland, the old part dating back to the thirteenth century, is spectacularly sited on the north-eastern shore of Dornoch Firth in Sutherlandshire, north-east Scotland. It was Edwina's first visit, and the brutish ancient battlements together with the nineteenth-century additions of batrizan turrets and dormer windows, contrasting with the beautiful gardens, appealed strongly to her.

The party was an oddly mixed one of youth and maturity, church and crown and aristocracy. Besides their host and hostess, George and Eileen, the Prince of Wales had already arrived with his younger brother Bertie – two future kings – and following soon was the Archbishop of Canterbury, Randall Davidson, Hélène Leveson-Gower and her sister Charlotte 'Baby' Demarest, William (Viscount Ednam) and Rosemary Ward, and several others whom Edwina had not met before.

Dickie Mountbatten was the last to arrive, at characteristic high speed in a car from Invergordon. He told everyone about the cruise with his father, how warmly he was welcomed on board and how kind all ranks had been to him. It had been perfect weather out of Invergordon and his father had enjoyed every minute of the cruise in this, the biggest warship he had ever sailed in. Unfortunately the North Sea September air had given him a chill and, on his last night, now ashore again at Invergordon, he had suffered somewhat from lumbago. Then Dickie had put him on the train to London after the naval doctor had pronounced him sufficiently recovered from his cold.

The Dunrobin house party was a huge success. The Prince of Wales fell for Edwina, as Dickie knew he would. She charmed everybody and uninhibitedly showed her rapidly developing love for Dickie. Then, on Sunday evening, 11 September, the flow of cheerfulness was stemmed. A telegram arrived late in the afternoon, addressed to Lieutenant Lord Louis Mountbatten - 'Deeply regret Papa died at 1.20 p.m.' The Admiral had been met by Victoria and his daughter Alice in London and they had gone to his club, the Naval and Military. He had said he was not feeling very well and had gone to bed, only to be found dead of a heart attack by a maid-servant a short time later.

On opening the telegram Dickie burst into tears. Edwina and the Prince of Wales attempted to console him. A servant looked up train times. There were no more that day, and it was too far to drive to London. Dickie said he would take the train the next morning. The Archbishop thought prayers before dinner might be appropriate. The entire house party was kneeling on cushions in the drawing-room, the Archbishop of Canterbury officiating, when the doors were thrown open and in walked the butler and two footmen with the usual evening cocktails. 'Everyone was rather put out,' Mountbatten recalled later, 'but I thought my father would have approved.'

It would also have been quite inappropriate 'to pop the question' (as Mountbatten put it) to Edwina. He decided to leave it until they next met in London. Meanwhile, the party broke up, and many of the guests also took the early morning train south. Dickie's elder brother was serving in the Mediterranean and it would be some days before he could get home. It was therefore Dickie's responsibility to look after the arrangements for the funeral and generally to support his mother.

Dickie Mountbatten's second attempt to propose to Edwina in London also failed as the result of another tragedy. Sir Ernest Cassel, whose winter sojourn in the South of France had been ordered by the doctors, had been poorly since he had returned. On the evening of the 20 September a dinner at Brook House, including Herbert Asquith, had to be cancelled. Cassel remained feeling seedy all day, but got up and was found dead by a servant at Brook House late in the afternoon of 21 September. Only a month earlier he had bought from King Leopold of the Belgians the beautiful Villa des Cèdres at Cap Ferrat for £88,000. Here he intended to spend much of the next winter on the Mediterranean. It was his last property purchase, the last big transaction of a lifetime of negotiating and buying and selling.

Cassel was, appropriately, at his desk when, like the Admiral, he had died suddenly of a heart attack. His hand was stretched out towards the three bell pushes that could summon servants. His had not been a happy life. For much of the time he had been lonely, with only the satisfaction of successful business, high honours and important friends for comfort. Only for the three years of his marriage had he found restful contentment and the joy of a fusion of minds. He had loved others, besides his wife and his parents. He had loved his sister and his only child. Perhaps, most of all, he had loved the evocative beauty and the youthful innocence and liveliness of mind and spirit of Edwina.

But he never saw Edwina after her return from Scotland, and never met her future husband. Exactly ten days after the death of Dickie's father, this fellow-German who had made his life and reputation in England had died swiftly in the mausoleum-like mansion which typified the belief in materialism which had dogged this extraordinary man's life. But his wealth had also enabled him to donate the gifts which had brought so much relief from suffering to so many people. Whether the last great gift to his granddaughter, framed in his will, would bring more happiness to her than his wealth had brought to Cassel himself remained to be seen.

Cassel had died as Edwina was on the train from Dunrobin, where she had remained after seeing off Dickie to his father's deathbed. Now she was met at the station by her grandfather's secretary, Miss Underhill, with the news of 'dear Grandpapa'. Her grief for the loss of her grandfather was as great as Dickie's on the death of his father. When they met they fell tearfully into one another's arms, bound by common grief.

In later years Lord Mountbatten always claimed, first, that neither he nor Edwina realized that she would inherit the greater part of the Cassel fortune, in fact three-fifths to her sister Mary's two-fifths, or rather more than £2 million (or about £30 million in 1983 terms); second, that his mother suddenly turned against the idea of his marrying Edwina – 'It never really works when the woman has so much more money than the man'; and third, that he himself judged that 'marriage was now out of the question' and that 'the question I was going to pop ... I didn't pop'. Edwina was, in fact, well aware that she was going to inherit a great deal of money and property from Cassel. He had made this perfectly clear to her, but had not specified the amount. It was not a subject that was discussed between the young couple, either, but Cassel was not a multi-millionaire who hid his wealth under a bushel. His complete lifestyle had long since told the world of his riches, from his vast contributions to charity to the splendour and opulence of his many properties.

It was also well known in Society that the Mountbattens were not all that rich. Their only home in England was Kent House on the Isle of Wight, which had been given to them by a member of the Royal Family because they had nowhere else after Louis had been forced to resign and they lost their Admiralty residence. Later, Dickie's mother caused some surprise by making a claim against the government 'for the return to be made to her because of an invention by her late husband which saved the Admiralty thousands of pounds', although everyone knew (as Prince Louis did when he was alive) that any device by a serving naval officer automatically became Admiralty property. Their German properties, which they had belatedly sold after the war, had been rendered less valuable by spiralling inflation. More of their wealth had been in Russia and had been swallowed up in the revolution and the assassination of the imperial family. Edwina and Dickie's friends encouraged the match not only because they made such a handsome and sparkling couple but also because it would provide Dickie with much-needed wealth and Edwina with less-needed but always welcome social status close to the Royal Family. Mountbatten shrank back from proposing, at least until a decent lapse of time between the death of Cassel – with front-page headlines pronouncing Edwina the world's richest heiress – and the announcement of a formal engagement.

For this reason, after the successive grand state funeral of Mountbatten's father, and the Kensal Green interment according to the rites of the Church of Rome for Ernest Cassel, Mountbatten made no reference to marriage but made amply clear his ardent love for Edwina, especially as it seemed likely that they were about to be separated for several months. His pride, let alone his heart, could not bear the thought that he might be jilted again while engaged on royal duties.

The final event of that summer and autumn, which was to complete the shape of the year 1921 satisfactorily rather than tragically, was the last and most important of the Prince of Wales's tours to India and Japan. It was also likely to be the most difficult, and the Prince wrote, 'I'm dreading India & I shall have a very difficult first month getting into the queer ways & getting to understand the queer life of the amazing country.' He had been told sternly by his father 'to do exactly as *they* tell you'.[3] The Prince badly wanted Dickie to come with him again, partly to take his mind off his father's death, and Dickie enthusiastically agreed to do so. For his part, the Prince was thankful to have his cheerful company, and wrote to Victoria from the *Renown*:

> You know how much his friendship means to me and that I just couldn't have done this trip if I hadn't got him with me. He means far more to me now than he ever did as he is now a man and not so much of a boy as he was last year which makes such a difference. He understands more, and of course I will help him in any way I possibly can in return for his wonderful friendship & devotion & more especially because you ask me to . . . he is so much older & wiser now.[4]

Before embarking in the battle cruiser with the Prince, Dickie had called on Edwina in the last week of October to say good-bye. Brook House was emptier and more mausoleum-like than ever now. 'I asked her if she would join me – that it would cheer things up if she did,' Mountbatten recalled, denying hotly that he knew that she would certainly come, and that the enterprise, including their engagement, was planned in detail from the start. 'Her trip to India was only very vaguely mentioned and I never thought she would pull it off.'

According to Edwina, it did take some 'pulling off'. For the present, unmarried and under twenty-one, she was literally the 'poor little rich girl', fated to remain on the same allowance of £300 a year that she had received before her grandfather's death. However, the first step was to winkle out of someone in Delhi an invitation to stay at the time when the royal party was in the capital. It was an early pointer to Edwina's ways of getting things done that, while there were several people high up in the Services or the civil government whom she could approach, she appealed first to the new Viceroy and his Vicereine, the Earl and Countess of Reading. 'Always start at the top' was one of Edwina's firmly held beliefs.

The Viceroy was Rufus Isaacs, who had been an old friend of Edwina's grandfather, and Edwina had been his hostess several times at Brook House. He was a lawyer, politician and financier of the first calibre and had been selected as Viceroy to replace the highly unsatisfactory Lord Chelmsford partly because 'a Jew, being in a sense an Oriental, had a natural bond with the Indians'. He was, in fact, the first and only Jew to be appointed Viceroy. Edwina's cable to Delhi produced an immediate welcoming reply: of course you must come and stay with us, and for as long as you like.

Next, Edwina needed money. It did not occur to her that as the imminent inheritor of some £2,000,000 she could approach her bank manager for £100 or so for a steamer ticket with a show of confidence. Edwina had been strictly brought up never to borrow money: only vulgar people borrowed money, and the working classes went to the pawnbroker. Although Cassel had created his fortune out of lending, borrowing and speculating he disapproved as strongly as Wilfrid Ashley of personal loans, which hinted at improvidence or extravagance. Edwina decided to 'touch' Aunty-Grannie, and went down to Bournemeouth for this purpose in the last days of October 1921. But dearly as she loved Edwina, even Cassel's sister was reluctant to lend Edwina the ticket money, and did so only after Edwina had pleaded that the reason for the journey came from the heart, and that – yes, she would find a chaperone. 'Well,' said Aunty-Grannie, 'he sounds a nice young man, and he's going where there are far too many anxious young women for my peace of mind. You shall have the money, my dear.'[5]

Ashley was strongly opposed to the whole madcap enterprise and he and Molly were extremely disagreeable before giving grudging permission, and then only because Edwina could show them the telegram from the Viceroy.

Next, Edwina invited herself to stay with Dickie's brother Georgie, now second Marquess of Milford Haven, at Lyndon Manor, the house they had acquired during the war. He and Nada now regarded Edwina as one of the family, and she got on well with them both – the gallant, handsome naval officer and his lively Russian wife. Their children, Tatiana aged four and David aged two, completed this agreeable family. But Edwina was beginning to feel that the whole enterprise was going sour. She had had only one letter from Dickie. Her meeting with her father and stepmother had depressed her, as always, and she had hated trading on Aunty-Grannie's good nature to acquire the money she needed.

The Milford Havens cheered her up. Georgie especially was 'flat out for us' as Mountbatten described their enthusiasm for the match. 'Of course you must go out and join him,' Georgie said. 'You really mustn't let him down. He'll think you're going to jilt him, and he couldn't bear that to happen again.' Nada, who was to become one of Edwina's closest friends, was equally pressing.

Edwina, eager to be encouraged, was soon converted back to the idea of the journey. In smart order she found a ship – a very cheap and primitive ship – and, she said, a chaperone. It was a cold mid-winter day when Georgie and Nada took Edwina down to Southampton and saw her into her poky little cabin. Georgie, who knew about ships in the tropics, forbore from telling Edwina that it would be hot in the Red Sea. They kissed her good-bye. 'Give our love to Dickie and David.'

The passage was exceedingly uncomfortable but Edwina, who never minded roughing it and had received plenty of training for it, was entranced with the whole experience – of shipboard life, of rough seas in the

Bay of Biscay, of the great solid rock of Gibraltar, and of Malta like a giant fortress rising above the horizon, an island new to her, like the Mediterranean itself. She always enjoyed hot weather and loved to tan her legs. She was thrilled by the Suez Canal, longed to explore the desert that fell away on either side of it, and found it as burning hot as Georgie had secretly feared it would be in the Red Sea. 'I just lay on my bunk with the ceiling fan slowly turning, and dreamed of the East,' Edwina recalled. And soon, in the early days of January 1922, they steamed into Bombay, and Edwina admired for the first time the massive and ornate fort, the long waterfront line of Gothic-Saracenic public buildings on the island, and the distant mountains on the mainland beyond.

Here Edwina parted from her chaperone, a mysterious grey figure of whom nothing is known – unless she was a convenient figment of Edwina's imagination. A porter put her into a gharry, which drove her automatically, as if there were no other destination, to the vast and luxurious Taj Mahal Hotel. After unpacking she took another gharry to the Victoria Station, which was swarming as it always is with thousands of Indians with their luggage and often their entire worldly goods.

'How much is the fare to Delhi?' she asked the booking clerk.

The clerk naturally quoted the first-class fare. Edwina was not in the least put out that she did not have enough money left. 'I'll go third then,' she told him. 'I think I've enough money for that. I wouldn't mind in the least.'[6]

The clerk shook his head, explaining that third class was for the poorest Indians, travelling fifty or sixty to a carriage, often with their livestock and spinning wheels. It was bare boards for two days. There was no question of Memsahib travelling third. Besides, it would be dangerous just now. There had been many riots and street fighting in Bombay between Moslems, Hindus and Parsees, and in the present mood there could be killings on the train, too.

Edwina gave up and returned to the hotel, asking for a trunk call to Lieutenant Lord Louis Mountbatten in Delhi. She got through eventually. His distant, crackling voice expressed delight and amazement. Then he laughed when she told him about trying to book third class. 'I'm stuck,' she said. 'The booking clerk, a very paternal gentleman, tells me it wouldn't do to travel third.'

Dickie laughed again. 'Good heavens, no! But book a berth on the Frontier Mail tomorrow. I'll get the money to you somehow.' And he rang off.

Edwina, who was soon to learn how Dickie relished resolving a crisis with speed and efficiency, recounted how an old Indian army colonel came to the Taj Mahal Hotel and asked for her. She came down to see him. 'Miss Ashley, I have just received a trunk telephone call from Delhi, from one of HRH's ADCs, a Royal Navy lieutenant, Lord Louis Mountbatten. He asked me to advance the necessary rupees for your railway ticket and other expenses at the request of the Viceroy.'

Edwina thanked him, and he added, 'You don't have to worry from now on. I hope you enjoy your stay with us. From what I hear they are having no end of a time in Delhi.'

It had certainly been a busy time for the royal party so far, nor had events always run smoothly. The organization of the polo matches, military parades, durbars and tournaments had been impeccably arranged by the Viceroy's staff. The travel and accommodation arrangements, ever since the Prince of Wales's party had arrived first at Bombay on 17 November 1921, had worked without failure, taking in some thirty-five destinations already. But no one had anticipated the ferment of revolution and threatened civil war that the arrival of the royal Prince would bring about. The Indian National Congress had organized a total boycott of the tour, which had been the cause of riots in Bombay and the killing of those Indian officials who had disobeyed it. The riots spread. Mahatma Gandhi, leader of Congress, had organized the boycott, not against the Prince of Wales personally but as a protest against British rule, and as an act of peaceful civil disobedience. Gandhi was appalled when he heard the news of the riots and began one of his first fasts in an effort to bring them to an end.

Meanwhile, the new Viceroy, following the advice of the Executive Council and the Council of State, ordered leading Indians to be arrested all over the country, though Gandhi himself escaped the order. Now, wherever the Prince of Wales's party rode through elaborately decorated streets, the painted signs of 'Welcome to HRH The Prince of Wales' made a hollow welcome. The local people remained at home and left the streets empty of onlookers, not even a single row of them. In Allahabad the young Jawaharlal Nehru and his father were both locked up in gaol when the royal party came through, depriving Dickie Mountbatten of the opportunity of meeting this remarkable young man.

The Prince and his ADC were aghast at what they saw, what they were not allowed to see, and the political and sometimes bloody consequences of their visit. The empty cities the Prince found 'a spooky experience'. Dickie took a more positive line. 'Why don't we go and talk to Gandhi?' he suggested. 'It would show that we understood and sympathized.

Between us we could convince him that we should be friends.'

Officialdom was outraged at this radical suggestion. Undismayed, Dickie asked if, instead, he could go alone. This idea was sharply rejected, too. Impenitent but resilient, Dickie took up some new distraction and, with his friend David, contrived to have fun between the heavy load of official functions. They became demons at croquet, and, with the enthusiastic backing of the Prince, Dickie began playing polo. He had never played it in his life and was an indifferent horseman. He also never contemplated doing things by halves. 'His initial appearance on a pony startled the Indian cavalry officers and my staff,' the Prince recalled. But he persevered and, though not a natural rider, later became an acceptably skilful and enormously aggressive polo player, who fell off with unusual frequency.

They visited Poona, Udaipur, Lucknow, Benares, Madras, Bangalore and many other cities, and at last the capital, Delhi. Lord Reading had made the most elaborate arrangements and laid on the most vivid pageantry for the royal visit. An enormous bungalow had been built in the grounds of the Viceregal Lodge to accommodate the Prince and his staff, with a paved courtyard, a fountain, and masses of bougainvillaea, palms, ferns, potted carnations and chrysanthemums, giving an impression not only of beauty and grandeur but also of a timeless quality as if the gardens had been there for centuries. The streets of the capital were decorated with triumphal arches, banners and flags. At night they were lit up and the most impressive buildings floodlit. All that was missing were the cheering crowds.

The tent-pegging tournaments and garden parties, the tiger shoots and pig-sticking, the military parades and the unveiling of memorials – all these were in full swing when Dickie Mountbatten contrived to slip away and greet Edwina at the station, where they fell into each other's arms and laughed a great deal while Dickie drove her to meet her host and hostess.

Not for one moment did Edwina Ashley consider that her arrival might be untimely and inconvenient. Instead, she threw herself at once into the social whirl and was an enthralled spectator at the sporting and ceremonial events. The Readings soon fell under her spell, and within a short time they, and everyone else, had accepted her as one of the royal party. She even received some curtseys. As for the Prince of Wales, he was enchanted that his friend's cup of happiness was now full, and that in his party there was a young woman who fell in with everything so gracefully and amusingly and embellished every event with her sparkling looks and laughter.

To ensure their privacy when they needed it amidst the formal and informal hurly-burly of the Delhi royal visit, the Prince of Wales slipped to Dickie a key to part of his bungalow where they could be alone together. The couple never forgot this gesture, and kept the key as a souvenir for all their married life.

By contrast with the formal duties of the party, and the depressingly hollow public functions empty of sound and spectators, the brief periods of recreation and the evenings in Delhi were marked by an exaggerated gaiety and light-heartedness. It was almost as if only champagne, pranks and idiotic games could keep up everyone's spirits. Not all of this evening noise and tumult was approved of by the stiffer members of the Executive Council and Council of State, like General Lord Rawlinson of Trent GCB, GCVO, Sir George Stapylton Barnes KCB and Major-General William Rice Edwards CB, CMG. But nothing could put a serious damper on the spirits of the Hon. Edward Pleydell-Bouverie, Flag Lieutenant to the Commander-in-Chief East Indies, the Hon. Bruce Ogilvy of the Prince of Wales's staff, his Assistant Private Secretary Captain Alan Lascelles, a number of the brighter young women - mainly daughters of the Delhi hierarchy - the Prince of Wales, Dickie Mountbatten and Edwina.

A young officer of the 2nd Queen Victoria's Own Regiment, detailed as guard of honour to the Prince, recalls a typical flirtatious prank at a ball - 'a marvellous spectacle, marvellous dress uniforms and dresses as well as beautiful ladies'. He was standing behind a pillar when he felt a touch on his shoulder. 'Do you know who I am?' It was the Prince, and when assured that he was correctly identified, he asked, pointing at Edwina and Dickie dancing, 'Now do you see that long chap with that beautiful girl? Well, next time they come round here, stop them dancing and tell him that I require him very urgently up in my room.' The Prince then slipped out of sight behind the pillar. The officer recalls:

> Now I felt that I was really for it. But as they approached round the ballroom floor I held up my hand. The tall chap began to expostulate, 'What the devil ...!', but the lady asked me what I wanted. I told them and the tall chap said, 'Sorry, Edwina, but I suppose I must go up and see what the so-and-so wants.' No sooner had he left than Edward P. appeared from behind the pillar and said, 'Edwina, my dear, I think this is our dance.' She grinned and off they went. And so did I - in the opposite direction!

At another dance a few evenings later on St Valentine's Day, 14 February, Dickie and the Prince danced in turn with Edwina, then Dickie drew her aside. They sat at an open window overlooking the garden.

When it happened, and he asked her to marry him and she said 'Yes, Dickie,' it was a confirmation of the inevitable – by no means lacking in romance and colour, as well as in the rich scents of the flowers below – but also a tick against one important item in the chronology of his life Dickie Mountbatten had prepared for himself.

Everything was in order. King George v had been telegraphed for his approval and had given it. The Prince of Wales 'was madly for it', and hugely enjoyed the spectacle of their being 'head over heels in love'. He also, more importantly, agreed to be Dickie's best man at the wedding. Even Mountbatten's mother had come round to the idea again.

This young, handsome and blessed couple would in effect now be gaining the freedom that a fortune always offers. The unrecognized irony lay in the fact that this personal liberty was achieved at the same time as Edwina's host, the Viceroy, signed the orders for the repression of India's Congress, and for the imprisonment of many more of India's future leaders than Jawaharlal Nehru.

5
The Wedding of the Year

Edwina and Dickie spent one week more in Delhi after their engagement, the rounds of official duties and evenings of entertainment continuing as before, except that the previous flirtatious manner of the young bucks and blades of the royal party – and of the Prince himself – subtly changed. The sex-related teasing that was a characteristic of these 'bright young people' ceased with betrothal. Things were different now, settled. The couple were looked at differently, just as Edwina and Dickie looked at the world and at each other differently. Edwina, the purpose of her presence so far from home now fulfilled, appeared to relax a little, while 'Dickie's cup of happiness was brimming over', as one observer remarked. 'It was a marvellous time but all too short,' Mountbatten recounted. 'My mother wrote to me to approve, and she wrote to Edwina, too, telling her that she knew she would make me happy. David was thrilled, of course, although he knew the inevitable outcome of Edwina's arrival in India.'

They said goodbye on 21 February when the Prince's party, like an Arab caravan of old, set off with its vast baggage and gifts for the rulers *en route*, making a circuitous journey via Karachi and thence on board the *Renown* to Colombo, Singapore, Hong Kong and Japan.

Edwina left Delhi a few days later, sailing from Bombay in as primitive a vessel as the one in which she had arrived. She was also without a chaperone, and there was, according to her younger sister, 'a terrible row about that later at Broadlands'. She was impatient to be home, impatient for the English spring and the preparations for her wedding. Then, when they were near Port Said, she read with shock and dismay on the ship's news bulletin that on 24 April, 'Lord L. Mountbatten, cousin of the King, died yesterday.'

So it was all over before it had begun! An Indian astrologer might have foreseen it: sudden death had haunted their relationship almost from the beginning – and now this. Edwina buried herself in her grief in her cabin and later emerged to ask the ship's wireless operator if he could discover the circumstances. 'I want to know the details.' There was some delay, then they came: 'Major Lord Leopold Mountbatten whose sister Ena was married to the King of Spain, has recently died....' Dickie's cousin! The fact that she had never even heard of him made her realize how little she knew about the family into which she was marrying.

The first roses were out when Edwina arrived at Broadlands. Her father and stepmother greeted her with unaccustomed warmth. They approved of the match, as well they might. Wilfrid Ashley could now write off one financial liability for ever, and the marriage virtually into the Royal Family pleased Molly, who was a great title snob. Now the Cassel trustees and lawyers opened up the coffers for Edwina, and for the first time in her life she was free to spend without restraint. She did so, at first held back by Puritan doubts and guilt, but then with rapidly growing lavishness. 'She now concentrated on filling her cupboards with the softest and sheerest lingerie,'[1] a friend wrote. Then she was off to Conduit Street, where Rolls-Royce sold their motors, and bought a 'Silver Ghost' model (the chassis alone cost £2,000 - or the price of four modest-sized houses) and ordered a cabriolet body by Barker to be fitted. This was Dickie's 'welcome home' present and wedding present, which Edwina used herself in the West End for shopping She enjoyed mastering this huge machine as she enjoyed driving all her life.

Dickie was not due home until 20 June. On the 18th Edwina set off for the Vicar-General's office in Creed Lane to acquire the licence. She enjoyed telling the story of that morning, of the registrar who was too busy at his desk to look up when she arrived in the office early in the morning, the bare boards being mopped down by a charlady.

'I wish to get married at St Margaret's Westminster,' she said.

'What is your name?'

'Edwina Cynthia Annette Ashley.'

'And your age?'

'Twenty.'

'You will require your parents' consent,' he said, looking up from his papers.

Edwina had the document and presented it.

'And who are you marrying?'

'Lord Louis Mountbatten, Lieutenant Royal Navy.'

The shock effect sent the official out of the room, murmuring apologies as he fled, to return a minute later with a pathetic piece of carpet. This he placed under Edwina's chair. A proper respect has to be maintained for members of the Royal Family, he told her with many apologies; and within a few minutes Edwina was walking out with the document.

Forty-eight hours later she was in Plymouth. A considerable crowd had already gathered to welcome home the heir to the throne on board the battle cruiser. For the first time, Edwina found herself caught up in naval ceremony and protocol, which for the heir to the throne was at the highest level.

Much of the light-heartedness of Dickie's first tour was absent from the Far East tour of 1921–2. From a political point of view, the Indian part of it, which was by far the most important, had been an unmitigated disaster. Instead of healing the wounds of the Amritsar massacre of 1919 and subsequent repression, and demonstrating Britain's gratitude for the Indian contribution to the war (over a million volunteers), it had worsened the situation. Both Gandhi and Nehru were now in prison, along with hundreds more who were working for independence. The response of the (now banned) Congress had been a slap in the face for the Prince of Wales and the British Government. There had indeed been plenty of private fun and games, much of it instigated by Dickie Mountbatten, but the Indian experience had been insulting, hateful and a complete waste of time and money. Some benefit had been gained by the visits to Singapore and Hong Kong, and no harm had been occasioned by the Japanese visit, but no benefit either.

Everyone cheered up as the *Renown* and her accompanying light cruiser neared home. Dickie asked for the banns for his wedding to be read in church on the last two Sundays before they arrived, 11 and 18 June. And now, on the afternoon of 20 June, the beat of the *Renown*'s turbines diminished in volume. The coast of Cornwall and Devon was in sight. It was a beautiful afternoon. Four seaplanes circled overhead as an aerial escort, and a flotilla of destroyers put out from Devonport, and stationed themselves a division on each quarter.

From the *Renown*'s bridge Dickie could make out the great crowds on the Hoe, and from Penlee Point all along Cawsand Bay to the mouth of the Hamoaze, and on both banks of the river. The royal salute crashed out, bands were playing, flags waving, church bells ringing, and the crowds cheering. 'It was a marvellous homecoming,' Mountbatten recalled. 'David and I and the rest of us were deeply moved.'

An hour after the massive battle cruiser had anchored, the Duke of York came out in a steam pinnace to welcome his older brother. Edwina and others, wives of the Prince's staff and the ship's senior officers, with the superintendent of the dockyard, followed after a discreet interval in a second boat. The *Renown*'s decks and below decks were loud with the sounds of greetings and exclamations. Edwina and Dickie contrived to find a moment of privacy. Dickie was bronzed from the tropics and the Mediterranean, and Edwina was 'looking lovelier than ever', as he described her. There was much to talk about, far too much for these circumstances. There was also much obligatory socializing on the quarterdeck on this long June evening, and then below where a formal dinner had been arranged by the Admiral's staff. The Prince replied to the speech of welcome. Everyone noted how tired he looked after the long tour.

The next morning there was a civic address and procession, and at 11 a.m. the royal train left Plymouth for London, slowing at several stations so that the Prince could wave to the crowds who turned out in thousands. London was *en fête*, too, with the King and Queen waiting at Paddington. Four carriages took the returning hero and his family through the packed streets. Dickie waved to them from the fourth carriage, which he shared with Lieutenant the Hon. Bruce Ogilvy, Captain E.D. 'Fruity' Metcalfe and Surgeon-Commander Alex Newport. Many of the women recognized him as the fiancé of an heiress and gave him a special cheer. Pausing briefly at Buckingham Palace, the procession continued down the Mall to the Prince's home at St James's Palace.

Dickie, his duties finally completed after eight months, was given leave to depart late in the evening. He went straight to Belgrave Place, where Edwina had installed herself with Marjorie, now Lady Brecknock. The talk and the champagne continued far into the night.

The next morning, a short distance away, Field-Marshal Sir Henry Wilson, one of the most famous soldiers of his day, was shot and killed by two members of the IRA as he left his house. Ignorant of what had occurred just round the corner, Dickie (one of the future best-known sailors of his day and IRA victim) climbed into his wedding-present Rolls-Royce for the first time. Although it was not a very nice day, he had the canvas top down so that large numbers of people, equally ignorant of the outrage in Belgravia, were allowed to glimpse the lofty 'Silver Ghost' and the striking and handsome couple in it, going shopping in the West End. In three days it would be his twenty-second birthday; Edwina would be twenty-one in November. That night, Dickie took Edwina to Claridge's, his favourite hotel, for dinner. Edwina was wearing 'one of her simplest trousseau dresses', and they toasted their reunion.

In the gossip columnists' style of the time, Edwina's clothes were as important as her movements. At Newmarket Races, which she had last visited with Grandpapa Ernest, she wore 'a bright red dress under a blue coat with red revers'. At the Duke and Duchess of Devonshire's ball she wore a white gown, in which she was photographed skipping up the steps of 2 Carlton Gardens, Dickie at her side. The shadow of the press – reporter and cameraman – was always close to them now, and neither gave the slightest sign of minding. There was a Buckingham Palace luncheon on 26 June. Most of the Royal Family were there, anxious for Edwina to feel at ease. They had no need to worry. Her own family experience from earliest childhood, and the two years at Brook House as hostess, ensured that. Her natural shyness and nervousness were well concealed. From early childhood, Edwina had possessed a natural social grace, charm and fluency of expression which almost everybody found enchanting. Queen Alexandra was among those who felt this as they talked of the Dowager Queen's husband and Edwina's grandfather and their close relationship.

There were other visits to Buckingham Palace and to Windsor Castle, too; and on 17 July, the day before the wedding, as a token of appreciation for acting as the Prince's ADC on two tours, Dickie was invested with the order of the KCVO (Knight Commander of the Royal Victorian Order). The ribbon completed the second row on his chest, which had recently been further embellished by the Japanese Order of the Rising Sun and the Grand Cross Order of the Nile.

The last weeks before the wedding were, in Edwina's words, 'sheer hell'. Stella Underhill, too, found it all a strain and a rush. She recalled:

> Sir Ernest's executors lent me to Lord Louis for these weeks before the wedding. I had had some experience the year before when Marjorie Jenkins had been married to the Earl of Brecknock and Sir Ernest had had the reception at Brook House. I sent out all the invitations – about 1,200 – except those to royalty which of course had to be sent out by Lord Louis personally. I kept lists of those invited as I sent the invitations out, and also of those who accepted.

Edwina's greatest problem was dealing with her fiancé. Instead of absenting himself from the scene while Edwina completed her trousseau, visited the hairdresser many times, organized the flowers, and with the help of her father and stepmother, Aunty-Grannie, Mrs Jenkins, and Marjorie and her friends, prepared for the reception at Brook House, he was very much present. 1,200 people were to be invited to the church, St Margaret's Westminster, nestling beside the Abbey, and most of them would be coming back to the house afterwards. But two tours with the Prince of Wales, nine years in the Royal Navy and an abiding confidence in his organizational abilities led Dickie to offer supervision at every level and at every stage of the wedding and reception arrangements, and his advice on matters of protocol. After all, the King and Queen, most of the rest of the Royal Family and a large number of dignitaries from home and abroad were to be present. Everything had to be Mountbatten-right.

Edwina was fully aware that Dickie's perfectionism, his need to command and impatience with anything or anyone who obstructed him might lead to stormy moments in their marriage. She had also been warned about pre-marital strife by friends who had experienced it. But their first rows – mostly about trivial detail on which she invariably gave way for the sake of peace and the need to get things done – came as a grave shock.

Meanwhile, the presents came pouring in during the first two weeks of July, many of them extravagantly grand, others more modest, and some extremely curious. Among the last was a set of no fewer than forty-four specially bound volumes of poems – any poems – from Sir Robert and Lady Kindersley. He was the immensely rich Chairman of Lazards; she had not learnt that neither Dickie nor Edwina was especially attached to verse, nor for that matter ever read at all if they could avoid it. Much more appropriate was the gift of Princess Victoria, who must have learned of their honeymoon itinerary and gave them a set of road maps of France in a leather case. As a reminder of past travels the Prince of Wales gave them a silver globe engraved with the tracks of the Australian and Indian tours. Somewhat pointed was the gift of the Viceroy and Vicereine, who had not failed to notice Edwina's shortsightedness in Delhi: they sent her a spectacles case.

Glittering among the massed array of presents set out at Brook House for the reception were sleeve links for Dickie with the royal cipher in diamonds from the King and Queen, the same from Queen Alexandra, who also gave a diamond pendant with the royal cipher in diamonds to Edwina, a diamond and platinum brooch from the Aga Khan together with a diamond tiara of five stars with a pearl in the centre, a diamond and turquoise brooch and earrings, and a bracelet of precious stones surrounded by diamonds. At the other end of the scale, the tenants of Broadlands clubbed together to buy them a silver fruit bowl. The Maharajah of Jaipur, a friend of Cassel's, arranged to send a superb horse. There were, most inappropriately, walking sticks for Dickie and some twenty-four umbrellas in all.

The morning of 18 July broke cool and cloudy. Soon the rain began to come down. But the more indefatigable wedding enthusiasts among the public were not to be deterred. The wedding had been built up by the popular press and the gossip columnists as 'the wedding of the year', and by mid-day Parliament Square was filling with hundreds of people, mostly women, and many seasoned campaigners with folding stools, picnic baskets and umbrellas. For them it was a fairy-tale wedding, its brightness quite undimmed by a splash of English summer weather.

But there were also a number of people, none in the crowds but some in the church, who were less certain about the suitability and less optimistic about the auguries of this wedding. Certainly jealousy played a part among some of these doubters, especially in the Navy. Many years earlier, back in 1875, Dickie's father, just naturalized and an eager young sub-lieutenant, had found himself heavily burdened with privileges heaped upon his unwilling shoulders by well-intentioned but shortsighted members of the British Royal Family. He, too, had toured India as a very young ADC of twenty-one to the then-Prince of Wales, and had later sailed round the world in company with two of the Prince's sons, one of them the future George V. Lieutenant Prince Louis of Battenberg had not improved his popularity in the wardroom as a result of these and many other marks of privilege. His younger son was now experiencing the same disapprobation and noticeably suspicious manner from his contemporaries and his superiors. In the eyes of some of his fellow officers, everything was going too sweetly and smoothly for the golden boy. Dickie succeeded in giving the impression that he did not notice the critical looks and hostility on shipboard, which did not improve matters. But he felt it very deeply, and recalled his father's similar difficulties. 'It was absolute hell,' Mountbatten said in later years.

In their own circle in Society, loosely called 'the Prince of Wales's Set', there was nothing but satisfaction and pleasure at the wedding. But there were many more circles within that closed Society world, each with its own suspicions and jealousies – the discreet and withdrawn inner circle of the old aristocracy, the uninhibited free-spenders among the more recently titled, the unashamedly super-rich who had done well in industry and out of the war, the old landed gentry and those who rode to hounds in too-new, too-correct hunting habits and had a dozen expensive hunters to draw on, those who were not as close to the Royal Family as they liked to think, and backwoodsmen peers and their often eccentric families who never came to London and scarcely knew what was going on. Among some of these variegated people, many of whom had never set eyes on Edwina or Dickie, there was suspicion about motives and suitability, the old class and money aggression doing its dirty work. 'I just wish they had waited and that there wasn't so much money about,' one of Edwina's friends remarked. Others thought they were too young. Lady Reading commented, 'I hoped she would have cared for someone older, with more of a career before him.'

Not a hint of these doubts, of this carping and cavilling, had reached the expectant crowds in Parliament Square. The pattern had already been set. Just as Dickie was and always would be popular and even loved among the lower deck in the Navy, so the working class and lower middle class in England loved and admired Edwina.

By 2 o'clock the police were having to move some of the crowds in order to keep the roads open for traffic and for the imminent royal arrival. It was still raining when the bridesmaids turned up. They were all in pale blue crêpe romaine with wide sleeves and Dutch bonnets of silver net, and carrying sheaves of delphiniums, making a brief cheering splash of colour before disappearing into the church, seven of them in all: Lady Mary Ashley-Cooper, Edwina's sister Mary, Joan Pakenham, and Dickie's four nieces, Princesses Margarita, Cecile, Sophie and Theodora. (Their one-year-old brother Philip of Greece had been left behind.)

A few minutes later the black royal Daimler drove into the Square and drew up outside St Margaret's. The King emerged, in non-festive black with bright carnation, followed by the Queen, according to the press, 'looking very handsome and stately in blue with a blue feather in her hat', her widowed mother-in-law appropriately less gaudy, three of George v's sons, and his daughter Princess Mary with her towering, glum-looking husband, Lord Lascelles.

Inside, they joined survivors of war-ruined imperial and grand-ducal families - the Dowager Tsarina of Russia, one of the few to escape, and the Hessians - and the packed congregation, straining for a view of the notables. Then to music from *Lohengrin* the groom appeared, in full-dress lieutenant's uniform, slim and tall, his sharp-chiselled face set in a solemn expression, walking with slightly splayed feet, the much shorter Prince of Wales at his side, both wearing swords.

According to the lady from *The Times*:

> A discreet murmur of admiration rose from the congregation as the bride entered on the arm of her father. The bride's gown was conspicuous by its combination of simplicity and richness. Of dull silver tissue cut on long, straight lines, with a waistless bodice, mitten sleeves and round neck, its effect was of subdued splendour. Narrow stole panels of unequal length, embroidered with crystal and diamanté, hung from either hip. The train, four yards in length, was of fifteenth-century point-lace mounted on cloth-of-silver edged with a heavier border of Spanish point-lace, forming a stole drapery across the shoulders. The

tissue foundation was turned back at the edge over the lace, so as to form, as it were, a frame for it.[2]

Like every important ceremonial with which Edwina and Dickie were to be associated, the first went off without a hitch. The prayers were read by the Rev. Frederick Long, who had once tutored Dickie, and the service performed by the rector, Canon Carnegie. Psalm XXIII was read: 'The Lord is my Shepherd; I shall not want . . .'; and it seemed as if they would not. The choir sang the Lord's Prayer set to music by Bortnianski; hymns 'Thine for Ever' and 'May the Grace of God our Saviour'; and Steiner's seven-fold Amen. Beethoven's 'Hallelujah' was sung during the signing of the register in the vestry. Then 'The Wedding March' was played as the bride and groom left by the east door.

The departure coincided with the first flash of sunshine of the day. A roar of cheering went up, the police linked arms, and some of the crowd shinned up lampposts. Edwina and Dickie emerged between the naval guard of honour, Edwina with her veil thrown back. But that was not all. There had to be the Mountbatten extra touch: a shining limousine, the driver a naval officer friend, the 'footman' holding the open door another naval officer, a party of naval ratings from the *Renown*, headed by petty officers and officers, ready to give a tow. Inevitably, an old shoe was tied on to the back.

The crowd, who had been ribbing the ratings during the ceremony, now gave a great cheer. Edwina and Dickie waved to them. The sun remained out, glinting on the brass buttons of the officers, the silver and paintwork of the limousine, the road along which it was towed at a spanking pace towards St James's Park, Buckingham Palace, Hyde Park Corner, Park Lane and Brook House. . . .

The arrangements at 'the marble mausoleum' (or MM) were as elaborate and ostentatious as befitted the occasion. The fashionable florist, the blind Captain Hope of Piccadilly, had been given *carte blanche* and had imported an avenue of potted orange trees, half in blossom, the others bearing fruit. The refreshment rooms were crowded with white and bronze lilies; in the hall massive vases of malmaisons had been placed like shrines to Cassel, whose favourite flower it was. But as in the church, blue delphiniums formed the *motif*; they were everywhere, in almost suffocating profusion. In keeping with this larger-than-life occasion, the cake required four husky men to lift it onto its table.

There were as many people outside the house as outside the church. The ratings, who had dropped their tow when out of sight, had leaped into taxis and were the first to arrive at Brook House. 'Here come the admirals!' shouted a wag.

Edwina and Dickie received their guests at the head of the orange avenue. There were hundreds and hundreds of them; nobody counted the total. By 5 p.m. the happy couple were worn out and could hardly get through the speeches. At last the Royal Family began to drift away and Edwina could flee upstairs to change into her going-away clothes, described as 'a coraline-coloured crêpe romaine worn under a coat of ruched crêpe romaine with a full round collar'.

No one was supposed to know where they were going, only that their honeymoon would begin at Broadlands, as Edwina's mother and father had begun their honeymoon. The splendid cabriolet 'Silver Ghost' Rolls was at the door, its luggage grid loaded high with new leather luggage. Dickie, now in lounge suit, climbed behind the wheel with Edwina beside him. The cheering faded as they moved into the traffic down Park Lane. The car made no more sound than its name implied, and they were so drained of everything except the need to get away from all those people that neither of them spoke for some time. The first hours of their honeymoon as they drove slowly down the A30 into Hampshire were, therefore, most uncharacteristic of their marriage.

A light supper had been laid on for them at Broadlands. Then they walked across the close-cut lawns beside the Test, and retired full of champagne, utterly happy if exhausted, to the large master bedroom where Wilfrid Ashley and his young bride had spent the first night of their honeymoon only twenty-one years before.

Robert Everett and his brother Henry, who had joined the Navy, caught a glimpse of them the next morning before they went off on their travels:

> The day following Edwina's wedding, my brother and I went over to Broadlands to see the old coachman. In the stable yard Dickie Mountbatten was tinkering with the Rolls-Royce that Edwina had given him. He recognized my brother and said Edwina would be delighted to see us. There was a lot of talk about the wedding at which my brother had been present and formed part of the guard of honour. I asked Edwina where they were going, and she said she was going to stay with Dickie's relations in Spain. I felt she had now really moved out of my circle.

Paris was the first destination. The Rolls was loaded onto the ferry at Southampton, and from Le Havre Dickie drove direct to the city at high speed. He was 'mad about' the car and loved to drive fast, always checking the mileage covered against the time, and deriving enormous satisfaction from calculating the average speed. On regular routes he would set out to break his own record, and many times claimed to have driven from London to Portsmouth in one hour twenty minutes. As if anyone minded very much, he would also add to this claim 'and remember, no front-wheel brakes'.

From Paris Dickie had laid out a precise itinerary, reserving rooms at the best hotels *en route* to Santander to stay with his cousin Queen Ena of Spain and King Alfonso. The bride and groom had not known one another for long enough to realize that this journey was bound to lead to conflicts; that Edwina with her more romantic notions of travel and her recently acquired freedom from chaperones and responsibility would want to wander down through this beautiful country, perhaps with a night at Tours, another at Amboise on the Loire, and so on. She had left the arrangements entirely to Dickie and not enquired further. It came as something of a shock, then, when she learned in Paris of their inflexible itinerary. There was a quarrel during which Dickie gave way. The bookings were cancelled; they would stop where the fancy took them.

The Rolls swept off south-west on the N10 and when darkness fell they found themselves in Tours. The Grand Hôtel de l'Univers, the Metropole, the Grand Hôtel de Bordeaux, the Hôtel du Croissant (to come down the scale) were all full. Neither had remembered that this was the French holiday season. The proprietor of a small pension finally took pity on the tired couple and offered them a hot, stuffy attic room with a small bed. It was not a successful night, and Dickie was always angered and humiliated by failure. This time Edwina gave way. Cancelled bookings were reconfirmed by telephone at great cost of time and patience, and the journey was resumed with Mountbatten clockwork precision. Edwina, as she was now rapidly learning, would be the one to make necessary adjustments in this marriage.

Ena (once a Battenberg) and Alfonso were a happy couple, and they welcomed Edwina and Dickie warmly after their long journey and gave them a good time in the palace and at the royal family's private beach at this northern Spanish port and resort. With the Grand Cross of Isabella Catolica safely in their luggage, they were back at the French frontier by 15 August, and were able to accelerate the Rolls again up to its maximum of 70 mph on the long straight *routes nationales* to Paris. They spent one night at the Ritz, and then drove east to Germany. This was all new country to Edwina, and most of it was new to Dickie, though he had made one fleeting visit to the Western Front during the last days of the fighting.

The Great War seemed very close again as they drove through the battlefield areas of Verdun, where France had been drained of her young men's blood, and Metz, into Germany and across to Darmstadt.

Edwina at once noticed the change that came over her husband as he neared the land of his fathers, the state of Hesse and the city of Darmstadt. He viewed the land and the people with a special proprietorial air, which this writer noticed when he travelled there with him fifty years later. To appreciate fully the all-consuming dynastic pride of this man, it was necessary to accompany him as he showed where he played as a boy; where the carriages drew up when the entire Russian imperial family arrived at Heiligenberg for their summer holidays before the First World War; where he tethered his pet lamb; where receptions were held in the grand-ducal palace in Darmstadt. With Ernie, Grand Duke Louis of Hesse, and Onor the Grand Duchess, Dickie showed Edwina the exquisite half-size house Ernie had built at Schloss Wolfsgarten for the doomed only daughter Elizabeth by his first marriage before she died in 1903.

The wayward, aesthetic and faintly decadent Grand Duke had been stripped of most of his powers but still managed to enjoy his title and diminished responsibilities, and was certainly a generous and happy host. Remembering Dickie's passion for fast cars, he had laid on a visit to the Opel test track nearby where the company was preparing its new Grand Prix cars, enormous machines which Dickie was allowed to drive. To Dickie's delight Edwina fell in love with the family and the beautiful wooded countryside, and was sorry to leave after only five days.

They were back at Brook House on 27 August. Most people were away on holiday or were shooting grouse in Scotland. Their honeymoon was not yet over; in fact for Edwina the most exciting part lay ahead. But meanwhile, Dickie was suddenly concerned about his career. When his mother had married Louis, he was already an established twenty-nine-year-old lieutenant. Nor did Victoria bring with her any great fortune. But when she saw her younger son married to this heiress whose wealth made it unnecessary for Dickie to do another stroke of work in his life, she showed herself anxious for his future. She even felt it necessary to write to Edwina hoping that she would take pride and interest in his career.

She need not have worried for either of them. Edwina, in whom the spirit of competition burned brightly, was almost as ambitious for his future as Dickie himself. Dickie understood as well as his mother the difficulties that lay ahead. 'Marriage to a very rich woman, as my mother pronounced, posed problems,' he said. 'I realized forcibly that the only hope of standing on my own legs was to work. I couldn't hope to produce the money that Edwina had. So I had to work very hard in the one profession where money doesn't count. I worked like a beaver to excel.'

Edwina was no threat to Dickie's career; the Navy, however, was. With the end of the war, the Navy had had to cut back great numbers of ships. Battleships and battle cruisers, for example, were to be reduced from around sixty to no more than fifteen under the terms of the recently signed Washington Naval Treaty with France, Italy, Japan and the USA. Personnel had to be reduced in proportion and hundreds of naval officers were asked to resign their commissions. When Dickie asked if he could extend his leave until the end of the year after his return from the Continent, he was surprised at the alacrity with which the Admiralty agreed. In fact Their Lordships were thankful to have officers on leave on half pay; and it now even appeared likely that on his return he might be asked to resign, especially as officers with private means were at the top of the list.

Lord Mountbatten always told people that he escaped 'the Geddes Axe' (as the thinning process was called) on merit and future worth. In fact, the Prince of Wales, knowing how damaging to his spirit it would be if he were asked to resign, and 'sensing that he possessed the potentialities of a sailor', intervened without Dickie's knowledge. 'He wouldn't starve if he were fired from the Navy,' the Prince (as the Duke of Windsor) once said. 'However, being related to my father, the Admiralty referred Dickie's case to King George V.... I and others recommended his retention in the Service. The King eventually agreed and in the light of things his decision in Dickie's favour has certainly been justified.'

Edwina was as relieved as Dickie when she learned that his naval career was safe. They had plans for an American visit and these now went ahead swiftly. There were brief last visits around the country: to Edwina's Aunty-Grannie at Bournemouth, where they found her not at all well with a bad heart; to Broadlands, where her stepmother was still spending nearly all her time and a great deal of money in renovating the house; and finally to the Sutherlands at Dunrobin. Back to London overnight, the boat train to Southampton, then aboard the *Majestic* for New York.

In later years Edwina lost count of the number of crossings of the Atlantic she made. The frequency of her visits never diminished her love for the country. 'I loved its sharpness and liveliness. Everybody was awake and alert,' she once commented, 'and ready for something new.' Mountbatten recalled her love for the jazz music in the New York night clubs, and of Negro spirituals in particular.

But Edwina's love affair with America began almost before the *Majestic* tied up in the East River docks, as she stood beside Dickie at the rails, staring up with that breathless feeling of wonder that assails everyone viewing massed skyscrapers for the first time.

As with most love affairs, Edwina always remembered that first meeting: the roar of Wall Street traffic as a background to the maritime sounds of a great liner docking, the tooting of the tugs, the accents of the porters and newspaper reporters and photographers as they came on board. The press wanted the Mountbattens, 'the handsome royal couple', 'the lovely Edwina', 'the fine, tall, royal Lord Louis'. There were plenty of show biz people on board, but it was the Mountbattens the press were after.

For half an hour Edwina and Dickie sat on a sofa, smoking and smiling, answering questions and asking some of their own. Yes, they had got engaged in India. No, not at the Taj Mahal by moonlight. And how did you find India, sir? Is there going to be a revolution there? Do you think there is going to be peace in Ireland now?

Dickie shook his head laughingly, 'It's no use asking me. It's not the Navy's business to talk.' And there were jokes about 'the silent Service'.

Edwina was equally discreet, equally disarming. While Dickie offered his monogrammed cigarettes to eager reporters, she patiently answered the usual questions about flappers and cocktails, divorce and the place of women in society. She was wearing a plain dark-blue serge dress and a long string of pearls. 'Oh, I just believe in being an old-fashioned wife,' she commented without a blush.

A limousine, which made the wedding Rolls look puny, whisked them with their luggage to their hotel suite overlooking Central Park. The lights were coming on, the leaves were still on the trees, the open horse-drawn carriages were clip-clopping round the park. Edwina had never seen anything to equal this urban spectacle. They changed, ready to go out to dinner at the New Amsterdam with Jerome and Eva Kern. Kern's recent smash hits included 'Cabaret Girl', 'Good Morning Dearie' and 'Sally', tunes to which Edwina had danced so often. The Kerns were great Anglophiles; Eva had been born in England, where Jerome had met her when he was studying there before the war. The evening was a wild success, ending with the Ziegfeld Follies.

All the famous and the rich people wanted to meet the young Mountbattens, whose reputation and connections – sometimes exaggerated – had preceded them. After a round of dinners and theatres in New York, they answered the call to the White House where President Harding entertained them. So did the US Navy Department, where Dickie was asked to speak at a Navy League dinner. The Navy also provided an aide to accompany them on their long and carefully planned journey across the States. His name was Lieutenant Frederick Neilson, and his wife Eulalia acted as *aide* to Edwina.

Wherever they went there were friends or friends of friends or relations anxious to show them everything. The Chairman of the Topeka, Aitchison and Santa Fé Railroad, Colonel George Thompson, had been a friend of Dickie's parents, and now provided them with a private luxury railroad car which took them first to Niagara Falls, then to Chicago, Salt Lake City and so to the destination which they expected would be the summit of their Grand Tour – Hollywood.

'Hollywood held everything for Edwina and me, and visiting it for the first time was a great thrill,' Mountbatten once said. The world of entertainment at the lighter level fascinated both of them. They enjoyed the music hall, cabaret, jazz music, comic actors, light comedy, almost everything that was done for fun and to entertain. In later years in their marriage Edwina was to do much for show business charities. They were both fascinated by the world of the cinema and by the technique of photography, still and moving.

In Hollywood in 1922 Mountbatten was at the outset of a lifetime's interest in the movies, but he already had a ciné camera and, as always, was determined to get top guidance on how best to use it, for fun and professionally. So Hollywood at the beginning of its Golden Age did indeed 'hold everything' for him. For Edwina the bright lights, glamour, creativity, novelty, the astonishingly vulgar and astonishingly interesting characters involved in the movie business – all these satisfied completely the lighter side of her nature.

The ever-ready limousine took them from the station to Pickfair, the remarkable creation of the remarkable couple, Mary Pickford and Douglas Fairbanks, who had invited them to use it for as long as they wished. They were away, but their friend Charlie Chaplin acted as host. Dickie liked him at once and they became life-long friends. For Edwina, Chaplin felt an even closer affection. She warmed at once to his mental and physical agility, his repartee, his eagerness to start new enterprises and see them through swiftly. At this great mansion, the brash modern equivalent in American Society to Dunrobin Castle in Scotland, they invented games, swam, talked and joked. They both had Jewish blood in their veins, they were both life-enhancers with bubbling senses of humour. And, as important as all this, they had experienced unhappy childhoods and each recognized a deep-lying melancholy in the other. They would have made a wonderful match, and perhaps they both recognized this. Chaplin's own first marriage, to Mildred Harris, had not prospered and he had not yet remarried.

Chaplin made a film for them. They shot it at Pickfair, and he persuaded Jackie Coogan to take part, co-starring Dickie and Edwina. It was called *Nice and Friendly* and it was all done professionally with make-up, props and camera crew; and it was done very quickly, in fact in less than a day, quick even for Charlie. Then Chaplin had it processed and cut, and gave it to them as a wedding present. He said he was sorry that Dickie was no actor and Dickie hung his head. But that, of course, was just a joke and all part of the fun. As a film director once commented on Mountbatten and Hollywood, 'If he had remained there in '22 he could have been a rival to Valentino – and would certainly have outlived him.' Chaplin, recalling those few relaxed days in his busy life, mentioned also *en passant*, 'Yes, and Edwina made a pass at me.'

During their last days in Hollywood, Cecil B. de Mille invited them to the studios and up into the hills where he was shooting a scene. The director's cameraman instructed Dickie on how to make best use of his new 35-mm movie camera. They had met most of the great stars on the day before they continued their tour to the Grand Canyon; and then they went on to Florida and back to New York. There it was more cabarets and musicals, a visit to Coney Island, duty visits to some of Cassel's cronies and – non-duty – a visit to 'The Dug Out' where disabled survivors from the war were taught vocational work.

Edwina and Dickie left for Europe early in December 1922, exhausted but with an amplitude of love for America and Americans, and with an over-sufficiency of gifts, which left them little room to move in their cabins. They had met everyone they had wished to meet and a few they had not. And there, unknown to them, lay the seeds of a self-inflicted mark that was to dog them both for all their young lives. Babe Ruth the baseball star, Charlie Chaplin, Jerome Kern, the President of the United States, all attracted this eager and ambitious young couple. They were name-seekers who were also hungry for fun. What they did not know, and what they did not consider, was that behind them from coast to coast they had left a trail of resentment and wounded pride. Chairmen and chairwomen of civic bodies, mayors of small towns, the leaders of local Society in small communities as well as leaders of the East Coast Four Hundred – Edwina was interested in none of them and snubbed many of them. She was after what she called 'the real America', the famous because they were famous, and the poor and sick because she had inherited, in enhanced form, the Cassel-Shaftesbury-Palmerston concern for the unfortunate and underprivileged. She was interested in Warren Harding because he was President of the United States, and interested in black roadsweepers on Fifth Avenue, New York City, waiters, porters, janitors, and obviously undernourished children on porches in the Deep South because they filled a need in her to succour the poor. This need, in tune with her age and the age she lived in, was still small and would take years to develop. But she still preferred to divert to a poverty-stricken Indian village in Colorado rather than receive a civic welcome from small-time officials in the next town.

Back in Britain, the Conservative Party had been returned to power, unemployment was rising, strikes were on the increase and workers were on hunger marches. Edwina went Christmas shopping from Brook House in the Rolls, wrapped in furs, the cabriolet top down against the winter cold. She was seen in Knightsbridge on 13 December after dancing the night away at the Chesham House ball the night before in a short diamanté dress.

Dickie was at the Admiralty seeing about his career. At the weekend they went down to Broadlands, where Edwina embraced her father and stepmother. Relations with her father had changed for the better now, and were to remain affectionate if somewhat distant. Wilfrid had stood as Conservative parliamentary candidate for the New Forest Division of Hampshire at the general election and had been returned with a handsome majority, to be appointed at once to the Ministry of Transport. Molly as lady of the manor carried out local duties and continued to supervise work on Broadlands and the gardens.

Christmas was spent with Georgie, Nada and the children, then back to London in the New Year. In the early months of 1923 the shape of their early married life was taking form. Now that his career in the Navy was safe, Dickie was using every influence to get an appointment to destroyers. An old friend of his father, Captain David Joel, agreed that Dickie should come as his first lieutenant.

Edwina, already proudly described by Dickie as 'definitely one of the leaders of the "smart set"', made her debut in this part. Apart from the occasional charity ball, her work for the underprivileged scarcely existed. At twenty-one she was hell-bent on having a good time and spending money on herself and Dickie. We catch occasional glimpses of her in photographs and paragraphs in the Society magazines and the Sunday newspaper gossip columns – out in the West End with Lord and Lady Blandford, Marjorie Brecknock and her husband John, Lord Brecknock, and the Duke and Duchess of Sutherland, Edwina in 'a straight frock of white marocain embroidered in crystals with a black marocain cloak with white embroidery, and three rows of large pearls'.

Dickie had expressed a wish for a speedboat and a faster car than the Rolls, perhaps a French Hispano-Suiza, the 37.2 model which could do 85 mph. Then they would need a country house, not too far from Portsmouth. There was already talk of polo and that meant stables and paddocks....

6
To Sea with the Fleet

1 January 1923 was the right day for the Mountbattens to take stock of their position and prospects, just as it can conveniently be seen now as the first day of their post-honeymoon married life. The future was relatively simple for Dickie even if it did call for hard work and the overcoming of numerous hazards and impediments in his chosen career. Like fighting a war or running a race, it may be difficult and dangerous but it has an ending, a conclusion: victory. At the age of twenty-two, Lieutenant Lord Louis Mountbatten was already into his stride, with successes behind him; and now he was going to the top. There was no more uncertainty in this than in the act of his entering the Royal Navy when still a boy. He was going to become an admiral, and he was going to become First Sea Lord, to emulate his father and correct the great injustice done to him and the slight to the family's pride.

For Edwina, who was in any case a much more complex, introverted, mercurial, and finally more intelligent character, the future was without any clear shape. Years of uncertainty faced her, and it is just and appropriate to take a measured look at this young woman and view any faults in her conduct with a full understanding of what she faced in 1923.

One of the few people who have written about Edwina said:

> The effect of the possession of great wealth is difficult to gauge in the abstract. For the first fifteen or so years of her married life, Lady Mountbatten enjoyed its fruits to the utmost. Yet running through the whole period there is an element of uncertainty, a search for horizons which she first needed to discover before she could measure them.[1]

Edwina's childhood was more unhappy than happy. She had known loneliness and neglect, had suffered harsh discipline and rigorous regimes – no more than many girls of her social class, it is true, but for the most important period she had lacked the support, the love, security and guidance of a mother. Moreover, we are concerned with an unusually sensitive personality. And then had come the sudden change in her fortunes, in every sense. Rapidly she had passed through the part-emancipation of life with her grandfather, the sudden brilliant light cast by her debutante days, the adjustment to the idea of extravagant personal wealth after the Ashleys' financial stringencies, and then the onrush of love and the even more fundamental adjustment to married life with an unusually demanding man, and the responsibilities it brought.

All these changes had occurred much too rapidly. Lady Reading had been right: she needed more time, and she had been denied it by her own impulsiveness and Dickie's urgent need to get everything done swiftly once he had made up his mind. Edwina was by nature excitable, and it was therefore unsuitable for her to be rushed. Her husband, however, was always a rusher; he could not help himself. And herein lay seeds of incompatibility.

We have to look, too, at the world in which Edwina was destined to begin her married life – a small world that in no way represented the social conduct and mores of the general public of the early 1920s. The 'bright young things' of the jazz age, their promiscuity, vices, tastes and enthusiasms; their snobbish special language and sham intellectualism pandered to by the unscrupulous fringe of bogus artists through neo-cubism, and writers through stream-of-consciousness novels; their excesses and cult of immorality and self-indulgence as they all read in Waugh's *Decline and Fall*: '... I don't believe one can ever be unhappy for long provided one does just exactly what one wants to and when one wants to' – this was the stage setting against which Edwina Mountbatten would act out her part for the early years of her married life. 'Everybody's doing it, doing it....' She had around £50,000 a year after tax when £1,000 a year less tax was a generous income, and the example of her late grandfather in her attitude towards spending money: extravagant in big ways, cautious in small ways – like tips, where the uneaten food went after parties, and the price of petrol.

The running of Brook House remained for the time being as it had been in Cassel's time, a joint operation with Stella Underhill for whom 'everything had to be so perfect, down to her clear signature "Stella J. Underhill"'. In fact, Miss Underhill became increasingly involved in the machinery for running the Cassel bequests, trusts and charities, an immensely complicated business which she understood better than anyone. Another figure now made her appearance at Brook House. Mary, her schooling over, was as unenthusiastic about living at Broadlands with the dreaded Molly as Edwina had been, and now that Edwina was married was invited to come and live with her among the bright lights, although, as Mary says today, 'Edwina took her chaperonage very seriously.' Looking back on this period, Lady Delamere asks, modestly but with a note of horror, 'Can you think of anything more horrible than to be married at twenty and twenty-one and to have acquired a lump tied round their neck like me - always with them? No privacy at *all*!'

The occurrence of a setback in the lives of the Mountbattens is rarely recorded, but there was one very early on in their married life, which much distressed Dickie. It had nothing to do with their domestic life, and certainly not with Mary, upon whom they both doted. His plot to serve in a destroyer under Captain Joel failed. The Admiralty decided that he had had enough of the good life, with two royal tours with the Prince of Wales and a six-month-long honeymoon with his rich wife. 'So they sent me to the battleship *Revenge* instead. It was the very last thing I wanted,' Mountbatten recalled. 'Not only did I not want a big ship, but the *Revenge* was a part of the International Fleet in the Dardanelles to deal with all the Balkan troubles at the time. And wives were not allowed - too dangerous.'[2]

So Dickie went to the Mediterranean for the first and last time without Edwina. She did not lapse into the stereotype figure of a naval wife moping at home and praying for her husband's safe return. She had no difficulty at all in filling her days, and half her nights; her movements in the country from house to house, and in London from restaurant to night-club to great ball, were closely followed and noted by the columnists, always with a mention of her clothes. She was seen 'in an Egyptian mummy dress with a sable stole' dining with the Prince of Wales and his party, pelting one another with cotton-wool balls provided by the management. Perhaps the next day she would be observed in her Rolls, her black retriever Simon at her side, off to the Knightsbridge shops. Brook House was closed for a while for redecorating while Dickie was away. Dark panelling was stripped from the walls, and Edwina's favourite colours of cream and pink replaced the sombre hues of Cassel's tenure. The heavy carpets were taken up from the main hall, the grand staircase and the gallery revealing the beautiful white marble. While Aunty-Grannie remained alive she was given use of the first and second floors; but when she died and the property became exclusively Edwina's, they moved down a floor and adapted Cassel's old vast bedroom suite into two bedrooms, a dressing-room for Dickie and two new bathrooms. Dickie contrived to be in London for the reopening party where the Prince of Wales and his brothers, Lady Elizabeth Bowes-Lyon, the Duke and Duchess of Sutherland, the Brecknocks and a select forty more danced to Paul Whiteman's already famous band. It was a typical noisy Mountbatten party that set the pattern for the years ahead.

Edwina, alone, was back at Nubia House for Cowes week. The house, as always during the Regatta, was full of guests. Edwina arrived with all her jewellery. She carried much of it everywhere, always finding it a comfort and reassurance, just as many women regard their handbags as indispensable. This practice had already led to some difficult moments, starting with the honeymoon when she insisted on bringing so much that Dickie felt obliged to carry a revolver. One afternoon at Nubia House a thief broke in during the quiet hour after lunch and lifted thousands of pounds' worth of valuables from the bedroom of another guest, Lady Crewe, and £6,000's-worth of Edwina's. Lady Baring intercepted the burglar, who was immaculately dressed, claimed to have 'Come to wind the clocks, my Lady,' and made an easy escape.

'Peggy Crewe was furious with my mother and never stopped grumbling about the loss,' Charles Baring recalls. 'But my poor mother was comforted by Edwina, who took a most generous view of the incident, which was typical of her kindness and strength of character.'

Dickie was back again for their Christmas with Georgie, Nada and their children. A week later they were with the Brecknocks, guests of Marjorie's father, and 'adding much to the excitement of the neighbourhood'. Edwina was pregnant and took very little notice of this fact so far as both diet and clothes were concerned. 'She had a dedicated resolve', her sister remembers, 'to continue her life in the normal way, which she always did in every direction. Physical illness was scarcely allowed to intervene.' She always treated her body like her cars, as if it were a machine to be driven flat out and reliable enough not to bother about, reserving her concern and affection for her pets and – intermittently – her children. Neither did she take much interest in what she ate or drank, and she never did either to excess. As to her clothes, she still gave the impression that she did not know what she was wearing; only that when opportunity allowed she wore casual clothes and as few as possible. But, such was her grace and bearing that everything looked well on her, and as she invariably went to the best couturiers and milliners and left everything to them regardless of expense, she soon qualified as one of the best-dressed women in London.

No one was a greater admirer of her appearance than her sister.

> She was chic, well-dressed, always suitably dressed. Nobody could look better turned out. She had a natural feel for clothes. I was so jealous. She could come

in at two or three in the morning and just put rollers in and tie a handkerchief round and go to bed. The next morning the rollers would come out in five minutes and her hair would be beautifully tucked under, and she would look perfect.

Dickie rejoined the *Revenge* at Gibraltar in the New Year. By late January Edwina was entering the last stage of her pregnancy and even she had to curtail her social life. Dickie, cruising with the Atlantic Fleet, was at Funchal, Madeira, when he received a signal informing him that he was the father of a girl, born on 14 February, St Valentine's Day and exactly two years after they became engaged, a coincidence that satisfied Mountbatten immensely. Everyone wanted to know her name, and Edwina told the press that she would first have to consult her husband. This she was able to do when, recovered from her confinement with amazing speed, she took the Blue Train to Cannes with her two nursemaids and secretary. Here she soon met Dickie, ashore from his battleship.

The Prince of Wales agreed to stand as one of the child's godfathers just as his grandfather had stood for Edwina. Mountbatten recalled:

> So, with his permission, we named her Edwina, too, after his name. That was her second name. Her first was Patricia after Patsy, Lady Patricia Ramsay, the Duke of Connaught's youngest daughter and Queen Victoria's granddaughter. And lastly we kept the name Victoria after my mother, who was of course named after *her* grandmother, the Queen.

Dickie got leave from his ship for the christening, which took place at the Chapel Royal with as much publicity as a really big party at Brook House. The numbers in the crowds outside came as no surprise. Several newspapers had already described Patricia as 'the richest baby in the world'. And those people attending the ceremony did, after all, represent the four elements most attractive to the people of England: wealth in abundance, royalty in numbers, aristocracy at the highest level, and show business personified by Mary Pickford and Douglas Fairbanks. Who could ask for anything more?

There were cheers when Edwina emerged holding Patricia, who was wrapped in a robe of Valenciennes lace and a lace-edged bonnet and cloak of white satin. Edwina was not wasting precious time nursing the baby, and she followed the rituals of the Season with the Brecknocks, the Milford Havens and her other friends and relations as if still childless: the Wimbledon finals, the Derby, Newmarket and Goodwood in early August; and with 'Poppy' Baring at Nubia House again for Regatta Week. She was at all the balls and dances, too, or so it seemed: the 'Heart of the Empire' ball;

Lady Pembroke's dance for her daughter; a dance at the 'Someries', the Regent's Park house of the mountainously rich Wernhers, George and Zia (Nada's sister); a party given by the Ashleys at Broadlands; and a weekend of parties and sessions at the gaming tables in Deauville.

By October 1924 Dickie was due to leave the *Revenge*. He had, in any case, hardly been an exile. Events like the christening of his daughter had brought him on leave to London; and he had seen more of his wife than any other married officer in the Atlantic Fleet. Now he was due to start a long signal course at Portsmouth, and the moment he heard he wired Edwina asking her to look for the suitable country house convenient to the naval base which they had discussed earlier.

This was the sort of task that Edwina enjoyed and performed efficiently and speedily. Agents, too, were quick off the mark and anxious to make a sale as soon as word got round that she was seeking property. For no more than a week she drove about West Sussex and Hampshire, and finally settled for a house and park called Adsdean, twenty miles from Portsmouth on the slopes of the Downs and with a beautiful view of the sea and Chichester harbour.

An architect would be hard-pressed to describe Adsdean, and it gives the impression that several failed architects had been employed during its construction. There were traces of mock-Gothic and Elizabethan influences and a touch of French château among the turrets and dormer windows. Its redeeming features were its generous and merciful covering of virginia creeper, and its situation. It was not for sale but for rent, which suited Edwina perfectly as it would not be an easy place to sell when Dickie moved on elsewhere. Dickie loved it when he saw it. 'I knew we were going to be happy there,' he said. 'It had plenty of stabling and the gardens were extensive enough for a paddock, a riding school and a small golf course. I also decided to build a special pit for practising polo.' There was, in addition, to be a hard tennis court.

The terms of the contract stated that Adsdean must be left exactly as it was found, but this did not deter Dickie from carrying out these substantial modifications and having everything 'all shipshape and Bristol fashion'. Inside, the place was soon fitted up with typical Mountbatten gadgetry, the type beloved of practical schoolboys: signalling devices as befitted his new speciality; a wireless (and these were in their infancy) even in the servants' quarters; and a signal clock on every guest room door to indicate the desired time for rousing, more often than not tampered with, to the sound of muffled giggles, in the small hours.

At Adsdean there were eight gardeners and eighteen indoor servants run by Frank Randall the butler. The Austrian cook who had been employed by Cassel and had known Edwina for almost all her life commanded the kitchens. There were houses with more servants than this up and down the country, but no servants were better looked after. With her natural concern for the less privileged, her own experiences at Alde House still fresh in her memory, Edwina saw to it that all the staff lived in healthy and comfortable conditions in their own private wing. Brook House was kept on as a fully running concern, complete with its own small regiment of servants, now more humanely cared for than under Cassel's regime, and was known ironically as 'the biggest *pied-à-terre* in Town'.

A further influence in the concern she felt for her staff was her new-found socialism. This had its roots in the radical-liberal strain of the Shaftesburys, which, in skipping her father's generation, seems to have gathered added impetus. Her grandfather on her mother's side, while the stoutest upholder of the principles of capitalism, was also at heart, and in his friends like Churchill and Lloyd George, a Liberal. This socialist strain was greatly strengthened by the advent of Dickie's mother in her life. Victoria, who was clear-headed, powerful and vocal in her socialism, had an immediate and lasting effect on Edwina, whose sharp mind was admired in turn by her mother-in-law.

Her friends tended to take a tolerant and even humorous view of Edwina's socialism. She did not at this time proclaim her political views strongly. 'We all knew she was a socialist, or thought she was,' said Barbara Cartland, who was a friend and contemporary. 'But we didn't mind. I mean to say, how could she be serious with all those millions and millions.'

Despite all those millions the overall management of this estate as well as Brook House was soon put in the unaided hands of Stella Underhill, with Edwina as no more than a supervisor. 'There was always a great deal to do,' Miss Underhill recalled mildly, 'with two houses and staff to run. There were also polo ponies and the yacht, and the wages of all these different staffs were paid through me!' In contrast to Cassel, Edwina was much loved by her staff; but in accordance with her policy they were also paid the strict minimum at a time when domestic jobs were hard to come by, and there was no over-manning in either of these two establishments. In the end it became clear that something would have to be done to relieve Miss Underhill, so Richard Crichton was called in as agent at Adsdean. Neither his family nor that of his wife Nona was blessed with private means, and the old soldier was thankful for the job.

'Colonel Crichton took over the running of the polo ponies and grooms, the yacht and her crew, the cars and the gardens at Adsdean with their staffs, and the outside improvements to the house,' wrote Stella Underhill. 'This left me with the running of the two houses together with all the private accounts.'

On a normal working week-day at Adsdean, Mountbatten got up early. A horse would be saddled up waiting for him and he rode for half an hour, or longer in the summer, ending up practising some polo strokes in his pit. Then he would have breakfast with Edwina in her room and drive off rather too fast to Portsmouth in his Rolls, later to be superseded by the Hispano-Suiza. In place of the regular mascot there was now a mascot in silver, a present from the Prince of Wales, depicting a naval signalman, arms outstretched, holding two flags. It was the talk of the officers on the signal course, most of whom did not own a motor car, and rather admired by the ratings.

Edwina spent most of the morning answering letters and on the telephone, and then took a vigorous ride on her favourite grey, Searchlight, often climbing onto the Downs and through the beech hangars above the house. Weekend guests who had arrived early or stayed late, which was common, were left to their own devices until luncheon. There was plenty to occupy their time, and Edwina would join them at a round of golf or a set of tennis in the afternoon. Dickie would appear up the gravel drive at around 6.30. 'Every detail of Lieutenant Mountbatten's day was planned,' wrote one biographer, 'with time allotted for his work, pleasure, friendship, exercise, feeding, study, invention, paternal duties and public relations.'[3]

Edwina found this rigid timetabling hard to bear, especially as he did not always keep to it. Something, or some person, might distract his attention and he would become interested and delayed and fall behind his self-imposed timetable. It never seemed to bother him, but it bothered her, especially when other irritations inevitable in married life for some people built up. Edwina's attitude to engagements and the observation of time were quite opposed to her husband's. Socially, she was extremely casual and preferred to make as few rigid arrangements as she could and turn up late. When, however, she was concerned with official functions and duties, public and private, her timing was impeccable. 'She had some sort of inner watch,' wrote a confederate of Edwina at a later period when her duties had multiplied many times over. 'She timed an inspection or a meeting with amazing precision while not seeming to do so.'

Edwina's easy-come-easy-go style in her recreational and social lives did not in any way interfere with the amount that she packed into a day and a week. 'The pace of the twenties suited her exactly. They might have been made for her,' a friend remarked. The visitors' book at Adsdean accumulated a growing list of names. As the 1924 Season died, Edwina and Dickie made up a party with the Prince of Wales to travel to America to keep the pace going during the dead season when there was not much to do except massacre birds and foxes.

The Prince of Wales was always trying to go to America. The freedom it offered him from protocol and formality, the country's freshness and welcome enthusiasm for new sports and distractions, jazz music and parties, all strongly appealed to his tastes and spirit of fun. Such was his love for America that he even affected a slight American accent. As often as he applied for permission from his father to go he was turned down. In September 1924 he used as an excuse the need to visit his ranch in Canada and to attend the important Anglo-American polo tournament on Long Island.

As soon as it was learned that the Prince and the Mountbattens - 'the Prince of Wales's Set' - were going, large numbers of their friends and a great many who would like to have been, booked passage in the liner *Berengaria* in which they were travelling. In the Prince's group were Dickie's brother Georgie and Nada Milford Haven, the Earl and Countess of Airlie (David and Alex), Harold and Lady Zia Wernher, the Duchess of Westminster, and Edwina's close friend Jean Norton who was married to Lord Grantley's heir, Richard. Lady Diana Cooper, *en route* to play again in *The Miracle* on Broadway, and her husband Duff, spanned the social and entertainment cliques on board, which also included Sophie Tucker, Vera Rubin and Ivor Novello's mother Clara.

The Prince spent the evening before embarking at Broadlands with the Mountbattens and the Ashleys, and the ship sailed the following morning. The *Berengaria* had once been the *Imperator*, intended as the German transatlantic flagship complete with an imperial suite for the Kaiser. Instead, his cousin occupied it, and it inevitably became the heart of the shipboard social goings-on. In fact, he spent a great part of the daylight hours during the passage playing mah-jong with Edwina and Dickie, a game to which he had recently become addicted. But he emerged on one afternoon to take part in the British tug-of-war team to play the Americans. This, of course, was organized by Dickie. Duff Cooper recalled:

> When it was objected that we were none of us either heavy or very muscular, he assured us that it all depended upon trying to pull in the right way and that under his instruction we would prove invincible. After some practice we took

on a team of the ship's crew, who certainly appeared much heavier and stronger than we were, but after a tough struggle we succeeded in defeating them. In our elation it never occurred to us that our opponents had probably received strict orders on no account to pull over the Prince of Wales's team.[4]

In the evenings the passengers saw rather more of the royal party - at a fancy-dress ball, the Prince as a Limehouse apache, and dancing to the ship's jazz band and the quieter ballroom orchestra.

The liner docked at New York on 30 August, reporters and photographers swarming up the gangways. Dickie, in blazer and yachting cap, the Prince in a grey double-breasted suit with wide lapels and tan-suede shoes, greeted them cheerfully. It was at once clear that this was decidedly a non-royal visit, and that the Prince and his party were out for a good time. 'After his long and strenuous years he was in holiday mood and his affinity with what had almost overnight become the richest and most undemanding society in the world was immediately apparent.'[5]

They were to be guests of Mr and Mrs James Burden of Syosset, Long Island, and over the following days the Prince and Edwina, Dickie and 'Fruity' Metcalfe, sometimes with other members of the party, had a richly varied and wholly self-indulgent time at race meetings (Belmont), polo meetings, dances and dinners, small private parties and parties with several hundred guests; or 'streaking it up Long Island in one of the fastest motor boats extant' as the *New York Times* described it, or dashing off in a borrowed car for a late night bathe in the Sound.

If it was not quite such a lurid experience as the New York newspapers reported, everybody was enjoying themselves, not least because the Prince was quite obviously happier and more relaxed than at any time in his life. Before he made the frequently postponed journey to Canada, and the rest of the party sailed home in the *Majestic*, the Prince's staff judged it advisable to issue a denial that HRH did not arise before noon after successions of three parties a night - or 'three straight'. He was always out of bed by 10 a.m., and into his host's swimming-pool, his staff emphasized. Moreover, he was going to visit a school in New York and the Museum of Natural History as well as the offices of the *New York Times* and Wall Street. None of this deceived George V when he heard. He had already made up his mind that none of his sons would again visit the New World during his lifetime.

If the King was not amused by his eldest son's carrying-on in the wicked USA, the effect of the Long Island holiday on Edwina was at once unsettling and depressing. There had been no more enthusiastic participant in the moonlight swims, the cocktail parties and the late-night parties that came to the edge of being out of hand. She enjoyed particularly the company of Nada, who had lesbian inclinations and whose marriage to George Milford Haven was no longer completely happy or fulfilled, and they were often seen together alone. These two young, rich and privileged women had married brothers who shared an enthusiasm for their careers and an abiding interest in the world outside the confines of domestic and social life.

Both Edwina and Nada came home to their families in the autumn of 1924 in a restless frame of mind. Beyond the estates and great houses they knew so well, beyond the new night-clubs of Mayfair, the Berkeley and Claridge's, the town houses of Belgravia, the resorts of Deauville and Cannes, the familiar castles and palaces of their Continental relations, there was a world which neither of them had explored. For Edwina the trip to India had first fired her curiosity to see more of the world. For both of them, the acute degree of restriction and confinement in their lives, as they saw it, had been spelt out clearly by this most recent voyage. They had sailed 7,000 miles and seen nothing beyond the estates and polo grounds of the rich and indulgently kind Americans of Long Island and New York. When Edwina returned to the newly acquired Adsdean, to be greeted by dogs and the nursemaid with eight-month-old Patricia in her arms, she brought with her toys for her child, gifts for the staff, photographs of shipboard life in the *Berengaria* (herself in Sophie Tucker's ample arms), Christmas presents bought on Fifth Avenue, and a stack of sheet music for the Charleston and Black Bottom. Her gifts and mementoes reflected clearly her life as a bright young thing of the mid-1920s; they did not reflect the restless dissatisfaction with her present way of life and the burning curiosity to indulge in experiences she had scarcely begun to explore. That she would soon begin to do this was inevitable. It was as inevitable as her husband's immersion in his signals course at Portsmouth to the exclusion of anything else – except of Edwina, who appeared as a dutiful item on his daily timetable and certainly not someone for whom he showed any depth of feeling or understanding.

While the Mountbattens had been engrossed in polo and parties out on Long Island, Noël Coward was busy on Broadway, staying at the Ritz (until he could no longer afford to do so), cultivating the famous ('I was at that period a bad celebrity snob'[6]) like the Kaufmanns, Alexander Woolcott, Douglas Fairbanks and Ethel Barrymore; and experiencing 'the mixed pain and pleasure of seeing Jack Buchanan bring the house down in the Charlot revue singing "Sentiment" '.[7]

A transatlantic liner could be an ideal venue for cultivating the famous, and it was not entirely by chance that Coward found himself in a first-class cabin on board the liner sailing for home with the Prince of Wales's Long Island set (minus HRH), the Fairbankses and many more who before long would be cultivating Coward. Thus began the long and fruitful relationship between the Mountbattens and 'the Master'.

They met again in London at a party given by the Fairbankses for the Prince of Wales. Edwina enjoyed keeping abreast of fashionable culture, so long as it did not entail reading more than a few lines, and Dickie had a keen calculating eye for the potentially famous. It was all part of the relentless game of remaining fashionable which did not permit any slackening of attention. Noël Coward was just beginning to be known for *I'll Leave it to You* and *The Young Idea* – 'moderately popular', as he defined his position, 'not yet "unspoiled by my great success", but in danger of being distinctly spoiled by the lack of it'.[8]

The Mountbattens, then, were in the front row of the stalls in the tiny Everyman Theatre on the night of 25 November 1924 for the first, tumultuous night of *The Vortex*. From that time the most fashionable playwright and the most fashionable socialites were seen at each other's parties, at the Ivy and Café Royal, and later at many royal occasions. Coward loved Dickie's royal connections and Edwina's sparkle and quick repartee. She embodied the scarcely concealed tense desperation, the striving for novelty which masked the real need for depth and substance in her life, and the staccato manner and speech affected by the spoilt young rich of her generation. In Coward's *Home and Colonial*, inspired by reading Evelyn Waugh's *Vile Bodies*, Lady 'Sandra' Magnus of Government House, Samolo, is a compound of Edwina and Lady Diana Cooper.

To show Mary something of Europe, now that finishing school was behind her, introduce her to skiing and assuage in small measure her own longing to travel, Edwina took her to Wengen in Switzerland at the end of January 1925, where they soon forsook the nursery slopes and began serious skiing with characteristic bravura. Back in England for Easter they were seen at Mrs Ernest Cunard's dance at her house in Portman Square, Mary in a 'blue dress which set off her wonderful red hair' and Edwina in 'soft pink lace'. Mary was shortly to come out and her movements and dresses were as closely followed as Edwina's. Mary, at eighteen, was described as the 'red-haired sister of Lady Louis Mountbatten' and 'almost as beautiful' as

Edwina, and, more crisply, as 'three-fifths as rich as Lady Louis'. Mary Ashley was presented at Court in the second week of May, and was embarking on a social life more than three-fifths as dazzling as Edwina's. The two blessed and beautiful young women were as close friends as they had been when Edwina had kept Mary's spirits up during that awful time when their mother was dying.

As for Edwina five years earlier, Brook House provided the setting for Mary's coming-out ball on 12 June 1925. Edwina threw all her organizational energies into making it a great success with all the grandest possible people present. Dickie's royal cousin had married Elizabeth Bowes-Lyon two years previously and, as the Duke and Duchess of York, headed the guest list, followed by Princess Mary and Prince Henry, 'besides all that's prettiest and smartest on the one hand, and good-looking and eligible on the other, of the younger generation in Society'.

The Season of 1925 was the last that Edwina followed assiduously, broken only by attendance at fashionable weddings such as that of 'Fruity' Metcalfe and Lady Alexandra Curzon on 21 July, and entertaining Dickie's Greek nieces, the Princesses Theodora and Margarita. She was at the Savoy ballroom to hear George Gershwin conduct his own 'Rhapsody in Blue', and dancing at the new Kit-Cat night-club, where she and Dickie were reported as 'having fallen victims to the tango's somewhat crowded charms'. And at Goodwood (Edwina 'in the shortest of skirts'), Cowes, Deauville – *La ronde impitoyable*.

But this was also the year when Dickie learned for the first time of Edwina's infidelities. 'I was terribly upset, and found it hard to believe,' he told this writer. 'It was an awful shock.'[9] Edwina's promiscuity was legendary among her friends and acquaintances, to whom moral discipline was foreign anyway. Besides being shocked Dickie could not understand it. Infidelity at this time was far from his thoughts, which were almost wholly concentrated on passing out not just well but supremely well from his course at Portsmouth. He accepted that his mind was elsewhere on some new naval problem or invention he was contriving. He was not often alone with Edwina. When they were together it was almost always with other people. It was only rarely that there was not someone else in the house, in London and the country, and people who amused them and had nothing else to do sometimes stayed for months, in one case for many years. They were called, quite simply, 'the stayers'.

For his part, Dickie, too, sought comfort elsewhere, although his demands were nothing like as powerful as Edwina's, and he was content with the company of one woman. This was Yola Letellier, the highly attractive and understanding wife of the French newspaper tycoon, Henri, the Mayor (eight times) of Deauville, who was a great deal older than she was. 'Dickie went to bed with Yola for thirty-five years,' recalls a member of the family. 'She was the one woman he had real affection for, and she understood his impatience and priorities and the fact that his mind was often elsewhere.' The importance of this relationship in Mountbatten's life cannot be overrated; at the time it was accepted quite naturally in the family's inner circle, Edwina liked to have her around and was genuinely fond of her, and Yola travelled freely with 'the Set' to social and sporting occasions.

Edwina's sister loyally tends to defend her morals, while conceding that she had her paramours –

> several but not all *that* many. Her very first was the multi-millionaire 'Laddy' Sandford. We were brought up to consider the media, the feelings of everybody and only a tight little coterie knew if there was a love relationship between individuals. Perhaps tactfully on a weekend in a big house, rooms would be arranged so that perhaps the gentlemen did not have to travel too far along the corridors.

Edwina at this time felt absolutely no constraints on her appetites – either for material possessions, which she treated carelessly (the robberies became something of a joke and she would leave priceless furs in restaurants), or for anything else, and certainly not her sexual needs, the gratification of which sometimes seemed to her partners as casual as lighting a cigarette or ordering another bottle of Dom Pérignon.

It is fruitless to speculate whether she would have been so extravagant and unrestrained in her behaviour if she had not inherited a fortune. But the possession of so much wealth and the manner of living in the tight little world into which she was thrust unquestionably conditioned her lifestyle. She embraced it, but was also too clever not to despise it and herself for her own enthusiastic participation. At the tables at Deauville, striding into Cartier or Boucheron impatient for instant attention, nodding acknowledgement of a head waiter's deep bow, the centre of attention in the royal enclosure at Epsom, she appeared the very essence of proud, patrician self-confidence. As a distinguished army officer recalled when she was older, 'She appeared to be someone determined to get her way in all respects, and always succeeded.' But a friend of hers at the time, who knew how dissatisfied she was in spite of her self-indulgent way of living, said, 'For Edwina, there was always something missing. She didn't know what it was or where it was but she was determined to find it.'

Dickie completed his course at Portsmouth and was so successful that he was accepted on the much tougher advance course at Greenwich, which meant moving to London. It was spring 1926. The miners' strike was developing into something more serious. Edwina went shopping in Paris and returned just before the General Strike, which threatened to paralyse the country. It may have seemed paradoxical, but to Edwina it seemed perfectly natural that, while espousing socialist views and deploring the unemployment and the conditions of the working classes, she should spend several thousand pounds in the rue de Rivoli and find herself strike-breaking in Fleet Street two weeks later. Lord Beaverbrook from time to time included himself in the Mountbattens' set, and had known Edwina through Cassel before she was married. He had quarrelled with Dickie in 1923 over a pretty girl, Kitty Kinloch, whom he quite wrongly supposed had become Dickie's mistress. 'Quite crazy and I told him so,' Mountbatten commented later. 'But he didn't believe me.' The Beaverbrook vendetta became notorious and damaging to both sides, but he never showed anything but affection for Edwina. So, when the *Daily Express*'s proprietor began appealing for volunteers to keep his office running (if not his newspaper), Edwina and Jean Norton thought it would be amusing to help run the switchboard. 'I was a freelance,' Lady Diana Cooper recalled in her autobiography, 'driving Duff, taking stranded workers home in my car, telephoning Max Beaverbrook for news and being connected by Edwina Mountbatten and Jean Norton. . . .'[10]

When all this was over, and the Fairbankses had arrived to stay at Brook House and had left in July, Edwina had to make preparations for renting out the Park Lane house (she did so the next year to the Argentine Ambassador) and buying one in Malta. Dickie had been appointed to the flagship of the Mediterranean Fleet as Assistant Fleet Wireless and Signals Officer from 16 December 1926.

Edwina welcomed this move. It promised sunshine and warmth, which she loved, a change of scene, a new life and new distractions, and an opportunity for travelling about the Mediterranean. Dickie was in his element. He revelled in the administrative work required to carry out the family move, and ordered an enormous motor yacht, the *Shrimp*, and a couple of motor cars along with his string of polo ponies to be delivered to Valletta in time for their arrival. Edwina saw to their house. She went out to Malta and found the nearest thing to Brook House on the island, a 'colossal marble monstrosity' Dickie called it, the Villa Refalo. It was not quite right for them as it stood, so she ordered an extensive rebuilding and decorating programme, and meanwhile rented three flats opposite Curzon House in Pieta.

Like all the big houses in Malta, Villa Refalo was built in the classical style of sandstone blocks, laid without mortar, white when freshly quarried but rapidly mellowing to the colour of butter in the wind, sun and sea air. An American described the house as it was when the Mountbattens first moved into it:

> The walls of the interior were painted in plain white distemper and the rooms were furnished with handsome pieces of Regency and early Victorian mahogany. Most of the windows were curtained with lemon-coloured linen, hanging from heavy antique mahogany cornices, and this yellow was echoed by a profusion of marigolds in vases, the only flower - apart from courage - that blooms on the island. Behind the house was a patio and beyond that lay the extensive stables where Lord Louis kept his polo ponies.[11]

By this time, Dickie had changed the name to Villa Medina after one of his brother's titles, the Earl of Medina. One of the many attractions of Malta for Edwina was the presence there of Nada. George was now a gunnery commander with the Fleet, and they had a large and extremely comfortable flat nearby.

During that last winter in London before moving to Malta Edwina followed her customary frenetic social programme in London and down at Adsdean. We see her at the Drury Lane theatre on 9 November for a 'big all-star Shakespeare charity matinée with George V, Queen Mary and most of the rest of the Royal Family'. She was raising funds for rebuilding the Shakespeare Memorial Theatre at Stratford, a highly fashionable cultural exercise. We see her dining as a fellow guest of the Wernhers with the Queen of Spain at Claridge's; and a few days later at a Claridge's ball for the League of the Helping Hand.

'Edwina is always excited about something,' one of her friends commented. 'But Malta is something special and she talks about nothing else except Mary's engagement. She is furious because she's got to have an operation on her foot. "Of all times, why now?" ' Edwina was referred to in *The Tatler* as one of several 'distinguished invalids' just before Christmas, the others being Lady Carnarvon, Lady Meux and Lady Adare.

Edwina was still limping and on a stick when she arrived at Adsdean for Christmas, unable to drive. The dogs came bounding out to meet her, and she received the usual warm welcome from the staff. Mary was with her, and her fiancé Captain Alec Cunningham-Reid, a war flying hero of great wealth and, like his future father-in-law, a Member of Parliament. Their engagement was not to be made public until January. The Ashleys came over from Broadlands for Christmas, too. Wilfrid was not pleased with the world. He had been expecting at least a knighthood if not a baronetcy in the New Year's Honours for his political work, but he knew he would have heard by now. Molly's chagrin was even deeper than her husband's.

With her foot better, Edwina resumed her social life for the last few weeks before sailing for Malta. Noël Coward caught the Mountbattens' world and style of living at this time in his light comedy *Hands Across the Sea*, although he did not write it until some years later. The Mountbattens, according to Coward, 'used to give cocktail parties and people used to arrive that nobody had ever heard of and sit about and go away again; somebody Dickie had met somewhere, or somebody Edwina had met – and nobody knew who they were. We all talked among ourselves, and it was really a very very good basis for a light comedy.'[12]

Noël Coward sent the Mountbattens free seats for the first night without hinting that they were the 'stars' of the show, and they took a party, puzzled by this unusual generosity. 'It was a bare-faced parody of our lives,' exclaimed Dickie. 'Absolutely outrageous, and certainly not worth six free tickets!' But of course they both loved it really. The plot is based on the wrong identification of a couple, the Rawlingsons, invited to Brook House. Commander Peter Gilpin RN (Mountbatten) was played by Coward himself, Lady Maureen 'Piggie' Gilpin (Edwina) was played by Gertrude Lawrence. In it Piggie is only briefly off the telephone and is on it at the beginning of this extract:

Piggie: No, darling, what is the use of having her – she only depresses you – oh – all right! (*Hangs up.*) Oh, dear –

Peter: It's quite easy for you – you can give them lunch on board.

Ally: We're in dry dock.

Peter: They won't mind. (*To Piggie.*) What is it?

Piggie: Robert – plunged in gloom – he's got to do a course at Greenwich – he ran into a tram in Devonport – and he's had a row with Molly – he wants me to have her for the weekend so that they can make it up all over everybody. Have you told Ally about the Rawlingsons?

Peter: Yes, he's taking them over the dockyard, lunching them on board and then he's going to show them a submarine –

Piggie: Marvellous! You're an angel, Ally – I must take off these clothes I'm going mad –

(*She goes out of the room at a run. There is the sound of the front-door bell.*)

Peter: Let's go into my room – I can show you the plans –

Ally: Already? They've been pretty quick with them.

Peter: I made a few alterations – there wasn't enough deck space – she ought to be ready by October, I shall have her sent straight out to Malta –

The man who took the real boat out to Malta, through the French canal system, was the *Shrimp*'s designer, Peter du Cane, with instructions to tuck her out of sight until Dickie arrived.

At the onset of his first important sea appointment, Dickie was well aware of the shoals and reefs that lay ahead of him in Malta. Edwina tended to pooh-pooh the difficulties posed by living abroad at a naval base with numerous other wives, few with a tenth of her wealth and most living very austerely. Dickie had the experience of his father with his close royal connections as a precedent, and in the 1920s the Service had far fewer officers with private means.

Edwina learned from Dickie in advance of the divisions that existed among the officers of Britain's premier fleet between the Pay Only officers (the 'PO's) and the Private Means officers (the 'PM's). She learned about the arrival of 'the fishing fleet' at Malta, the unmarried young women who at once obtained a copy of the Navy List and ran through the names of all those unmarried young officers marking them 'PO' or 'PM'. The married officer PMs lived very different lives ashore at Malta, but the difference was especially marked ashore when the Fleet was cruising. The 'expensive lot' of wives would turn up at Cannes or Brindisi, Alexandria or Crete according to the movements of the Fleet. They mostly came, in style, by liner or train. Edwina would be among the relatively few who had their own steam yacht, yet her husband was still only a lieutenant.

The less privileged 'PO' officers came ashore and made their own amusements among themselves. A retired captain explained:

> On cruises the 'expensive lot' took their wives. The POs never met the PMs ashore. There were no hard feelings. We didn't regard them as royalty, nor envy them, we just thought the women were rather stupid, giggling and making funny faces. Most POs disregarded the high jinks of the rich, but the lower deck was not all that pleased, not because they were rich, but because they were seldom on board arranging sports etc. for the sailors and taking an interest in their men. Mountbatten was an exception. Firstly, he was regarded as a royal and therefore he got the same loyalty from the lower deck as has always been given to the monarchy. Secondly he was very clever, and thirdly he was an excellent seaman. Later, however, his hand-picked crew and his perpetual advertisement that his was the only destroyer of note, lowered their estimation.

Unlike the Army and the RAF the Royal Navy made no provision for married quarters ashore at Malta, and many junior officers could not afford the passage or the rent money for their wives. Now here was a twenty-six-year-old lieutenant coming to live in the highest style with his family, with his own 'bloody great yacht' as another lieutenant described it and his own string of polo ponies. 'We didn't bother about the fellow,' was a characteristic comment after the Mountbattens' arrival. 'I was not one of the stable lads.' (This was the ironic term used for some junior officers who were asked by PMs with polo ponies to help exercise them in their free time as the local population could not be entrusted with this task.)

Edwina was completely confident that any difficulties they might meet could at once be charmed away. She flattered herself that she was equally at home with all classes and all levels of income. Five years earlier she would have been daunted by the task. Now, as Sir Charles Baring has attested, she was an entirely different woman. She was twenty-five, self-assured and perfectly prepared for any problems life in Malta might pose for her.

'She was certainly the most beautiful woman in Malta,' a young officer at this time remembers. 'She had quite a "fast" reputation already, and to tell you the truth we were all looking forward to her parties.'

At the end of March 1927 Edwina and Mary left for Paris on a buying spree, including part of Mary's trousseau, and then rendezvoused with Patricia, nannies, secretaries and the rest of her entourage in the South of France. Dickie's ship *Warspite* was due to make a courtesy visit to Villefranche, and the moment when the great battleship, a veteran of the Battle of Jutland, dropped anchor in the bay and Dickie and other members of the staff came ashore in the Admiral's barge can be regarded as the beginning of Edwina's overseas service as a naval wife.

7
The Restless Heart

There is a certain similarity between Admiral Lord Nelson and Emma at a naval port in the Mediterranean and Lieutenant Lord Mountbatten and Edwina at Malta a century and a quarter later. There is a disparity in rank and age and Mountbatten was not yet a Nelsonian hero, whatever his reputation may have been at Mayfair's Kit-Cat Club. But wherever he went eyes turned towards him, and Edwina's looks and reputation attracted as much curiosity as Emma had received from the sailors in Naples Bay in 1798.

Most of the officers had already made their minds up about Dickie Mountbatten. Those who had not yet met him during his eleven years' service had learned of his reputation and reacted accordingly. No one questioned his qualities as a seaman, but a lot of officers of all ranks questioned his style and manner. He began with this huge disadvantage of privilege or presumed privilege, and from that point became his own worst enemy. Perhaps he could not help it, perhaps his German antecedents and family background blinded him to the folly of flaunting his sharp competitiveness, and not only in gunnery practice or inter-ship regattas. Nor did the exhibitionism and the evident conviction that he was right in everything he did endear him to many officers. His father had suffered from these self-inflicted disabilities in exactly the same way, and made very few friends. In Dickie's case there were some officers in the wardroom who had the perception to recognize that they had in their midst an agreeable, intelligent and amusing young man who was making the best of a very awkward position. But they were not many, and in later years Mountbatten would often complain of the uphill task he had to establish himself in a new ship. He was never a man's man, only, later, a young man's man, when there was no competitive element.

One of Edwina's important and little-acknowledged contributions to her husband's success in his career was made in these early difficult days.

'It was Edwina who took him in hand when he complained of injustice and having to fight with one hand tied behind his back,' a contemporary and friend of Mountbatten claimed. 'Of course it was tough for him, but she would rally him and tell him to "Rise above it, Dickie! Worse things happen at sea."' This affectionate, crisply simple recipe was just what was needed. He did indeed 'rise above it', sustained by the knowledge that his father had done just that; and, paradoxically, by the wounding knowledge that 'they' had got his father in the end. They were not going to get Dickie Mountbatten. But they might well have done so had Edwina not been there behind him, advising, guiding and encouraging a strong line.

For Edwina herself during these difficult years, a strong line came naturally. The unhappy, scruffy, eighteen-year-old girl Charles Baring had talked to for long hours back in the winter of 1920 still could not see where destiny was going to take her. But her conviction that it would carry her far and high was stronger than ever, and the mastery of organization and administration that came with the inheritance of wealth, the control of large households and the creation of a family, had given her a new sense of authority and self-confidence. Anyone could see that in her step and her manner of conducting herself.

There were no terrors for Edwina in facing the curiosity of Service wives who had gossiped about her past and her reputation long before she arrived, and long after her arrival. Some of these wives, and their husbands, looked forward to the Mountbatten descent upon the island, half expecting that they might introduce into a relatively staid and established social scene a touch of the more abandoned gaiety of Brook House, especially as Edwina had brought along her sister, whose reputation was quite as colourful as her own. (Mary adored Malta. 'Some of the happiest days of my life have been spent there with Edwina and Dickie,' she says today.) The officers and their wives were 'curious and anxious to meet those "well-known society people",' wrote one commentator, 'hoping they would give an unending series of large and lavish cocktail and dinner parties.'[1]

It was not like that. There was nothing spectacular about the beginning of the Mountbatten social era on Malta. With un-showy bustle, the family settled in to their flat – nursemaids, chauffeur, secretary, cook, housemaids, gardeners, grooms: a miniature Adsdean. The Mountbattens gathered about them their own coterie, led by the Milford Havens. Visitors arrived and departed: the Spanish royal family, the Casa Maurys – Paula (*née* Gellibrand) and the Marquis – friends from the South of France, the Brecknocks, Dickie's mother and the Greek princesses.

Above left: En route to the tennis finals at Wimbledon, 1924; *above:* and at rest against the marble of Brook House, 1925

Left: With Marjorie Brecknock at the Metcalfe-Curzon wedding, Chapel Royal, 1925

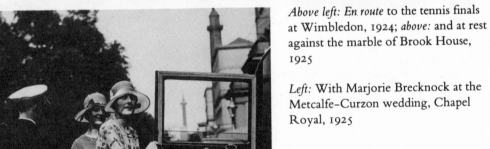

Left: With Mary at the seaside; *above:* and with Dickie at the Grand National, 1926

Below: Cowes Regatta, 1926. Edwina at the helm of her bull-nose Morris with her all-girl crew, including Lady Loughborough next to her and 'Poppy' Baring and her sister in the dickie

Newly promoted
Lieutenant-Commander
Lord Louis Mountbatten,
1928

Patricia, aged three, with
Edwina, 1927

Above: Douglas Fairbanks and Mary Pickford, Edwina's guests, 1929

Below: Mary, now the Hon. Mrs Alec Cunningham-Reid

Right: With King Alfonso of Spain

LADY LOUIS MOUNTBATTEN AND "THE PEOPLE"

LIBEL ACTION SETTLED: APOLOGY IN COURT

Lady Louis Mountbatten was the plaintiff in a libel action, Mountbatten v. Odhams Press Limited and Another, before the Lord Chief Justice in the King's Bench Division on Friday.

Mr. Birkett, K.C., announced that the action had been settled.

He said that Odhams Press Limited were the proprietors of "The People," the editor of which, Mr. Harry Ainsworth, was also a defendant in the action.

Defendants had submitted to every demand made upon them by the plaintiff, and after the statements which would be made in court he would ask that the record be withdrawn on terms he would state publicly.

Plaintiff was the wife of Lord Louis Mountbatten, a naval officer, at present attached to the Mediterranean Fleet. In August, 1931, he was ordered with his ship to Malta for an appointment which in the ordinary way would be for two years.

As was only natural and right, Lady Louis decided to go with him, taking her children with her. She intended to make her home in Malta for the period of her husband's service.

That inevitable and natural desire on her part to be with her husband gave rise, it would appear, to the most atrocious and most abominable rumours.

Lady Louis took a prominent part in the social life of London, and her departure, which was stated in the Press at the time to be for about two years, gave the opportunity for the malignant, poisonous and lying tongues of scandal to wag.

LORD AND LADY LOUIS MOUNTBATTEN.

"It is, of course," went on Mr. Birkett, "always a matter of acute difficulty to ascertain the actual author of a dastardly rumour, and even now, though the most rigorous steps are being taken to track these rumours to their source, I do desire to say publicly that if the author, or indeed the repeater, of these rumours is discovered, no mercy will be shown and no consideration of any kind will be extended."

Mr. Birkett added that in this case they dealt only with the newspaper.

Before reading the libel, Mr. Birkett said:

The Libel

"The practice on these occasions is not to read the libel in order to avoid giving further publicity to it, but after the most careful consideration, and indeed at the express request of Lady Louis Mountbatten, I propose to read the libel.

"I will do that in order that its full enormity may be known."

The libel, he said, was headed "Behind the Scenes," and was signed "The Watcher."

Underneath was the headline in large type "Famous Hostess Exiled."

Lord Hewart: You have not been able to find out who "The Watcher" is?

Mr. Birkett: We have not.

Mr. Birkett said that another headline to the article was "Society Shaken by Terrible Scandal."

The article read:

"I am able to reveal to-day the sequel to a scandal which has shaken society to the very depths. It concerns one of the leading hostesses in the country—a woman highly connected and immensely rich.

"Her associations with a coloured man became so marked that they were the talk of the West End. Then one day the couple were caught in compromising circumstances.

"The sequel is that the society woman has been given hints to clear out of England for a couple of years to let the affair blow over, and the hint comes from a quarter which cannot be ignored."

"Your lordship will observe," continued Mr. Birkett, "that 'The Watcher' gives no name.

"There are many witnesses here this morning ready to go into the witness-box and say that when they read the paragraphs in this paper they believed that they pointed unmistakably to Lady Louis Mountbatten.

"They were horrified and shocked to find this loathsome allegation coupled with her name.

"Lady Louis Mountbatten is a famous hostess; she is one of the leading hostesses of society; she is highly connected; she is immensely rich, and she has gone to Malta for two years.

"Your lordship may think that the word 'Exiled' at the top of the article, coupled with the words, 'The hint comes from a quarter which cannot be ignored,' puts it beyond all doubt that the writer deliberately intended to defame Lady Louis Mountbatten.

"It is unnecessary to say that there is not one syllable of truth in these horrible allegations, nor is there the faintest ground upon which these lying rumours could be brought into existence at all.

"Lady Louis has been informed by her friends of the identity of the coloured man supposed to be referred to in this article. She has never even met him nor had anything whatsoever to do with him in any shape or form.

"As soon as the libel appeared in print every endeavour was made to track down the originator of this foul rumour.

"Lady Louis Mountbatten was compelled to bring the proceedings publicly to vindicate her good name. If the case had been fought out in court it would have been the right of Lady Louis Mountbatten to go into the box to deal with those matters on oath.

"She desires this morning," added Mr. Birkett, "to ask your lordship's permission, despite the course the defendants have taken, to go into the box to deny upon oath these poisonous allegations.

"Defendants had never sought to defend the action. Immediately complaint was made that the name of Lady Louis Mountbatten was being associated with this article they did everything in their power to mitigate the very grievous wrong which had been committed.

"The defendants had given to Lady Louis Mountbatten the fullest indemnity for the costs and expenses to which she had been put, and an unqualified apology and withdrawal which they intended to repeat again in court through Sir Patrick Hastings.

"There is one further matter of some importance," added Mr. Birkett. "Your lordship will appreciate from what I have already said in this undefended case that Lady Louis Mountbatten was in a position to demand not only damages, but exceedingly heavy damages from the defendants.

Without Doubt

"Without the smallest doubt a jury would have awarded very heavy damages, and there are no limits to the sum which a jury might have awarded in this case.

"Lady Louis desired it to be made plain that in the circumstances of this case no money that could be named would be adequate to compensate her for the anguish, misery and distress which this libel has caused.

"To accept one single penny would be to her in the highest degree distasteful. What she did desire was that she should have a speedy and public vindication of her name, and that would be done in the fullest possible manner."

Lord Louis Mountbatten gave evidence of his appointment abroad which, he said, was announced in the public press at the time. He made arrangements for his wife and children to accompany him a little later.

Mr. Birkett: And have you returned on special leave simply and solely in order to go into the witness-box?—Yes.

Lady Louis Mountbatten followed her husband in the witness-box and said she had come back from Malta solely for that purpose.

Mr. Birkett: The second paragraph in this publication deals with a coloured man. Is there one single word of truth in the allegations there made?—Not one single word. In fact I have never in the whole course of my life ever met the man referred to.

Your friends have named to you the coloured man supposed to be referred to in the paragraph?—They have.

Do you tell my lord you have never met him?—I have never met him.

K.C.'s Statement

And you have never had anything to do with him in any shape or form?—The whole thing is a preposterous story.

Sir Patrick Hastings, K.C., for the defendants, said that having regard to what had been said the only reason for his appearance on behalf of the proprietors was to do everything he could to put right what undoubtedly was a very grievous injustice which had been done to Lady Louis.

From the moment the defendants' notice was drawn to the matter their only object was to accede to every request made and to volunteer all the assistance they could give in a genuine desire to make it clear to everyone who might be interested that defendants had nothing but the most sincere and genuine regrets for the publication.

Defendants now understood it to be a rumour of which they themselves had never heard.

"It is quite idle for me," said Sir Patrick, "merely to express regrets. What I am anxious to say is that everyone who has heard Lady Louis's denial of these atrocious rumours and everyone who in future will read her denial, must be satisfied once and for all that there was no ground for the rumour and no truth in the suggestion underlying it.

"The defendants desire to express to her and to Lord Louis Mountbatten their genuine and deep regrets for the publication and to ask them to believe that these expressions are not only genuine but sincere.

"Had Lady Louis desired that damages should be paid, we would have been most anxious and willing to pay them."

Lord Hewart: What is it I am asked to do?

Mr. Birkett: I ask that the record be withdrawn on the terms I have indicated.

"With considerable doubt and hesitation," continued Lord Hewart, "I assent to the request that the record be withdrawn, but I don't exclude another possibility from my mind. A copy of the paper will remain in the custody of the Court. I should indeed have been surprised if the plaintiff had accepted pecuniary damages in such a case as this."

The record was accordingly withdrawn on the terms mentioned.

(Mr. Henry Moore, of "The Watcher's Weekly," asks us to state that he is in no way connected with "The Watcher" who, until last week, signed our gossip column.)

Top left: Paul Robeson with Peggy Ashcroft in *Othello* at the Savoy Theatre, 1930

Above: The *People* report on the libel action, 1932, which had such a shattering effect on Edwina

Left: On the way to Buckingham Palace for lunch on the day after the libel action in the King's Bench Division

Left: With Jean Norton at Brioni, August 1932

Below: Balmoral, August 1936. Edward VIII dressed as a peasant, with Dickie; and on the right, Wallis Simpson and Edwina

Above: On her return from the Pacific

Left: Edwina's travels: Polynesia, 1935; the copra boat in which she served as a crew member

With Dickie at the Miami Biltmore Country Club, 1938

LAURENCE OLIVIER SOPHIE STEWAR
TREATMENT SUGGESTED BY J.M. BARRIE

Top: With Noël Coward at the first nig of *As You Like It*, September 1936

Left: 'Society women play their part in the war effort', as the original caption reads. With Lady Forbes in Edwina's new role with the WVS sorting out comforts for the Forces

Above: Edwina joins the St John Ambulance soon after the outbreak of the Second World War

Those who had waited so expectantly for a new and spectacular dimension to Valletta's social life noted the unexpected quietness of the coterie, and also its restlessness. Officers' wives found it difficult enough to subsist there at all, and rarely had visitors or other members of their family to stay. Mobility was governed by wealth, and few naval families were wealthy in 1927. The Mountbatten crowd were so peripatetic! Every week people were coming and going, disembarking from the ferry or from ocean liners or their own yachts and re-embarking for the French Riviera or Rome or Brindisi, cars and taxis making something of a Piccadilly of their street. The locals loved it. Not only were the Mountbatten set spending lavishly and employing local labour, but this family was so polite, especially milady.

And then suddenly, in early May 1927, they all disappeared, everyone except the resident local servants. Mary was to be married and Edwina was to be hostess, beside her father, at the reception. Edwina took a house in Upper Belgrave Street for the Season because Brook House was let, although the Argentine Ambassador gladly agreed to allow the reception to be held there.

The wedding was like a repeat of the Mountbattens'. 'All London was there.' 'The bride was lovely. Her beauty is not quite so striking perhaps as her sister's, but it is more ethereal.' 'Lady Mountbatten seemed to have achieved a new dignity to add to her beauty as she received her guests,' noted another observer. 'She has certainly been the perfect elder sister.' And Patricia appeared for the first time in an active role, as a bridesmaid. There were a thousand guests and a thousand presents. It was another spectacular wedding, this time in perfect weather. Everyone claimed that it was 'a real love match'. The Cunningham-Reids left for the South of France, and then for America in the *Olympic* and a world tour.

There is no hint of contentment or serenity of mind in Edwina over the following years. Her beautiful home in Malta did not see her for more than a few days until she returned with Patricia to be with Dickie over Christmas 1927. Those whose business it was to follow the travels of the rich and famous had great difficulty in keeping up with Edwina's movements. 'She seems to move about Europe faster than anyone else,' one of them wrote from France, 'being in Malta at one moment, London the next, Brioni for the polo, and now probably miles away from Dinard.' And another: 'Lady Louis Mountbatten is said to be in Genoa, but she is so ubiquitous that one can't be sure.' *The Times* reported her as being on her way to America in the *Majestic*, others denied this. In November she and

Marjorie Brecknock were at another Noël Coward first night, *Home Chat*. 'She had hardly arrived from Malta when she dashed off to Paris, and last week she was at the Aintree National.'

A constant characteristic of Edwina's movements, which was later noted by the newspapers, was that she was nearly always seen with women – women, of course, of her own rank and means. Besides her sister, these were Nada, Jean Norton, Lady Katherine Brownlow, Lady Daphne Weymouth, Lady Alexandra Metcalfe, Marjorie Brecknock, Paula Casa Maury, and one or two others. At one polo meeting in the summer of 1928, a reporter observed 'our four most lovely women together, Lady Mountbatten, Lady Alexandra Metcalfe, Mrs Richard Norton and the Marchesa de Casa Maury. Why has no one invented a name for this quartet, they go about so much together?'

Also in that same year Edwina, Marjorie Brecknock and Alexandra Metcalfe opened an all-women's club, ironically called 'Masters', in Savile Row, 'somewhere where they could have cocktails, luncheon and perhaps dinner before the theatre'. Four more women, including the Duchess of Sutherland, stepped in to form a committee. In the end men were also reluctantly admitted, 'being necessary and desirable for financial as well as other reasons', as an 'intimate gossip columnist' recounted to his readers.

In September 1928 Edwina sailed for America in the *Leviathan* to stay with Gloria Vanderbilt. It was on this trip that she fell in love with Harlem. Ever since her first visit to India in 1922 she had acquired a special attraction for people with dark skins. It was not only because Edwina instinctively questioned and then very often turned her back upon received opinion and prejudice, although that would have been enough for her to take her own stand on the colour question. At mixed-colour gatherings – few in London, more in New York – she naturally gravitated towards black people. She seems to have been born with a love of people with dark skins and this affection remained with her for all her life. Their presence, whether the skin was light dusky Indian or West African deep black, seemed to comfort and reassure her. At a time when colour distinction was not regarded as prejudice but normal and commonplace, and the reverse regarded as eccentric, Edwina communicated with black people as easily as with white people, and they always responded as sympathetically, a factor that was to be of supreme importance later in her life. She trusted black people, loved their art and their music, whether mournful soul and blues or hot jazz as played by Louis Armstrong. Above all, conscious as she always was of her Jewish blood and background, and of the Jewish history of persecution, she related to black people everywhere as the downtrodden of the world.

The subject of archaeology was also at this time beginning to take a serious grip on her, and she acquired numerous books on the subject. Not to read, of course. She persuaded her friends to do that for her, reading them and picking out the salient points. She never could find time, she would tell her sister, to read them herself. The first attraction of archaeology was that it offered her a justification for getting away from home, and for adventurous exploration in out-of-the-way places. It all started in a modest enough way. After returning to Malta for Christmas 1928, Edwina, with her sixty-five-year-old but game mother-in-law, made her first archaeological trip to Algeria, working along the sites of the North African coast. She was pregnant again, but was quite undeterred by this inconvenience. She joined Dickie at Gibraltar when his ship anchored. There were the usual dinners and receptions for the arrival of the flagship; then, with a few days' leave due to him, Dickie took Edwina to stay in Morocco, where they were, naturally, received by the Sultan. When Dickie was due back, the Straits were suffering such appalling weather that the regular ferry could not put to sea. With his ship about to sail, Dickie resorted to chartering an open launch at Tangiers and they endured a wretchedly rough and even rather dangerous passage back to Gibraltar.

The flagship's next port of call was Barcelona. Edwina's Rolls-Royce was available, but not the *Shrimp* or the chauffeur. 'So Edwina insisted on driving herself the 600 miles or so to Barcelona,' Mountbatten later recounted, his mother having now returned directly to England. 'The roads were terrible.' To Edwina the journey meant nothing. She had complete confidence in her car and in herself as a driver. She was, in fact, by contrast with her husband, now well known as a superb driver. Kenelm Lee Guinness (of the brewing family), who started the K.L.G. spark plug company and was a notable racing driver, once described Edwina's driving as 'better than any man I've ever known'. When asked about Dickie as a driver, he answered, after a pause, 'The worst'. Edwina was, however, now eight months pregnant and the jolting had its predictable effect. By the time she reached the Ritz Hotel in Barcelona the pains had begun, and she greeted Dickie with the news. He was delighted and reached for the telephone. It was an automatic response for him to make contact with the most important available person if he had news or required advice. So he asked for the King in Madrid.

The events that followed made a contribution to the large fund of stock stories Mountbatten might recite at the appropriate moment. The telephone line was bad and King Alfonso thought the Mountbattens were requiring protection rather than a doctor. So in no time at all the hotel was surrounded by soldiers to herald the arrival of the Military Governor of Barcelona. There was, of course, a happy outcome. A doctor and nun were found, and on 19 April 1929 Edwina gave birth to Pamela Carmen Louise Mountbatten. Marjorie Brecknock, summoned from England, arrived the next day.

It says much for Edwina's physical toughness and resilient spirit that the baby survived the last weeks of racketing about Africa and Gibraltar. Such was the nature of Edwina's life after the age of thirty that she had no more children. It was never a source of regret to her, but Dickie's hopes of having a male heir were dashed as a result and this became a subject of much bitterness between them.

Edwina returned to London late in April with her two children. She had Brook House again as a base between trips to the Continent, and in August she and Jean Norton with Arnold Bennett, Beaverbrook's aide Brigadier Michael Wardell, and several others were invited on a cruise by Beaverbrook. It took in the northern capitals and Leningrad and Moscow. They lived in such protected splendour that Edwina was unable to satisfy her curiosity about the real Russia and the lives of the ordinary people. She merely remained approving of the socialist experiment, quite undeterred by the fact that the Russians kept a particularly wary eye on her in the mistaken belief that she was a sister of the Tsar they had assassinated twelve years earlier.

She returned happily and eagerly to the social whirl. The Fairbankses came to stay at Brook House; Dickie arrived for a lot of polo; and there was a splendid evening with Prince George, the future Duke of Kent, at the first night of Coward's *Bitter Sweet*.

The Cunningham-Reids had bought a house in Upper Brook Street, just round the corner from Brook House. While it was being internally stripped and virtually rebuilt, Mary and Alec lived, in total harmony with their host and hostess, in a capacious suite in Brook House. When the work was complete they held a large-scale house-warming party in the New Year. Edwina was reported to be in a beaded white frock with matching coat which she kept on the whole evening, even when dancing, which was considered very recherché.

Early in 1930, before taking up a home shore appointment, Dickie went on to half pay in order to make another long visit to America. They had talked about doing this with the Brecknocks many times. Dickie wanted to re-establish his contacts in Hollywood with Sam Goldwyn, Cecil B. de Mille, Charlie Chaplin and others. His interest in show business, and in the movies in particular, was more intense than ever. He wanted to initiate a

Royal Naval Film Corporation – as it came to be called – to provide entertainment on men-of-war and encourage the making of films for recreation and for improving many professional aspects of naval practice. The four of them made a light-hearted compatible party. They again hired a special coach on the train for crossing the continent and ever-hospitable Hollywood welcomed them as warmly as before.

In April 1930 one of the glossy magazines chiefly concerned with the movements, the clothes, the births and marriages, the houses and the tittle-tattle of society people reported that 'Lady Mountbatten is expected back from America soon. Her many friends must often regret the wanderlust which takes her away so often and so far, leaving her such short intervals to spend in London.' This had been noted many times before by this and other magazines and newspapers, and it was true that of course she was always missed by her friends when she was away. But there is a certain significance in this comment, for 1930 was the last year until the war when she did not make one of the expeditions that became remarkable for their duration and adventurousness. The wanderlust of the past was nothing compared with the wanderlust of the future.

Edwina Mountbatten's married life can conveniently be divided into three phases. For the first ten years she found herself in the world in which circumstances had placed her, a small world of the rich, privileged, titled, with networks to all centres of influence, cushioned from the realities of everyday life for ordinary people, guarded by the bastions of power. There were rules of behaviour which were generously flexible, though Edwina came close to breaking them. It was a fevered, fantasy world really, depicted by Michael Arlen, Noël Coward and Evelyn Waugh whose dramatis personae were Margot Metroland, Paul Pennyfeather, Lottie Crump, Peter Pastmaster and Lily Christine (in real life Mrs Richard Norton). It has been called decadent, meaningless and self-indulgent. It was all these things, but its worst evil was its wastefulness.

Edwina has often been referred to as the poor little rich girl of this era. But there was nothing to be pitied. She could have swum away if she did not like the beach upon which she had been cast. Or she could have chartered the *Berengaria*. But she loved it. Her pleasure can be observed in what she wrote, what she said, in what people remember of her, in the countless photographs of her, at Deauville and Cannes, dancing the Black Bottom, at sea in the *Shrimp*. As general social behaviour had reacted against the restraints of Victorian codes, so Edwina relished the freedom from childhood constraints her class and wealth offered her. She loved spending money on over-priced dresses and motor cars. She loved rushing from here to there. She loved having affairs and hearing of the affairs of others, travelling and relaxing with women friends, experimenting with drugs and from time to time gambling and drinking too much.

There was nothing pathetic about Edwina Mountbatten during this period. The only pathetic thing was the waste. Edwina was willing to be profligate in all things, and that included the waste of her brain and the years of her prime. She was much too intelligent not to recognize that, for example, it was not enough to pay only lip service to the arts, go to first nights of experimental plays, cultivate promising and amusing young artists, especially if they were surrealists, and hang Miró drawings up her stairs. This might be the smart thing to do. But it was not enough. Nothing was enough. The more she satiated her appetites, the faster she fled from one distraction to another and one bed to another, the more she realized that the greatest need of all was not being satisfied: to discover who she was and what she was here for. What was it all about? What *was* her destiny? Edwina was not the poor little rich girl; she was the rich little lost girl.

She began to discover what life was all about in the second phase of her married life. She found her destiny and completed her mission in the final phase, although she never recognized that she had done so. She never found peace, but she was not looking for it. She was not looking for it because she did not know that it was attainable.

The real broadening of Edwina's horizons, the renewed search, began in 1931. She had told her friends in 1928 that she was going to North Africa to visit archaeological sites. Archaeology and the study of ancient civilizations was indeed a spur to her travels. But more than anything else she wanted to learn about people and places, the more distant and little known the better. Nor did she in the least mind dangers and discomforts; she never even considered them. And so, after the comforts and relative security of Southern California, Edwina and Marjorie Brecknock disappeared into the wilds of Mexico, Guatemala and Honduras to study Mayan art and civilization in the Yucatan peninsula. Then they chartered a boat and made their way about the islands of the West Indies, enjoying the swimming and the sun. They were back in London by May, suntanned and full of their adventures.

In 1932 Edwina turned to the East. This time she took Nada as a companion. Dickie's sister-in-law did not have a mind to match Edwina's, but she relished danger, was game for anything, and always preferred the company of women. They rendezvoused in Germany and then proceeded on what the press described as a 'lengthy trip into the wilds of Arabia'. Their route took in Jerusalem and Damascus, Akaba in Transjordania, Baghdad and Tehran; they travelled with basic camping equipment, wearing shorts and shirt for the rougher times, and formal clothes for the more formal occasions. For, while this was an informal expedition, without any strict itinerary, Edwina alerted kings, sheiks and sultans as well as British ambassadors along their route. This course of action was as much second nature to her as it was to Dickie.

In Transjordania Edwina chartered a light aeroplane for hopping about the desert, camping beside it at night. In Damascus they bought an ancient car and drove 600 miles across rough desert to Baghdad. The British Minister there invited them to dinner and tried to dissuade them from continuing: savage mountains, hostile tribes and other fearful dangers lay between Baghdad and Tehran, he warned them. But the spirit of Lady Hester Stanhope, and more recently Ethel Mannin and Freya Stark, burnt brightly in the hearts of these two women and they refused all offers of help or escort.

The car held together for this, the roughest stretch of their journey, and they made Tehran in good time. Here, according to Edwina's friend Madeleine Masson, 'In the grottoes of Tak-i-Bostan they admired angels with Coptic faces and, as the sky deepened into azure dusk, they were enveloped in the inimitable blue which is the colour of Persia, and is reflected in the sky, the water, the water jars, and often in the clothes of the women.'[2]

Before leaving Europe, Edwina had contacted Dr Ernst Herzfeld, the distinguished German-born archaeologist who had first worked in Kurdistan in 1905 and had for some years been excavating at Persepolis, the buried city he had discovered. Herzfeld was jealous of his privacy and did not care for visitors as a rule, but had invited Edwina to study some of his findings. She and Nada spent a fascinating week there with this unsurpassed guide, and Edwina always called it 'the most interesting time in my life'. At the end of November they were back in Baghdad, where they dined with King Faisal, and on 5 December flew back to Jerusalem.

They were home for Christmas at Adsdean, showing off rock carvings, statuettes, icons and a memento from every part of their spectacular journey.

The years 1934 and 1935 showed that Edwina's desperate need to be on the move resulted in her rarely being with Dickie or the children or at home, either in Malta or in England. 'I don't know what it was,' one of her friends speculated. 'Something kept driving her on. It was as if she was tied into one of her fast cars and it had no brakes.' At the end of January 1934 she persuaded Marjorie Brecknock to come and explore South America with her, and they started off from Lisbon for Rio de Janeiro via Las Palmas and Pernambuco. Friends and acquaintances whisked them about the hinterland and they swam and sunbathed before heading for Buenos Aires.

Edwina was determined that they should trek over the Andes and down to the Chilean side. This was a rougher trek than either of them had encountered before, not just testing but downright dangerous. They had a guide who appears to have treated them rather like two of his pack horses; and in jodhpurs and numerous layers of woollies, knives stuck into their belts, they rode up through rain and snow and freezing wind, sleeping rough, and then down to Puyehue, across the lake, heading for Osorno.

The two women, both in their early thirties, then worked their way more rapidly up the coastline of Chile to Antofagasta and by train to La Paz in Bolivia, where they suffered from mountain sickness and became closely involved in a local uprising, with shooting in the streets – and at them. The Inca ruins drew them to Macchu Pichu, and by mid-April they were back in the Yucatan, again studying the Mayan civilization.

One man who knew Edwina particularly well at this time says today:

> Edwina's travels were a great mystery to me, and to a good many other men who knew her intimately. It was as if she wanted to get away from men for a while. She always travelled with women and she always seemed to go out of her way to live 'posh' or very primitively, risking her neck sometimes. She used to write letters, I believe, but I don't think she kept a diary or anything like that. She took a camera and she used to show me her pictures when she got home – very good, too. But she didn't seem to learn anything much – or rather not for long. She picked up an awful lot about archaeology but never followed it up with any reading, and after a few years she was on to something else.

After being away for four months, Marjorie and Edwina separated at Miami, Florida, and Edwina joined Dickie for a week or two on Malta. The children, though pleased to see her, seemed perfectly content with their nursemaid and Patricia's governess. The girls, now aged five and ten, were quite contrasting in appearance. Patricia was tall for her age, already held herself well, and was the more serious of the two, while Pammy was a plump giggler, more fun-loving than her sister had been at this age. They were both brown and Patricia was already a strong swimmer.

A stream of visitors now appeared at the Villa Medina. Wherever Edwina remained for more than a few days they always arrived in numbers like medieval barons paying court to some royal progress. Among them on this occasion were King Alfonso and Noël Coward and a chirpy fair-haired boy of rising thirteen, Prince Philip of Greece, the future Duke of Edinburgh.

Edwina was off again before summer had much advanced in the Mediterranean, now to Indo-China, the first time she had travelled to the Far East, visiting ruins and temples and the ancient site of Angkor. The following year she was away for many more months, this time with the intention of exploring the Pacific and studying Polynesian culture and history. In Papeete, Tahiti, she signed on with two other Europeans as crew of an ancient fifty-ton schooner trading copra for beads and trinkets as Captain Cook had once traded for fresh food 150 years earlier. No one heard from her for four months while she roughed it, standing watch, scrubbing down decks and trimming the sails through fair weather and many foul squalls. She returned to Tahiti invigorated, almost as black as the natives, hands hardened and calloused. She returned to Europe via Australia as passenger number one on the first ever Sydney–London commercial flight, dropping off at Malta.

It had been a tougher experience than any before it, and this time she had no woman friend or relation with her, almost as if she hoped for greater success in finding herself while freed of any association with her home life.

As on all her travels, once she arrived at any point of civilization her life was transformed. Not only did she herself command suites in the best hotels, but officials from governors and ambassadors downwards, and rich locals, came to see if they could do anything for her. And there she would be, as likely as not in a faded cotton dress or old jodhpurs, showing pleasure at her welcome, modestly, even casually, reciting her adventures, showing her mementoes, retracing her route on her maps, something she always particularly enjoyed as a great map enthusiast. Then, the next morning she would be away again, by the first train or ship or – increasingly through the 1930s – by plane.

Early in 1936, while it was still cold in England, she suddenly took herself off to Vladivostock alone, travelling in a luxury private car on the Trans-Siberian Railway. Then she embarked on a primitive steamer to Vancouver and made her way across Canada.

'How was your holiday?' Stella Underhill asked her on her return. 'Rather cold,' replied Edwina. 'Well, milady, if you will go to Siberia in mid-winter. . . .' Miss Underhill was always ready with the sound, practical comment.

As for Mountbattan, such was the deplorable state of their marriage, he was content for her to be away for as long as she wished. At the same time, even to his closest friends and family, he assumed a considerable pride in Edwina's travels, in accordance with his immutable policy of finding total satisfaction in every aspect and every detail of the life of every Mountbatten. Later, he ordered a large and beautiful coffee table upon the glass top of which was engraved a map of the world with every one of Edwina's journeys traced on it, to which the attention of visitors was drawn.

During the spells in London between these long voyages and treks about the world, Edwina continued her social-cultural rounds as relentlessly as before, and her friends agreed that the more she tried to wear herself out clambering over the Andes the more energy she seemed to generate for late nights out in London. There she would be, tanned and fashionably dressed – a touch *outreé* but no more – chatting and laughing with her close circle of women friends at first nights, at private views of *avant-garde* artists, shopping at lightning speed in Bond Street and Knightsbridge, dancing with the Duke of Kent at the Cavendish, myopically scanning the card at Ascot.

In May 1930, while Douglas Fairbanks was staying at Brook House and Dickie was doing a signal course at Portsmouth, there was a sensational first night at the Savoy Theatre of a new production of *Othello*. Peggy Ashcroft played Desdemona, Sybil Thorndike Emilia, Maurice Browne was Iago and the singer Paul Robeson played the part of Othello. Robeson had had a tough time becoming established in the USA and was the subject of much of what was then called 'anti-Negro prejudice'. Later, it did not help him that he was pro-Soviet in his views and let his communism be widely known. Edwina was fascinated by this brilliant actor-singer with his deep, sonorous voice and magnificent physique, as well as his lively and intelligent mind. Their friendship was widely known in Society, and many people today remember him at Brook House parties. He stood out not only because he was tall, courteous and charming, but because it was not commonplace to see blacks in fashionable company in London in the early 1930s.

Edwina was only one of many people who admired Robeson. Sybil Thorndike said, 'He is the nicest man I have ever acted with.' As for Robeson, his biographer writes of him at this time: 'He felt he understood the British people and felt himself to be part of the English scene. Each month, the easy, personal tempo of life had seeped deeper into his consciousness.'[3]

'I was made a fuss of by Mayfair,' Robeson himself recalled. And the fuss intensified after the success of the experimental show at the Savoy, *The Emperor Jones*, the second half of which was devoted to Negro spirituals and a song by Beethoven.

In May 1932, some weeks before she left with Nada for the Middle East expedition, Edwina was in Malta, the King of Spain among her guests. She had recently been skiing at St Moritz with the Cunningham-Reids, and the gossip columns had been full of notes on her clothes – 'She sports the best curly fur jacket yet seen in the Engadine'. But there was more malicious gossip, too, concerning her lifestyle when last in London, with hints and innuendos about 'dark-skinned gentlemen'.

One of these was 'Hutch', Leslie Hutchinson, the immensely popular night-club singer and pianist. He was uniquely charming and accomplished, and was often bidden (for a fat fee) to private parties, including those held at Brook House. Edwina was extremely fond of 'Hutch' and did not attempt to conceal her affection. It was typically indiscreet of her to present him with a gold cigarette case engraved with her name and a loving message, and it would have been extraordinary for Leslie Hutchinson not to show this with some pride to his friends.

Neither Paul Robeson nor Leslie Hutchinson was ever mentioned by name in print in connection with Edwina for fear of libel proceedings, but on a Sunday late in May the *People*, greatly daring, headed its gossip column 'Behind the Scenes' with a story, heavy with innuendo: 'SOCIETY SHAKEN BY TERRIBLE SCANDAL'. So widespread was Edwina's reputation that few people, even in the lower echelons of society, could fail to identify her and her 'associate'. The story ran:

> I am able to reveal today the sequel to a scandal which has shaken Society to the very depths. It concerns one of the leading hostesses in the country, a woman highly connected and immensely rich.
>
> Associations with a coloured man became so marked that they were the talk of the West End. Then one day the couple were caught in compromising circumstances.
>
> The sequel is that the Society woman has been given the hint to clear out of England for a couple of years to let the affair blow over, and the hint comes from a quarter which cannot be ignored.

The 'quarter which cannot be ignored' was, of course, Buckingham Palace; and, when the attention of the King and Queen was drawn to the article, a request was issued and dispatched to Malta – and this could not be ignored either. Edwina and Dickie had been warned by a friend in London about the publication, and a copy of the *People* was sent to them by express post. Meanwhile, Dickie had exchanged long cables with the family solicitors, who advised about the likely outcome of proceedings. The Mountbattens had, in fact, no choice in the matter. The Palace required them to institute proceedings in order to deny the imputation on two counts: that Edwina was having an association with a coloured man, and that the Palace had suggested she should live abroad.

Edwina and Dickie arrived in London on 6 July 1932. They had already taken out proceedings for libel against Odhams Newspapers, who published the *People*. Members of the Bar not connected with the case observed that it had certain curious aspects. For a start, they were surprised that the Lord Chief Justice's court was opened at the unusual hour of 9.30 a.m. and that the case was over before anyone – including representatives of the press – knew about it, which resulted in its being heard virtually 'in camera'.

One of the greatest advocates of the day, Norman Birkett, acting for the Mountbattens, opened the case: 'It is not too much to say that it is the most monstrous and most atrocious libel of which I have ever heard.' He also prevailed upon the judge, Lord Hewart, to make an exception and allow the Mountbattens to go into the witness box. This display of co-operation allowed Edwina herself to stand up and state strongly that she had never in her life even met the man referred to, who had been identified by her friends; and for Dickie to explain that the reason why Edwina had come out to Malta was that he was serving there as an officer in the Royal Navy, and that she had certainly not flown from scandal in London.

For the defendants, Sir Patrick Hastings could only make an unqualified apology – 'genuine and deep regrets'. A denial and apology would be given prominence in the newspaper. Edwina refused all damages.

The case attracted a lot of attention, and millions of people learned of the scandal who would not otherwise have done so. It also attracted a lot of attention in the Inns of Court. In addition to the early opening of the court without notice, and the privilege granted to the Mountbattens to give evidence themselves, could Edwina really have succeeded in proving that she was the person referred to barristers asked one another. If Odhams Newspapers had been informed beforehand that Edwina would not accept any damages, would they not have been strongly tempted to give the required apology anyway, whether or not they were guilty of libel, especially if Edwina, or the Privy Purse indirectly, had agreed to pay all the costs?

The case led to damages of another kind all round, with long-lasting effects.

The day after the hearing Edwina and Dickie lunched with George v and Queen Mary at Buckingham Palace, and this was widely reported. It was intended to show that there was nothing to forgive and that solidarity prevailed, rather than that all was forgiven. It did nothing of the kind. The Palace was not pleased that it had had to take the extreme step of obliging the Mountbattens to appear in court in order to teach Edwina a lesson. As for Edwina, she was outraged at the whole business, its covertness, hypocrisy and censoriousness, and the way she had cravenly submitted to the royal demand. She was not accustomed to being censured and disliked it the more because she could take no direct and immediate counter-action. She never forgave the Palace, nor the King and Queen, and from being a soft republican, like her mother-in-law, she became a strong and vocal anti-monarchist. It also hardened her politics, and her friends recounted that while prior to her libel case only the *Daily Herald* was allowed inside Brook House, now it was only the *Daily Worker*. And when it became clear that Edwina was virtually barred from the Court during the remainder of George v's reign, she was reported as declaring, 'I don't give a rap!' Naturally, Edwina also became harder and more cynical. The last traces of that rather wistful *naïveté* which partly concealed her sharp judgement disappeared for ever.

The figure most seriously damaged, however, was not Edwina but Paul Robeson. For Edwina to stand up in court and declare that she had never met him when their relationship had been so close, and when he had been invited to her house frequently and been seen there by dozens of her friends, deeply wounded him and he never got over it. He believed until the end of his days that the proceedings were taken only because of the colour of his skin. The disillusionment went far beyond Edwina and his loss of her. He saw it as evidence that colour prejudice in England, which had always seemed to him relatively mild by comparison with the USA, was really as strong and prevalent. English hypocrites were just better at concealing it.

And what of Mountbatten's views of the proceedings and of Edwina's behaviour? There was a great row, of course. There had been rows from the mid-1920s, but they were both aware of the need to keep them private, and they were both adept at doing this. He had now become reconciled to her behaviour, so long as he was not bothered, and to the fact that he did not really understand her and why she behaved as she did.

A friend of the young Edwina, who also knew Dickie well, recalled: 'For Dickie, women were just passing things. He liked to be surrounded by women but he never thought or worried about them. He was very good with them but he once told me, "Quite honestly I know nothing about women."'

This same friend recalls an episode at Palma, Majorca, in the year of the libel case, 1932.

> I was invited on board Dickie's ship for drinks and we went down to the wardroom where there were lots of two-and-a-half stripers [lieutenant-commanders] gossiping away. It was nothing but bitchy talk about promotions and they were damning everyone not present wholesale. I asked Dickie something about Edwina, whom he hadn't seen for some time, and he brushed the subject aside as if it was of no importance. It came as a great shock to me. But I suppose I had always believed that Dickie reckoned that it would be a very good marriage but at the back of his mind was the belief that it would help his career. That was the only thing he really cared about.

The Paul Robeson case was especially unwelcome to Mountbatten because it directed his attention to Edwina's behaviour when he had long since reasoned to himself that there was nothing he could do about it so he had better concentrate on getting to the next stage up the ladder – three stripes on his sleeve – which he did the next year. Now he was sorely afraid that this exposure of his wife's reputation, if not of her carryings-on, might prejudice his promotion. And *that* he would never forgive. It also risked his delicately poised but all-important relations with the Palace, which had saved his career in the past and would certainly support it in the future so long as the record sheet was clean.

The case, then, was an unwelcome occasion for both of them. Relations became so strained that now they could no longer always conceal how bad they were from their friends. When they returned to Malta, there was not a naval wife who had not heard about the case, and when together the Mountbattens were watched with much curiosity. One naval wife remembers a command ball at the Queen's Hall in the summer of 1932. She recalls:

> When the Mountbattens arrived it was fairly obvious that the atmosphere was rather strained. A long line of sailors formed up to take part in the Palais Glide and Lady Mountbatten spontaneously joined the line, and obviously enjoyed it, being the only lady. However, her husband was not amused! When she

returned to her party after the dance it looked as though a few unkind words were exchanged.

Late in 1934 Edwina disappeared without notice from the social scene in London and Malta. She had suddenly decided to go back to the USA by herself for a long period. Her love for the big country had steadily increased since her honeymoon. In England she felt confined and Malta brought on claustrophobia after a short time. America offered her the freedom she always ached for, and she loved it for its multi-racialism as well as for its black people. Harlem was her spiritual home, but she had another and more spacious and comfortable home in Joshua Cosden's estate on Long Island.

Her friends afterwards called this absence 'Edwina's black period', although whether or not this special definition had a double meaning no one today seems quite sure. She never talked about these months in America even, it seems, to her closest friends. 'Edwina's black period' remains a mystery in her life. There was, of course, a great deal of speculation at the time, but no hard fact, only doubtful gossip, which did include quite frequently the name of Prince Obolensky.

She was back on Malta by early summer 1935, dashing off to Cannes and Rome. Her trips to the mainland were nippier than ever now. 'Lady Louis Mountbatten always "uses the air" on her journeyings to and from this island,' reported the *Times of Malta*. Several of these journeyings were to ports and resorts along the coasts of France, Italy and Dalmatia to rendezvous with the Prince of Wales and Mrs Wallis Simpson, the Prince's mistress.

8
Relationships and Reappraisals

Dickie and Edwina were among the first to learn of the Prince of Wales's liaison, which began in 1931, with Mrs Simpson, the fascinating and ambitious American woman. Over the years, since Edwina and Dickie had become engaged out in India, they had kept in regular touch with the Prince, dining with him, visiting night-clubs with him, and exchanging visits. Like other of his friends, they had seen David through a number of love affairs, none of which was wholly satisfactory. Like Mountbatten, the Prince loved to be surrounded by pretty, flattering women, but those with whom he had a closer relationship, like the loyal and long-suffering Mrs Dudley Ward, failed in one way or another to satisfy him. Wallis Simpson was different, and the Mountbattens were relieved and delighted to find him fulfilled and happy in his relationship with her.

At first the affair appeared relatively innocuous. George v and Queen Mary heartily disapproved, of course, but they disapproved of almost everything about their eldest son just as the King's grandmother had disapproved of almost everything about her eldest son. A few people who knew the Prince well and had met Wallis felt uneasy and predicted trouble ahead. Among them were Edwina and Dickie's mother, Victoria. But the relationship did not in the least degree cool the Mountbatten-Prince of Wales friendship, and they saw a great deal of one another, as the foreign press especially noted. On summer holidays in the Mediterranean and Adriatic the foursome were much photographed in swimsuits on the decks of yachts, on beaches and enjoying the new sport of water skiing.

With the death of George v in January 1936, and the accession of the Prince of Wales as Edward viii, Edwina's relations with the Palace naturally improved. She had never held a very high opinion of David, regarding him as weak if amiable and sometimes amusing company, and she was sorry for him because he was a man not best fitted to carry heavy responsibilities. By early 1936, she was also full of forebodings on the eventual outcome of his affair with Mrs Simpson with all its seemingly insoluble constitutional problems. Mountbatten was not nearly so concerned; and, when he was proved wrong, declared after the abdication that if George V had lived one more year the Prince of Wales would have summoned up the courage to tell him that he was going to marry Wallis Simpson as soon as her divorce was through and that he was prepared to sacrifice the succession in order to do so.

Never were Mountbatten's balancing powers more severely tested than during the Abdication crisis and its aftermath. There is no doubt that he felt a genuine affection for David, even if his oft-repeated claim that 'he was my best friend all my life' was characteristic hyperbole. There is also no doubt that the advancement of Mountbatten's own career figured above all other considerations, and that this advancement depended to a great extent on three factors: his royal connection, his own skill, dedication and pertinacity, and Edwina's wealth. Edwina's less tangible support remained unrecognized by the blinkered eyes which were focused ahead on the glittering peak of the Royal Navy's summit.

For the first months of the new reign the waters appeared clear of hazards, and for Mountbatten it was 'Full steam ahead' – a state that he always relished, on land or at sea. Edward VIII appointed him Personal Naval ADC, and in thanking him Mountbatten (23 June 1936) said that he could not have been given a nicer honour. Mountbatten, alone in London, dined with the King a number of times at St James's Palace. On 31 May there was a dinner party which was to become notorious for several reasons. The carefully selected guests included the Lindberghs, the society hostess Emerald Cunard, Colonel the Lord Wigram, Keeper of the King's Archives, and Lady Wigram, Wallis and her husband, the Mountbattens, the Duff Coopers, Admiral Sir Ernle Chatfield, First Sea Lord, and the Prime Minister, Stanley Baldwin, and his wife. Charles Lindbergh was there because he had recently been in Germany and shared the King's interest in the Nazi regime; Emerald Cunard because she had done so much to smooth Wallis's path into top Society; and the Mountbattens because (as the King wished them to be seen) they were part of his family. Ernest Simpson was present to add respectability to his wife's presence, and the Prime Minister was there to prepare him for the coming matrimonial event.

Before the guests arrived, the King, in explanation of the Baldwins' inclusion, said to Wallis, 'It's got to be done. Sooner or later my Prime Minister must meet my future wife.' This was indeed accomplished, and it made Stanley Baldwin very uneasy about the relationship. In the Court

Circular the next morning, there were the names of Ernest and Wallis, as Frances Donaldson has commented, 'an official and wholly unusual method of announcing his friendship with the Simpsons'.[1] It was, according to the future Duchess of Windsor, 'the last time Ernest and I were publicly together in David's company'.

Between 27 and 30 September, the Mountbattens were two of a spirited house party at Balmoral, an autumn gathering very different from those stiff and formal affairs of George v. Besides the Mountbattens, the Court Circular published the names of the Americans, Mr and Mrs Hermann Rogers, the Harmsworths, Lieutenant-Commander and Mrs Colin Buist and Mrs Simpson, without her husband this time. On the surface the King appeared relaxed after his long cruise on a chartered yacht in the Mediterranean with Mrs Simpson and was behaving like a young man in love for the first time instead of a bachelor forty-year-old King-Emperor. But awaiting his attention were hundreds of letters and telegrams of protest, mainly from British citizens abroad and addressed directly to Buckingham Palace as well as to the Prime Minister, Queen Mary and the Archbishop of Canterbury. There were also press cuttings from American and Continental newspapers gossiping about the relationship and speculating about the future. Among these, the *New York Woman* revealed to its readers that under English law the King could not be sued (by Ernest Simpson) for adultery.

Edwina's close knowledge of the mind of the King and the depth of his passion convinced her that catastrophe was now imminent, and she at last convinced Mountbatten of this. But what could either of them do or say as house guests of a host who was in a state of exaltation? Mountbatten once said, 'I know it was terrible for David. Winston was among those who believed he couldn't live without her. I didn't think that, but I know it was a terrible decision for him. I always thought it was his duty to remain King, and told him that he ought to give up Wallis if that was the only alternative.'[2]

It is extremely doubtful if Mountbatten used much, if any, pressure on the King. His tightrope was very unstable at this point of the crossing. Edwina never mentioned the matter to the King, according to her friends. But it was not the delicacy of the issue, nor the risks involved in trying to persuade the King to give up Mrs Simpson, that led her to remain silent. Ever the pragmatist and fatalist, she knew there was nothing to be done, by the Prime Minister, the Archbishop of Canterbury, Edwina Mountbatten, or the most loyal of the King's subjects taken at random from the street. David was going to marry Wallis and that was that, Edwina reasoned. It was no longer any use worrying. If it led to the downfall of the monarchy, the nation would probably be the better for it anyway. And good luck to them both.

'Edwina was not in the least affectionate towards Mrs Simpson,' Edwina's sister recounts today. 'She was playing a very difficult role. The King was her husband's best friend, and she knew of the disapproval of the other royals at the time. Edwina may have had rather an admiration for her - and so did I - but no more.'

On the evening of her return to London she went to the premiere of the film *My Man Godfrey* wearing a diamond star in her hair and another holding in place a short black taffeta cape. Both she and Wallis Simpson were busy settling into new homes. Mrs Simpson had taken a Nash house in Regent's Park, 16 Cumberland Terrace, while her divorce came through; Edwina was at this time encouraging exciting new young artists and was shrewdly buying the paintings of Joan Miró. She and Mountbatten went to a lunch party in honour of the Polish Foreign Minister at the Edens' with Duff Cooper, Churchill and the Austen Chamberlains.

The Wallis Simpson crisis was fast approaching its climax at this time, and by the beginning of December it seemed that all was lost. Edwina held small cocktail parties to show off her seeming insouciance about the whole business. Mountbatten was deeply troubled and was seen about socially very little. On 1 December he wrote an agonized letter to the King in what he described as his terrible trouble, reminding him of how many loyal citizens he had, and enclosing letters of support from Lord Lymington (who had just been through his own divorce) and Sir Geoffrey Congreve, a naval contemporary of Mountbatten's. Mountbatten emphasized to his cousin that, as a friend of Wallis, if he wanted his company at any time he had only to telephone.[3]

The King finally abdicated on 10 December. While the nation mourned as if there had been a royal death, or remained stunned by the shock, Edwina went briskly about her business. The new Royal Family cancelled all invitations, as did many London hostesses. At Lady Cunard's musical party for Sir Thomas Beecham, most women wore black, but according to one report, 'Lady Mountbatten looked almost startlingly gay in a dress of aquamarine blue, pailettes matching her aquamarine necklace and a wrap of bright blue ostrich feathers'.

Almost from the start it appeared that Mountbatten was going to cross the chasm safely from one reign to the next. His relations with the new King, George VI, had never been as close as with his older brother. The Queen, who was a shrewd judge of people and possessed the advantage of a Scottish rather than a German background, and a sensible, non-royal upbringing, tended to watch Mountbatten's lifestyle with reservations. Ever-protective of her husband, who had been thrust unwillingly onto the throne, she found it hard to forgive her brother-in-law, and for this reason alone regarded his close friends with some degree of suspicion. But family solidarity came first, especially in 1937 of all years, and on 1 January Mountbatten was appointed Personal Naval ADC to the new King and was invested with the GCVO (Knight Grand Cross of the Royal Victorian Order).

In this same month Edwina went off to Davos with her sister, who had reverted to the name Mary Ashley pending her divorce, and returned for the christening of the Duke and Duchess of Kent's first born in the Royal Chapel. All the Royal Family, including Princesses Elizabeth and Margaret Rose were at the lunch in Belgrave Square afterwards; and to complete the royal day and span the two reigns, Mountbatten took Edwina for tea with Queen Mary at Marlborough House.

On Edwina's return from one of her extensive trips with Nada she learned the latest state of the Mountbatten transition from the reign of Edward VIII to George VI, and of David's (now the Duke of Windsor) marriage plans. The Duke was living at Schloss Enzesfeld outside Vienna, the home of Baron Eugene de Rothschild and his wife Kitty. He was barred from visiting Wallis in case the pending divorce with Ernest should be compromised. The 'freezing-out' process by the Palace establishment was well under way, and anyone who visited him was sure to be included in some sort of list, which might lead to embarrassment and difficulties. Mountbatten was longing to see him and offer himself as best man at his wedding, but it was not until the Duke of Kent went out with his elder brother's permission at the end of February 1937 that Mountbatten felt safe in making the journey. On 11 March Mountbatten had tea with his cousin at the British Legation in Vienna, and then drove with him to the Schloss where he stayed with him for several days and had many talks.

Reports on these talks between the two cousins about the forthcoming wedding are at variance. Mountbatten confirmed to this writer that he had twice offered to act as best man but had been turned down by the Duke, who explained that the wedding was to be a royal occasion at which there was no best man, and that his two younger brothers (the Dukes of Gloucester and Kent) would attend as 'supporters' in accordance with tradition.

The Duke of Windsor did not recall this conversation, only that in the event Mountbatten did not attend his wedding at all, which led to quite bitter recrimination and a break in their friendship - although such a break was not acknowledged by Mountbatten, who never accepted that there could be any sort of discord between himself and members of the Royal Family.

However, documentary evidence in the Duke of Windsor's archives suggests that Mountbatten was indeed invited to the wedding and was discouraged from attending, as were the Duke's two youngest brothers. A letter from Mountbatten to his cousin dated 5 May 1937 states quite clearly that this was the case but that he hopes to reverse the decision. There is nothing to show whether or not he succeeded. What is certain is that he would have loved to have gone, and to have stood as best man. In the event, the ever-willing 'Fruity' Metcalfe stepped in and was best man at the wedding in June.

'The unspoken order had gone out,' wrote the Duchess of Windsor in her memoirs. 'Buckingham Palace would ignore our wedding. There would be no reconciliation, no gesture of recognition.'[4] When the Duke learned that his wife could not be addressed as Her Royal Highness, he referred with bitter irony to the 'nice wedding present'. For both of them the cup of bitterness was full, and many snubs as bad as this were to follow. Edwina was sorry about the virtual severance of relations with 'David and Wallis' created by the abdication and their marriage, and regarded it as one more manifestation of the silliness of a monarchy.

Meanwhile other family events, some royal and festive and some tragic, occupied the remaining months of this eventful year, 1937. First, there was the May Coronation. This was to be a great spectacle as well as a great demonstration of unity, and although Edwina did not entertain any enthusiasm for the national effort being made to recover the reputation, domestically as well as world-wide, of the British monarchy, she entered into the occasion with a fair show of enthusiasm. She knew her duty drew her beside Dickie, and that as the most colourful and controversial members of the Royal Family, many eyes would be watching them keenly.

The gossip columns followed Edwina particularly closely at this time, noting her dresses, her company and her movements. As one newspaper reported:

> By accompanying the Duke and Duchess of Kent to the Westminster rehearsal last week, Lord and Lady Louis Mountbatten showed how skilfully they had maintained their position in the new social reign, despite a long-standing friendship with the King who was never crowned.... When Lady Louis emerged to public view, she was seen chatting vivaciously to the Duke of Kent, while her husband shared a joke with Duchess Marina of Kent.

At the end of May 1937 the Mountbattens held a dinner party with the newly crowned King and Queen as guests. The dinner was to welcome to London Prince Louis of Hesse, the younger son of Mountbatten's uncle, the Grand Duke. 'Lu' had met on a skiing holiday the Hon. Margaret 'Peg' Geddes, the daughter of Lord and Lady Geddes; they had fallen in love and were to marry later in the year. Meanwhile, Lu had been appointed honorary cultural attaché at the German Embassy. Popular royal enthusiasm following the Coronation remained high, and on that evening of 31 May a large crowd gathered to watch the arrival of the guests – the Duke and Duchess of Sutherland, Lord and Lady Plunket, Mrs Ronald Greville, Sir Philip Sassoon, and then the King and Queen just before 8 o'clock. The only person missing was the guest of honour. The Hessian Prince had been prohibited at the last moment from attending by his Ambassador, von Ribbentrop. It was not a good evening for Anglo-German relations.

However, the Anglo-German wedding went ahead as planned and was due to take place in London in November 1937. Mountbatten was deeply concerned in the plans for his cousin and had worked out his usual minutely detailed programme. Except for one infant daughter and Lu who awaited them in London, the entire Hessian family took off by air from Frankfurt. The Sabena Fokker tri-motor was scheduled to land at Ostend, but failed to do so. Thick fog had suddenly descended and the pilot lost his bearings on the final approach, striking a tall chimney. Everyone on board was killed.

Edwina was with Dickie and the betrothed pair at Croydon to meet the party. It was a fine early winter afternoon, crystal clear. They watched a big Imperial Airways machine take off, and then, after a long delay, were told of the crash. Everyone rallied round. There were consultations with the bride's family, at which Mountbatten's mother was present. She proposed that the wedding should go ahead immediately, the next morning, before everyone emerged from their state of shock and recognized the enormity of the tragedy. Victoria was a wise old bird. It was certainly the best way of coping, not least for the unfortunate bride and groom.

Mountbatten's mother, now aged seventy-four, still had many family responsibilities at this time. Edwina, who remained close to her until Victoria's death in 1950, shared them as far as she was able to, and when Edwina was in London there was always much to-ing and fro-ing across Hyde Park. One of the shared responsibilities was – and had been for many years – for Prince Philip, Mountbatten's youngest nephew.

Prince Philip's mother remained intermittently unwell for most of the years between the wars, and was usually abroad, in Paris, staying at Darmstadt or elsewhere. His father was living in Monte Carlo and Prince Philip rarely saw him. His sisters were much older, and one had been killed in the Ostend air crash. He was brought up by a number of members of the family, with George and Dickie Mountbatten and their wives chiefly responsible, and his grandmother Victoria as a sensible surrogate mother. 'Kensington Palace was a sort of base where I kept my things,' Prince Philip told this writer when discussing the late 1930s. 'I liked my grandmother very much and she was very helpful. She was very good with children. Like my own mother, she took the practical approach to them. She treated them in the right way – the right combination of the rational and the emotional.'

Prince Philip also owed a great deal to Edwina. Their relationship was always very cordial and relaxed, and he admired the way her mind worked and her way of dealing with problems as they arose. They also laughed at the same things. Mountbatten, whose contribution to Prince Philip's upbringing is widely acknowledged, and who remained a close supporter, adviser and friend all his life, greatly valued Edwina's relationship with his nephew. 'Oh, she was marvellous with him!' he once exclaimed.

Until 1938, of the two brothers, George took the greater share of responsibility for Prince Philip's upbringing. 'I was away a lot,' Mountbatten once explained, 'and my brother after he resigned his commission was much more available than I was.' At the end of 1937 George was forty-five, a rich and successful businessman, fit and only just past his prime. Born Prince George of Battenberg, he had become Lieutenant Lord George Mountbatten RN in 1917, and Earl Medina, Marquis of Milford Haven, on his father's death. He was a modest man who did not seek or attract the public eye very much, and had, Mountbatten believed, a brain far sharper than his own. He was, according to the memory of many people, including the present Queen, a very nice and very kind person. He was not, however, a very happy man. The wide reputation of his wife, Nada, for preferring women's company, was a great sadness, and he often regretted his decision to leave the Royal Navy, which Nada had pressed on him.

Then, in the winter of 1937–8, George became crippled after falling down and breaking his leg. The bone would not heal and, after protracted and painful treatment, he died of cancer on 8 April 1938. This new blow badly shook the whole family, and especially his mother. From this time, Mountbatten became even more closely responsible for Prince Philip, although he was now an unusually self-sufficient sixteen-year-old schoolboy at Gordonstoun School.

Dickie and Edwina's supervision of Prince Philip's education and upbringing had been facilitated by Mountbatten's appointment to the Admiralty in 1936. In the previous summer the relaxed yachting holidays, the ritzy shore excursions and Riviera visits to the rich and famous had been cut short by the looming Italian crisis and threat of war. The Italian dictator, Benito Mussolini, had resolved to extend his empire to emulate Julius Caesar and bring greatness back to Rome. The invasion of Abyssinia on 2 October brought war with Britain and France close, and with it brought an imminent threat to the security of Malta. The British Mediterranean Fleet was considered to be too vulnerable to Italian air power at Malta and was moved to the eastern Mediterranean, leaving behind a flotilla of old destroyers, including Mountbatten's, as a sort of suicide squad - the 'do-or-die boys' as they were named. Wives were evacuated, too, but not Edwina. She had recently taken up the hobby of radio announcing, which she loved, and was judged to be clear-voiced and incisive. 'Her job was really to keep our spirits up,' recalls one listener. 'And she did it very well. I always listened to her in the mornings.'

The crisis blew over, wafted away on the gentle breeze of appeasement; Edwina closed down the villa, and she and Dickie made their separate ways to London. Their return coincided with the completion of a giant change in Mountbatten domestic arrangements in London. Adsdean continued to be maintained, at prodigious cost, as the country seat, though rarely lived in. In London an economy, of a sort, had been put in train. The mere suggestion of demolishing Brook House was regarded as sacrilegious by the upper echelons of Society in the early 1930s. But the Cassel executors and trustees did not share this veneration for the Mountbatten marble mausoleum and suggested to Edwina that £17,000–£20,000 a year for maintenance alone was perhaps a needless expense when one or both of them were abroad for much of the time. Brook House had indeed become a gross anachronism. After much discussion and consideration of alternative plans, it was sold to Coutts and Co. the bankers, who leased it to a property company.

The last days of the old Brook House symbolically marked the end of an era, the end of more than a decade of celebrations and parties: of coming-out balls for Ernest Cassel's two prized granddaughters, receptions after their weddings, parties with jazz bands, parties for Paul Robeson, ('. . . Masked parties, Savage parties, Victorian parties, Greek parties, Wild

West parties, Russian parties, Circus parties, parties where one had to dress as somebody else, almost naked parties in St John's Wood, parties in flats and studios and houses and ships and hotels and night clubs, all that succession and repetition of massed humanity. . . . Those vile bodies. . . .') as Evelyn Waugh so graphically related.

For Edwina, who had first tasted a sort of freedom there before she married, and run it with Stella Underhill as efficiently as any of Mountbatten's men-of-war, the loss of Brook House might have been cause for sadness. It was nothing of the kind. Only the loss of Broadlands could have caused Edwina any sense of deprivation. She walked out of it for the last time, down the steps to her car in Park Lane, and was away without a backward glance. 'All right, that's over – now let's get on with the next item,' she might have said aloud in her rapid-speaking, clipped voice.

For some time the house remained empty; the furniture was stored and only the bronzes and Dresden china, which Edwina did not want, were left to be auctioned. The Mountbattens were in Malta and Stella Underhill was in charge of the great echoing curtainless rooms and uncarpeted corridors with their trace of cigar smoke and the faintest echoes of deep patrician voices from another age. Queen Mary had all her life been a keen collector of Dresden, her collection much augmented from houses in which she stayed and where her outsize handbag was much feared. (Nubia House had suffered severe losses in the early 1920s.) When she heard about this sale she said she would like to see the collection, and Miss Underhill was deputed as guide. Miss Underhill wrote of this difficult occasion:

> One of the ladies-in-waiting, Lady Elizabeth Motion, was a sister of Lady Helen Cassel whom I knew, so this made things easier. When Queen Mary had examined all the china she turned to me and said she would like to see the bedrooms. I had to tell her that they were all empty, but she wished to see them all the same, especially the one that HM King Alfonso [a notorious womanizer] had had when he was staying at Brook House.

The marble, pannelling and chandeliers also went under the hammer, and on this site in Park Lane there now arose a block of luxury flats, surmounted by a penthouse on two floors, set back to give a spacious verandah overlooking Hyde Park. This the Mountbattens rented for £4,200 a year, and everything was to their own design, including the exclusive high-speed lift of which Mountbatten was inordinately proud, even after Queen Mary (who did not like lifts) got stuck in it.

Stella Underhill was much concerned with all the preparations for moving in in August 1936. Mountbatten was now working at the Admiralty, and when Edwina was in London she lived with her mother-in-law in her Kensington Palace chambers. Miss Underhill's secretarial department at the penthouse had two rooms on the north side of the lower floor. She recalled:

> The rest of that floor was taken up by the morning-room, drawing-room and dining-room, all of which faced the park and could be thrown open into one large room. Also the children's wing was on the south side and the kitchen and men's rooms along the north side. On the floor above and along the front were Lord and Lady Louis's bedrooms, bathrooms and private sitting-rooms. Over the children's wing were the two visitors' rooms, and over the men's side in the north wing were the maids' rooms. It was a beautiful place.

In all the penthouse boasted thirty rooms, the five reception-rooms ingeniously arranged with collapsing walls so that they could be converted into a single entertaining room for parties, or a 150-seat cinema. Edwina's American friend Mrs Joshua Cosden, a well-known decorator and designer, dealt with the interior decoration, with Victor Proetz, the famous designer, acting as consultant. Of the drawing-room, an art magazine wrote, 'The ceiling is overlaid with tarnished silver leaf in a bold herring-bone pattern that contributes the dull metallic glint of steel armour and pewter tankards in the glowing velvet of the paintings.'

Among Edwina's friends and acquaintances there was much curiosity about the interior of the penthouse, much angling for invitations, and numerous jokes about the austerities Edwina must be suffering in the confined space of a mere flat. Privileged friends were taken to see the Rex Whistler murals in Edwina's boudoir – 'his designs are rustic, with corn, scythes and rakes in silver against a delicate blue background'.

In the months before the war finally closed it down, all members of the Royal Family were visitors on a number of occasions. Edwina had her socialist friends, including Bernard Shaw, as guests, and Mountbatten his Service and political friends, among them Winston Churchill, to whom he was confiding secrets about the shortcomings of the Royal Navy. Noël Coward found it cosy after Brook House, *avant-garde* artists thought it vulgar and bourgeois. The attention of passers-by in Hyde Park and Park Lane after dark was irresistibly drawn to the penthouse by the uncompromising power of the floodlighting.

The completion of the decorations of the penthouse and parties to show it to friends and relations had to be squeezed in to the brief intervals between Edwina's trips abroad – to Austria, France, Germany, Spain, and longer expeditions to America and exotic corners of Africa and Asia. Archaeology seems to have been replaced among her enthusiasms by the study of wild life and straight exploration. For example, in early 1937, after the usual urgent public announcement in the newspapers that she would be away for a long period and please would people not write to her, she left with Nada for East Africa, exploring and photographing wild life in Kenya, Rhodesia and elsewhere.

As always, the two women were treated solicitously and as almost-royals in the capitals, and then disappeared for weeks on end into the bush, perhaps with a guide or two and full camping equipment. They left Salisbury, Rhodesia, on 10 April and arrived at Croydon airport, London, a few days later. In her arms Edwina carried a not-very-small lion cub. She had named it Sabi, after the river in present-day Zimbabwe. At Adsdean it roamed freely, to the alarm of the servants, playing in the golf-course bunkers and once eating most of the golf clubs of a weekend guest, Lord Duncannon.

Edwina's last expedition before the war was to the Far East again, this time with two women friends. While in Sumatra they learned that the Burma Road had been completed, and they decided to buy a car and drive the length of it. The 800-mile-long road had been built painstakingly and with the most primitive equipment over hundreds of miles of fearful terrain to provide a back-door supply link with the outside world for the hard-pressed Chinese in their war against Japan. It was regarded as a prodigious achievement by the Western world, and also as a most dangerous road – dangerous not only from the Japanese, who were certain to do all they could to destroy it, but from natural hazards. No one but Chinese truck drivers had driven the length of it. This suited Edwina very well, providing as it did satisfaction for the pioneer in her, her love of flirting with danger and of accomplishing what were regarded as impossible feats.

Edwina had always enjoyed setting herself difficult targets. Time and again she had demonstrated that when given authoritative warning advice she would certainly disregard it and derive the greater satisfaction in doing so. She had a keener eye for a challenge than anyone who knew her had ever seen. 'Dear Edwina, she did so love confounding those who thought they knew best,' one of her friends remarked. The word 'impossible' was sheer nectar to Edwina, just as danger was a heady scent that she could not resist. 'She was utterly fearless', this same friend added, 'and didn't understand danger.'

As usual, Edwina experienced no health problems that she would acknowledge as such on this long and testing trip high into the mountains, through remote old walled towns and miles of anchusas, azaleas and flowering cherries. From Yunnanfu they flew out to Hanoi in an ancient Junkers plane, which was shot down by the Japanese on its next trip, and then to Saigon and home by May. It was as rapid a trip back to England as Edwina could make it for at every halt *en route* she learned of the worsening political situation in Europe. There was now every reason to believe that this would be the last adventurous journey she would make for a long time. The dug-outs beside the Burma Road, the anti-aircraft batteries guarding the airfields, the scores of military trucks, the aircraft factory they had seen under construction at Yunnanfu – all these warlike sights among the scarlet rhododendrons and Buddhist temples pointed towards the imminence of world catastrophe.

In the last months before the Second World War broke out in September 1939, Edwina's father showed signs of failing health. Wilfrid Ashley had led a life that appeared coldly detached from his fellow men and women, even his two wives. Certainly his marriage to Cassel's daughter surprised many people at the time – this lively, excitable, clever and beautiful half-Jewish girl and the stiff, untalkative Guards officer and landowner. It was an odd match, but Maudie must have loved him for she could have married almost any eligible young man in the country.

As a working partnership, his marriage to Molly Forbes-Sempill seems to have worked well. She was socially ambitious, and politically ambitious for her husband, who was a fine public speaker but no more than fairly able as a Member of Parliament. She entertained the right people widely at Broadlands and in London, although a brief reference in a magazine article in 1932 does not suggest a relaxed weekend for her guests: 'Broadlands is about one of the best-run houses in England. The weekend guests receive a post-card before arriving, with the times of trains, dinner and the cautionary note: "Don't ring the bell more than once; the servants are well trained."' 'She was not at all popular among the local people,' Robert Everett recalls.

Wilfrid Ashley's politics were always to the far right of the Conservative Party, and in the rise of the Nazi Party he foresaw a return to discipline and financial and social order in Germany which ought to be supported in England. He formed the Anglo-German Fellowship and became its President in 1935, and was Chairman of The Comrades of the Great War. Robert Bruce Lockhart, journalist and Beaverbrook protégé, noted in his diary on 5 December 1935:

> In the evening went to the inaugural Anglo-German Fellowship banquet ... Mount Temple (who is the father of two half-Jewesses in Lady Louis Mountbatten and Mrs Cunningham-Reid by his first wife, Cassel's daughter) made a very indiscreet remark: 'We know Germany "fought fair"' after a long eulogy of traditional friendship between England and Germany – 'and I hope that in the next war – well, I mustn't say what I was going to say!'

On a more prosaic level, Mount Temple was a competent Minister of Transport, and during his time was responsible for introducing many road improvement schemes including 'arterial roads' (precursors of motorways) and the notorious roundabout, alive and flourishing to this day.

Her father's anti-socialist, anti-semitic and pro-Nazi views did not help his relations with Edwina. However, Wilfrid Ashley, grandson of that great libertarian the seventh Earl of Shaftesbury, repented before his death on 3 July 1939. To Molly's chagrin, Edwina now inherited Broadlands and its thousands of acres, and Classiebawn Castle and its estate in Ireland, which had been much neglected and visited by her only twice since her marriage. In spite of her unhappy childhood at Broadlands, this house remained her favourite home for the rest of her life, the place she was anxious to show first to visitors to England – including, little more than ten years hence, the Indian Prime Minister, Jawaharlal Nehru.

In looking back over an important and accomplished life it is difficult to imagine what its shape would have been if one cornerstone in the edifice had been removed.

A woman who knew Edwina well has said that she would have found her true role in life in her forties regardless of a world war. 'The war merely gave it a deeper and more effectual expression. All that rushing about was finished anyway. She was like a bluebottle that is driven nearly frantic in a room and suddenly finds the open window.'

While both Edwina and Mountbatten were still alive, one biographer wrote of this time – the late 1930s:

> Fortunate in everything, the Mountbattens even picked the right generation in which to live. They got the best of the century. War overtook them in the very prime of their lives, after they had had their fun at a time when great wealth was something that could be enjoyed and they were both young enough to enjoy it. War swept away the gay life, and many of their set still living emotionally in the thirties were swept away with it.[5]

In the event, Edwina's recognition of her destiny occurred before the bombs began to fall. Its timing approximates with the Munich Agreement of September 1938, and from the details Edwina acquired from Mountbatten's German relations of the true horrors of the Nazi persecution of the Jews and of conditions in the concentration camps. According to one of her closest friends, she began by 'bringing over from Germany all her Jewish relatives and housing them in suites in the Ritz'. Before leaving for the Far East, she wrote to her now reformed father, 'It is such a ghastly nightmare the Jewish question . . .', and told him that, in a small way, she was doing something to help the refugees. Here is the first hint of the new Edwina, although it took the actuality of war to complete the conversion from pleasure-seeker to crusader.

Their friends noticed that relations between Edwina and Dickie, which had run from bad to worse during the 1930s, showed signs of improving in the last months before the Second World War as if the forthcoming crisis demanded a closing of the ranks. 'They were seen about together much more when they were both in England,' one friend reported. 'We were all thankful to see this as it did look at one time that the rift might be final. I really believe that there would have been a divorce but for the children – and, more important still – the damage it might do to Dickie's career. Then, of course, there was Peter Murphy.'

Peter Murphy was one of the Mountbattens' 'stayers', the longest stayer of them all. He was an *éminence grise* in the Mountbatten household for many years, remembered today for popping up ubiquitously on numerous occasions, at parties, in the conversation of friends and in photographs. When both Mountbattens were at home he formed with them a *ménage à trois*. His functions were never quite clear to outsiders but he seemed equally loved by Edwina and Dickie. Ludovic Kennedy, the biographer and historian, describes him as a left-wing ex-Guards officer whose friendship with Mountbatten was long and important.

Lady Delamere speaks of him affectionately. She recalls:

> He was in the Guards and then he was at Cambridge with Dickie. They became great pals. He was no bone of contention in the family because he was a homosexual. He was extremely well read and it's my honest conviction that he was equally fond of them both. It was good for them to have somebody like that around who was pleasant, most intelligent and sang for his supper in the sense that he got his food and drink and was comfortable and all that. I think you could call him an affectionate ADC to them both. They both respected his opinion enormously. When he died in 1969 Dickie was terribly upset.

We get a brief glimpse of him in 1945, immediately after the Japanese surrender. Peter Murphy's namesake, a journalist called Ray Murphy, had just arrived in Singapore hoping to write an official biography of the 'Supremo', as Mountbatten was at that time called – Supreme Commander South East Asia. He got an interview with Mountbatten, who characteristically told him that he could not authorize an official biography and proceeded to give him extensive unofficial assistance in numerous interviews with the offer of numerous introductions.

Peter Murphy strolled in while Ray Murphy was waiting to see Mountbatten, 'a tanned, rather heavy man, clad in corduroy trousers and a checked sports shirt'. He was 'as bald as a bust of Caesar,' and referred to Mountbatten as 'the old boy'.[6] He then asked Ray Murphy whether *Cannery Row* by John Steinbeck would make a good aeroplane read for Mountbatten on his imminent flight to Delhi. Later he joined them both for dinner.

Peter Murphy was, in Ray Murphy's judgement, clearly on close and familiar terms with Mountbatten. But Peter Murphy's most important role was to act as a third-party buffer between Dickie and Edwina in the 1930s, reducing the acrimony which was never far beneath the surface, and offering them both amusing conversation and the benefit of a shrewd and well-informed mind. When one was away, he provided company for the other, and was equally at ease with either of them. As Yola Letellier was the unsung heroine, Peter Murphy was the unsung hero of the Mountbatten dynasty, steadying the ship, keeping it off the reefs. Without his presence and influence, Mountbatten might well have lost Edwina's strength and wise counsel before the Second World War, and have enjoyed a less brilliant career. It is certainly difficult to visualize Mountbatten as the last Viceroy without Edwina beside him as Vicereine, supporting and guiding him through the intricacies of those last imperial weeks in India.

The *rapprochement* between the Mountbattens was seen most markedly on the polo field. Edwina enjoyed watching polo, with its thunderous beating of hooves, thudding impact of contesting players and the lurid language which is inseparable from the game. She was almost invariably asked to present the cups, though by no means frequently to Mountbatten's Adsdean team. In February 1938 she and Yola both accompanied Mountbatten's team to Jamaica, where they played four major tournaments at Knutsford Park.

The year 1938 was the last in which Edwina conformed to the party-giving, Season-following round of the decades between the wars, the last during which she could with reason be called 'the perfect social butterfly', as one of her daughters described her. In July she gave a ball for 600 guests at the penthouse, and then another ball for Sarah Norton, the debutante daughter of her old friend Jean. There was Cowes, and then Monte Carlo in August; autumn parties, more polo, and pheasant shooting at Six Mile Bottom with the Kents, with Mary as hostess in Cassel's vast shooting lodge.

Finally, there was the last premiere of the year - and of an age: the bright lights of Leicester Square, the sparkle of diamonds in the foyer, sister Mary in a full-length silver fox fur coat ('it took one year to collect the skins'). It was one of the great Fred Astaire/Ginger Rogers musicals, its title wistfully appropriate, *Carefree*.

9
Crusader at War

The *Carefree* life of Astaire and Rogers had ceased for Edwina and most responsible, clear-thinking British people a few weeks earlier, in late September 1938 with the signature of the Munich Agreement. Mary, a great Chamberlain admirer, was at Heston airport to greet the returning Prime Minister waving his bit of paper. Edwina saw that war was now inevitable. Just as her husband was helping to prepare the Royal Navy for a renewal of war at sea – at the Admiralty with a staff appointment in the Naval Air Service – Edwina now threw herself into her own preparations.

Late in the autumn of 1938 new faces, unrecognized in the social world of Park Lane, appeared at the Brook Street entrance of Edwina's home, and were whisked up to the penthouse in 'the fastest lift in London'. They had come to instruct Edwina in first aid and the care of the sick. Word of Edwina struggling with tourniquets and splints on the deep carpets of the penthouse caused a good deal of uncharitable mirth in her social set, and it was popularly supposed that this was one more of her passing fads of which she would quickly tire. Her closest friends – Marjorie Brecknock (who was to become very high up in the ATS [Auxiliary Territorial Service]), Jean Norton, Nada, sister Mary – were quick to recognize an entirely new Edwina. 'She was getting to grips with something useful for the first time in her life,' one friend remarked. 'To Edwina had come a moment of unique clarity,' Madeline Masson has written. 'The bombs would drop and then, for the first time in her life, she might be needed.'[1]

Lying dormant like a cold seed, the concern for others in need which she felt on her honeymoon for poverty-stricken Mexican villagers – and elsewhere during her travels – now began to germinate strongly. Soon its growth was to be scarcely controllable.

Edwina's quick mind picked up the basic essentials of first aid in no time. Unconcerned with her own health all her life and believing that it was weak and self-indulgent to give thought to bodily well-being, she suddenly found it necessary to study anatomy and learn about disease, common injuries and drugs. This did not affect in the slightest degree her indifference to her own health, which would have repaid study and care. She had never been a very fit person. Her circulation was not good, she felt the cold badly, her digestive processes were not strong, she needed sedatives for a good night's sleep, and she suffered from neuralgia and migraine, which were not eased by her short-sightedness. She rose above these handicaps and hated even to be asked how she was. Before starting her training, the health of others was equally of no interest to her, and woe betide her daughters if they complained. Now, in this entirely new Florence Nightingale world of casualty wards and operating theatres, she was giving herself up wholly to the health and well-being of others. It was indeed a curious metamorphosis.

Early in 1939 she joined the WVS (Women's Voluntary Services) and began a six months' training course at Westminster Hospital. All her natural squeamishness had to be concealed by self-discipline. Previously, Edwina's contact with hospitals had been limited to lavish charity balls. She was now viewing physical suffering extensively and for the first time. Like some newly converted fanatic or Christian martyr, the appetite for her own suffering fed upon itself, and every wound to be dressed and soiled bed to be changed increased the degree of her enthusiasm. 'She knew that there was much worse to come so that she might as well get over this part without fuss,' recalled one of her friends.

The brief release from this training provided by her expedition to bomb-shattered Chinese cities became a salutary preview of what Britain was soon to suffer. On her return, and at the suggestion of members of the hierarchy of the St John Ambulance Brigade, she joined that great and historic organization. Just as Edwina learned pot-scrubbing at Alde House before she became a great hostess, she now knew the fundamentals of nursing practice. But she also knew all the time, as contemporaries and seniors knew, that with her semi-royal social standing, her wealth, authority and powers of organization, even the middle ranks of the St John Ambulance were not going to hold her for long. And, for their part, the Brigade's hierarchy knew that they were blessed with a pricelessly valuable recruit. 'Looking back on those days now,' a senior officer at the time recalls, 'it seemed as if she just swept into HQ and took over everything – and thank goodness for it too.'

The St John Ambulance Association had been created by the 'English langue' of the Order of St John of Jerusalem, which had its origins in

Jerusalem and Acre as an international co-fraternity for the relief of crusaders. In the late nineteenth century, the Prince of Wales was the Grand Prior. He introduced Cassel to the Order and Edwina's grandfather was appointed a Knight of St John. Edwina was familiar with the aims of the Order, which encouraged and promoted 'all works of humanity and charity for the relief of persons in sickness, distress, suffering and danger, without distinction of race, class or creed, and the extension of the great principle of the Order embodied in the motto "*Pro utilitate hominum*"'. It was manned entirely by volunteers and possessed a high standard of discipline, skill and *esprit de corps*. In November 1939 Edwina was appointed County President for London of the St John Ambulance. The post had in the past been largely nominal. It was no longer to be so. Edwina no more believed in figureheads than in monarchs.

War had scattered her family, and the whole Mountbatten lifestyle had altered as radically as Edwina's by the autumn of 1939. Patricia and Pamela had been sent to New York to live with the Vanderbilts, sailing in the liner *Washington* with other privileged children - Duff and Diana Cooper's son among them - six weeks before hostilities actually began. There was a great deal of public criticism of this evacuation of wealthy children at the time when less privileged or more responsible parents, including the King and Queen, thought it their duty to keep families together. Edwina did not take any notice of this outcry, which was anyway very transient. Characteristically, Mountbatten bridled and remained defensive about it. 'With their Jewish blood, they would have been the first for the gas ovens if the Germans had invaded,' he would say in justification.

The Park Lane penthouse was closed down and the valuables sent for storage to Broadlands. Edwina moved into Kensington Palace with her mother-in-law and drove to her office at the singularly early hour of 8 a.m., which became the practice for the rest of her life. Mountbatten was with his destroyer flotilla at the outset of his brief and eventful sea-going wartime career in which most of his eight ships were to be sunk, including his own flotilla leader, HMS *Kelly*. By March 1940 Edwina was St John Ambulance President for London, Hampshire and the Isle of Wight. Her promotion was proving as dazzlingly swift as her husband's was to be later in the war.

Pre-war predictions had foretold an instant and annihilating descent of German bombers on London and other great cities. When these attacks failed to occur, the defensive measures were slackened and children returned from their evacuation areas in the country. Now in the late spring of 1940, with the German invasion of Denmark and Norway, and then of

France and the Low Countries, the threat recurred, the 'phoney war' was over. One of Edwina's contemporaries has written:

> It seems now as if the pattern of events concerning the Brigade in London in 1940 had been pre-ordained by some divine power. By the beginning of the autumn Blitz, we were deeply involved in all the London ARP [Air Raid Precautions] operations with Ambulance men and women represented in almost all the shelters, rest centres and first aid posts. Then along came Lady Louis like Florence Nightingale herself to see that it all worked.

Edwina's authority as deputy Superintendent-in-Chief of the entire Brigade from June 1940, and as co-ordinator and commander of all St John personnel working with the London ARP services, marked the real beginning of her life of dedication and relief of the suffering of others for which she will always be remembered. Now, said her friends, there were no further doubts of her destiny.

One of the cruel aspects of the bombing campaigns of the Second World War was the far worse relative suffering of the poorer-paid manual worker, whether of Dortmund and Essen, London or Coventry. The poorer people lived close together and close to their places of work, which in turn were the prime targets of the bombers. The rich got out, the middle classes were more scattered and often distant from targets. London exemplified this injustice. The Germans were not bombing indiscriminately in 1940, either in London or Coventry. In London the first target in the early days was dockland, where the dockers and their families of the East End lived next door to their work – the people of Bermondsey, Whitechapel, the Isle of Dogs and Stepney. Their agony during the autumn and winter of 1940–41 was appalling and on a different scale from anything experienced in west, north and south London, where life at first was uncomfortable and noisy but nothing like as dangerous as the east of the city.

Edwina's first great crusade was in the East End of London during this bombing period, when she became not another lady-with-the-lamp but a woman with a cause and the power to sustain it. Shelters had been designated in preparation for mass bombing, but it seemed that no one had possessed the imagination to visualize what they would become after weeks of nightly occupation while the buildings and streets above were blown up.

In early September, with the first daylight and then night bombing of London, Edwina began her series of tours of inspection which were to become such a notable feature of the Blitz. For night after night, as the bombs came down, she drove her small car with hooded lights over broken glass and scattered rubble from shelter to first aid and medical posts and again to the next shelter, covering as many as ten in one night. Pockmarked with shell splinters and flying debris, and filthy dirty with mud and dust, her car became a recognized feature parked outside Brigade HQ or Kensington Palace among the spotless limousines.

A fellow worker recalls a typical night during the early stage of the Blitz:

> We went first to a warehouse off the Commercial Road. It was still quite early in the night but every inch of space had been taken up - whole families with children who ought to have been evacuated, and probably had been once but had been brought back home again. In the half light it was like something out of Dante's *Inferno* - people trying to sleep on deck chairs, on the wooden floor, on old crates, anywhere and everywhere. We were told that there were no lavatories for the ten thousand or so people and that was why the floor was already awash with urine and there were piles of excrement. Later Edwina managed to discover the lavatories - no more than buckets really - behind some sacking. Two of them! The bombing hadn't started when we were there. I can't imagine what it would be like when it did. Edwina talked to some of the people as she walked about, touching some of the old people, reassuring them that things would be improved. And so they were - with incredible speed.

Stepney had thirty-four shelters, every one packed with frightened men, women and children, without sanitation or anything except the concrete floor to sit or lie on. The bombing of so many old buildings brought out hordes of rats, which were attracted to the warmth and stench and scuttled over the people lying in the darkness. As a formula for widespread disease - a plague to match anything conceived by H.G. Wells in *The Shape of Things to Come* - the conditions were ideal. Here, too, was the ideal cause for the crusading and reforming zeal of Edwina, at the very outset of her new life.

Most of the divisional superintendents of this area of east London had made efforts to improve conditions, but were hopelessly hamstrung by bureaucratic obstructionism charged now with that doom-laden excuse, 'Don't you know there's a war on?' Edwina never had any truck with petty bureaucrats and officials. She traded unscrupulously on her charm, rank and connections, and also, it must be added, on her ability to strike the fear of God into lesser mortals. She brushed machinery and officials aside with equal disdain and briskness, and went to the top - in this case to the Minister of Health himself, Malcolm MacDonald, whose life was made a misery by memoranda, telephone calls and personal visits from Edwina; although, characteristically, she also became one of his closest friends.

Another account of a typical 'lady-of-the-shelters' night, written while Edwina was still alive, has been left by an early biographer. It was, it seems, a cold evening in November 1940:

> It was seven-thirty, very dark and the raid had started. Stitcher [Mr B. Stitcher, the superintendent] met her at the entrance of St Mary's Shelter in Whitechapel Road (since demolished by bombs), and down they went immediately into the shelter below the cinema. She met the First Aid staff of two ambulancemen and two nurses, inspected the first-aid room and their equipment. She spoke to shelterers, asking how they were getting along, without being so fatuous as to ask if they were comfortable. The bombed-out were her special concern. One old man was very upset; she sat by him on the floor in her clean uniform and tried to comfort him.
>
> From St Mary's they drove down to the Watney Street Shelter, under the railway arches. The raid had reached one of its peaks. Bombs were falling all round them, and on the way over the car was hit again and again by falling debris.
>
> 'I think we'd better take cover till it eases off a bit,' Stitcher suggested.
>
> 'No,' she said quietly. 'Let's get on with the job.'[2]

One of her lieutenants, Miss Myrtle Tuckwell, who often accompanied Edwina on her night tours, recalls how 'her hat was just at the right angle, and there was never a hair out of place. She'd go down into those filthy shelters, so dainty and clean herself, with a smile for everybody; and you should have seen their faces light up.'

She never wore the standard tin helmet everyone else wore on duty, relying instead on a St Christopher medal for protection. No one ever observed a trace of fear and yet she was at as great a risk as any fireman or warden who remained above ground. Everyone had their Blitz story, funny, ribald or tragic. Edwina did not care much for talking about those days, but someone once prevailed upon her to tell of the evening when she visited a shelter, found it in a distressed state, prevailed upon everyone to start singing, and later left to the refrain of 'Daisy! Daisy!' She could still hear the voices when a heavy bomb screamed down and extinguished all sound. There was not one survivor. Edwina had just reached the right side of a brick wall.

'My wife's courage was fantastic during the Blitz,' Mountbatten claimed proudly. 'She really didn't know what fear was about. A lot of people used to say "If it's got my name on it, it'll get me" about the bombs. Somehow she knew she would survive and get on with her work. Amazing!'

It may have been incredible luck that led Edwina to go through the worst of London's Blitz without suffering more than a few scratches. But her superstitious and fatalistic characteristics told her that it was the badge that saved her – the St Christopher with her name and address on the back.

Edwina saw Dickie only intermittently during this time. He was awaiting the repair of the *Kelly* which had been torpedoed and dragged back safely to a dockyard, earning him the DSO (Distinguished Service Order). Edwina had travelled up to Hebburn-on-Tyne with other anxious wives to console the survivors and honour the twenty-seven dead. The destroyer's company loved her for it. When the *Kelly* had been damaged by a mine earlier, she had paid for everyone's Christmas leave railway fare so that they all got home. In those days nobody regarded that sort of gesture as patronizing.

The Germans finally finished off the *Kelly* on 23 May 1941 in the Mediterranean. Edwina had felt certain that, after the two earlier escapes from destruction, Dickie's ship would not survive a third time. She also knew that he was certain to be in the thick of the fighting off Crete. When the Admiralty telephoned her in London with the simultaneous news that the *Kelly* had gone down but that Dickie was safe, it was an immense relief. But the next news, that more than half the ship's company had been lost, grieved her terribly. By this time she knew many of them by name. She was also told that Prince Philip, who was serving in this theatre, was safe, too.

In London, Edwina had sent Dickie's mother away from the bombing down to Broadlands, which had now become largely a hospital again. Brigade headquarters had moved to 43 Belgrave Square, where it was to be joined by the British Red Cross Society, and Edwina took a lease on a modest house, 15 Chester Street, which was to remain the Mountbatten London HQ for the rest of the war, with an attic room reserved for Prince Philip whenever he happened to be in London.

Dickie returned home by the fastest possible means and arrived, typically, in time for what he regarded as the best news of the war – the German attack on Soviet Russia on 22 June 1941. The experiences of war had gone a long way now towards healing the breach between Dickie and Edwina. Someone who had known them before the war and met them again said they were like Russia and Britain, uneasy allies 'but to the outside world stout friends in the face of adversity'. According to Sir Henry 'Chips' Channon, Edwina 'looked a dream of beauty and seemed fond of Dickie'.[3] No one would have made this second comment five years earlier, and certainly neither the observant Noël Coward nor sister Mary.

The friendship between Coward and the Mountbattens had prospered in spite of Coward's satirical one-act play and other faintly waspish references to them. Dickie and Noël were both too realistic and too good actors to allow small rifts to widen. Coward had been a frequent visitor to Malta in the late 1920s and during Mountbatten's second tour of duty there in the mid-1930s. Like Peter Murphy, his presence always had a healing effect on relations between Dickie and Edwina, because they both loved and admired him and he always amused them. For his part, Coward's love for the Royal Navy was widely known. 'I love the Navy,' he once wrote. 'I inherited my affection for it. All my mother's family were Navy.... I love anything to do with the Navy. To start with they've got the best manners in the world and I love the sea and Navy discipline.... I would have loved to have been in the Navy.'[4]

A few days after Mountbatten's safe return from the Mediterranean, Coward dined with him and Edwina. 'Dickie told the whole story of the sinking of *Kelly*,' Coward wrote in his diary. 'Absolutely heartbreaking and so magnificent. He told the whole saga without frill and with a sincerity that was very moving. He is a pretty wonderful man, I think.'[5]

From this evening there eventually emerged the film *In Which We Serve*. When Coward made the first approaches to Mountbatten he was given provisional approval 'provided that it couldn't be traced back in any way to the *Kelly* - and above all to me'. In the first script Edwina became Lady Celia Kinross living in a huge country house larger than Broadlands, and of course with a Rolls-Royce and driver. Mountbatten would not have that, so the title was dropped, along with the limousine and country estate. No one who saw the film was fooled for a minute, but Mountbatten was able to point to the disparity when defending himself against accusations - particularly by the Beaverbrook Press - of self-glorification in partnership with Coward.

Between July and September 1941 the Mountbattens saw more of one another than at any other time during the war, although Edwina continued to fill a ten-hour day at her office and Mountbatten was becoming more and more drawn into the war in the higher levels of power. In August he was appointed to the command of the aircraft carrier *Illustrious*. She had been badly damaged in the Mediterranean and was undergoing repairs at the US Navy Yard at Norfolk, Virginia. This gave him the excellent excuse to travel to America to supervise the repairs, and Edwina agreed to combine work with pleasure and to accompany him on their first trip together for many years to the country they both loved.

It was a curious experience to be back in New York again after the rigours and dangers of two years of war. On the surface, little had changed since that magical honeymoon arrival back in 1922 when they had been so warmly fêted as the representatives of extravagant and regal youth. In fact, the skyscrapers were taller, the avenues more brilliantly lit, the traffic heavier and faster than ever. Invitations to shows and parties poured in to their hotel suite as before. The telephone rang before they were unpacked. But when they began to meet their old friends they recognized the difference in outlook and attitude at once. 'Everyone looked at us as if we were patients recovering from a serious operation,' Mountbatten once related. 'We used to laugh because they were so kind and *gentle*. They also wanted to know everything.' One or two less sensitive people mistook the mood and invited them to bright weekend parties to cheer them up, as they put it, and take them out of themselves. Edwina took a very firm line with them. They weren't even on leave, she would explain. They had come to do a job of war work. Even their children would see them only briefly.

Edwina's work was to travel the country in order to thank personally those people and organizations which had contributed so generously – over £5 million – to Britain's war charities. She was there at the invitation of the American Red Cross, who were as anxious to know what the effects were of bombing on a civilian population as Edwina was to express Britain's gratitude. She knew that she would have to make speeches in numerous cities, in twenty-eight states in all, and she was not a natural speaker and had little experience.

Mountbatten knew that Edwina was dreading what she regarded as an extended ordeal. Like any good actor, shyness on a platform was quite beyond his comprehension, but he answered Edwina's appeal for help willingly enough, beginning by tearing up the set speech she had painstakingly composed. 'It's got to come from the heart, not from a piece of paper.' It was like Cecil B. de Mille showing them both how to make a film nineteen years before – the master instructing. He explained to her the basic and finer points of public speaking, and how – above all – to relax and feel at one with her audience. Edwina's self-discipline and clever practical mind did the rest. After this brief and highly effective course, Edwina never read a word of the countless speeches she made and never made a speech which did not arouse the admiration of her audience.

On this gruelling tour the pattern was set for the tours that were to feature so frequently for the rest of her life. Always in perfectly tailored uniform, well-groomed, a touch of rouge on her cheeks (something she had never needed in peacetime) and lipstick, she would answer the greetings of her hosts and hostesses with her charming smile and express immediate and spontaneous enthusiasm for everyone and everything she was shown and told. Her memory was a match for Mountbatten's, and she was always thoroughly briefed with the names, status and duties of everyone she met. If she had met anyone before, however fleetingly, she would remember the name, occasion and any special circumstances so that they were at once made to feel like a personal friend. She would often follow this up by remarking, 'Do come and see us when you are in London any time.' A young naval wife recalls the occasion when a friend summoned up the courage to do just that and 'drop in': 'She was very nice but Lord Mountbatten was furious!'

A friend has written of this tour:

> She spoke from the heart, and her audiences were moved. Her speeches were unadorned, but the men and women who listened to this unvarnished prose learned how the British hospitals and ARP and voluntary societies functioned, what had become of the thousands of garments, dressings, bandages, tons of food, and other comforts sent by them to Britain, and they understood, as never before, what a solace their gifts and supplies had given to the suffering and bombed-out population of Britain.[6]

A characteristic of Edwina's, which made itself evident for the first time in this 1941 tour, was to set herself a gruelling programme and then, with every sign of satisfaction, extend it still further, like a long-distance runner intent on breaking his own record. It was as if she enjoyed testing herself to the limit and then seeing how far beyond it she could go. It was not done out of any sort of public bravado, but only for personal pleasure of a nature most people find hard to understand.

Before the completion of her American tour, Edwina insisted on extending it to include a number of cities in Canada. She was completely exhausted by the time she reached Montreal, but she diplomatically and effectively repeated her speech in French at a dinner given in her honour by the Quebec Provincial Council of the St John Ambulance Association; after which she proceeded with a smile to inspect, with no evidence of haste or weariness, the Montreal Corps of the Brigade.

Edwina was back in England before Pearl Harbor, and she was able to celebrate with Dickie the entry of the country she loved into the war. He had inspected the American naval base a few weeks before it was bombed, and told Edwina of the words of warning about its pitiable unpreparedness he had given to Admiral Harold Stark, Chief of Naval Staff, on his return. Mountbatten had been relieved of command of the *Illustrious* before she had completed repairs in order to take up a new and highly important appointment at Combined Operations. Soon he was an acting Vice-Admiral and a member of the Combined Chiefs of Staff. Edwina was also promoted. Her rise was even more rocket-like than Dickie's: after less than two years she was appointed Superintendent-in-Chief of St John Ambulance Brigade, with an 'army' of almost 100,000 volunteers. And in the 1942 New Year's Honours she was made a CBE (Commander of the British Empire).

Edwina's appetite for medals did not by any means match Mountbatten's, but she was not so modest that she did not derive satisfaction from receiving them and watching the numbers above her uniform breast pocket grow with the passing years until there were three rows comprising among them the DCVO (Dame Commander of the Royal Victorian Order), the Brilliant Star of China and the Belgian, Netherlands and American Red Cross Medals.

Edwina had her enemies, in peace and war. It was inevitable that she made them; it was amazing that she made so few. Before 1939 she made enemies among those she slighted, and those who considered themselves slighted by her offhand manner. People she had met, perhaps on unimportant occasions, might be ignored the second time. Very often, but not always, this was occasioned by her short-sightedness. (On war duty she wore her spectacles to avoid these mishaps.) With people who did not commend themselves to her she could be ruthless, and then her manner could be as fierce as her grandfather's when crossed. And, like her husband, she did not – in that contemporary phrase – suffer fools gladly. Sometimes she was cruel, without intending to be. Her victims might be women, rarely men, who could not keep up and did not respond quickly enough.

Edwina loathed 'commonness' and the attributes of the middle classes and could be very scathing about them. 'She liked the "top" and the "bottom" but wasn't so good with the in-betweens who she thought were unamusing and suspected were all social climbers,' remarked one of her friends. This sweeping condemnation of those who were neither out of the top drawer nor deserving of her attention as the underprivileged and needy was Edwina's least likeable characteristic. But she was a product of her age, and this snobbery, which could cause distress to decent people, was a widespread consequence of Victorian-Edwardian social attitudes.

Edwina also, and more agreeably, loathed pomposity and could be mischievous when she met it, although she was sometimes accused of it herself. Later in the war, when the Brigade moved to 3 Belgrave Square from Grosvenor Crescent and shared premises with the British Red Cross, she sat on selection boards with her opposite number, Dame Beryl Oliver, an admiral's wife who was Commandant-in-Chief. Edwina clearly found her insufferable. Dame Beryl was very austere, rather frightening and very pompous, according to many who worked with her, although she was also highly competent and 'her heart was in the right place'. One of her staff officers recalls the invariable preliminaries to a selection board meeting:

> Edwina would always come in after Lady Oliver, specially dressed for the occasion with huge diamond earrings although she was otherwise strictly in uniform. The whole situation was very tense. Lady Oliver had never put make-up on her face from the moment she was born. Edwina had on rouge as she was so very pale without. She had the charming habit of coming in, sitting down next to Lady Oliver, taking a powder compact out of her pocket and shaking powder all over Lady Oliver's uniform. This did not please her.

Among the middle ranks in the Brigade Edwina's disapproval could manifest itself more sharply. Her first thought was for the successful care of the sick and injured, and she saw inefficiency as much of an enemy as lack of supplies and other shortcomings. She also had a marvellous talent for spotting it. When she did, heads rolled, and she did not give much, or any, thought to what happened later to those she disposed of. In some cases, but not often, they had a valid defence which was left unheard.

Her call for speed, her natural impatience, her crusading zeal, all resulted in casualties left on the road behind her. What is remarkable, however, is that they were so few. And what cannot be questioned is that Edwina was never deliberately motivated by malice. The processes of imagination had not been much exercised in the ivory tower which she had inhabited for so long, insulated as she had been from the realities of life. A rebuff was as foreign to Edwina as the need to do without something she wanted. She could claim to be a socialist, and sometimes claimed to be a communist. 'Edwina M is now a complete Socialist, which for anybody in the position of a millionairess, a semi-royalty, and a famous fashionable figure, is too ridiculous.' That was in 1942. Eighteen months later, 'Chips' Channon, a very shrewd observer, noted in his diary again: 'Politically [Edwina] talked tripe and pretended to be against all monarchy, she who is cousin to every monarch on earth. According to her they must all be abolished. How easy it seems for a semi-royal millionairess, who has exhausted all the pleasures of money and position, to turn almost Communist!'[7]

Most people laughed and shrugged off Edwina's extreme political views. 'Quaint' was a word often used by her friends to describe them. In fact Edwina knew nothing of the levelling-down process, nor of the realities of the lives of those who would benefit from her egalitarianism.

Not a breath of socialist politics ever entered the portals of 3 Belgrave Square. There, whatever mixed feelings some of those who served under her might feel, none could deny that the honours she really rather enjoyed were deserved – even if, as one of those who passed through HQ recalled, 'There was a slight feeling of envy among some of the staff because her uniform was so very smart and clearly tailored to her own needs by her dressmaker.'

After Edwina's return from America at the end of 1941, her professional life for the following two years assumed for the first time a coherent shape. At HQ in London she worked like any hard-pressed administrator, taxing to the utmost the staff closest to her, and especially her private secretary, Nancie Lees, who deserved a damehood herself for the hours she kept and the pressures to which she was subjected. Only slightly less hard-pressed were her two senior staff officers, Muriel Watson and Moya Lumley Smith, who was killed with her father in the Guards Chapel flying bomb disaster.

In addition, Edwina was also involved at any one time in a number of campaigns, which kept her on the move from one end of the country to the other. The most unrelenting of these was recruiting for volunteers, and this took her to every centre in Britain. Clubs, ambulance units, canteens, hospitals, convalescent homes all demanded her attention, too. Her performance on a platform had now become a byword throughout all the charities in the land, and she received a steady flow of appeals to open this and attend that. She did so, far above the call of duty. In addition, she started up campaigns of her own, including 'Salute the Soldier Week'. Her work inevitably became self-multiplying. She slept worse than ever and showed signs of the strain she was experiencing.

'Late in the day before she went home she would sometimes look awful,' said one of her staff. 'It was hard to believe that before the war she was reckoned to be one of the most beautiful women in England. She was grey and haggard and lined. Even her beautiful eyes looked tired behind her thick spectacles.'

'She was absolutely indefatigable,' recalled another staff officer who worked closely with her. 'At weekends she would come in to the office in mufti with armfuls of papers and two dogs on leads. She had walked from

Chester Street. We worried about her in the traffic as she was so blind. I know she wore glasses, but all the same. . . . She wasn't careful of herself at all.'

There were few parties in those days and social life was very circumscribed. Occasionally she dined out with Sibyl Colefax and other of her pre-war friends, and very occasionally went to the theatre or the cinema. The film which of necessity occupied some of her precious spare time, was *In Which We Serve*. Coward had been working on this while the Mountbattens had been in America. He recalled 'a proud and pleasant day' in April 1942 when 'the King and Queen arrived with the two Princesses, Dickie and Edwina'[8] to visit the film set where it was being made. There were other visits, too, and numerous meetings between Dickie and Coward at Chester Street as the film progressed. The premiere was on 17 September 1942.

However, the most time-consuming aspect of the film for Edwina was the soothing of Dickie's ruffled feathers over the attacks made on him and Coward by Beaverbrook and his newspapers. Beaverbrook's hostility to the Mountbattens had greatly diminished with the war but was violently rearoused by the Dieppe raid, followed closely by *In Which We Serve*. The press baron believed that Mountbatten had squandered Canadian lives at the 'fiasco' of Dieppe. With more substance, a shot from the film could be construed as an attack on the *Daily Express*. The Beaverbrook vendetta (as Mountbatten saw it) against him, which never quite ceased even after Beaverbrook died, greatly distressed Mountbatten, and was the worst cross he had to bear in all his life. For a man as vain as he was, for a man who valued public esteem so highly, it was unremitting torment – no less.

It was Edwina's duty, as she saw it, to try to contain the damaging effect on Mountbatten when he was so deeply involved in the war effort at the top, and to reassure him of its relative unimportance. Later, she wearied of his pained preoccupation with Beaverbrook and his newspapers, saying it was boring and something he should rise above.

It was said at the time that Edwina met Dickie only once a week, on the stairs when he was running up and she was running down. It was more frequent than this, before Mountbatten took up the appointment as Supreme Allied Commander in South-East Asia in September 1943. But it is doubtful if they once put their feet up at 9 o'clock like everyone else to listen to the evening news on the radio. They certainly never went to bed together; that had ceased years ago. When they did meet it would be on some formal occasion or, like a divorced couple, at weddings or funerals.

For example, they were both at the Duke of Kent's funeral on 29 August 1942. Mountbatten's cousin and the King's youngest brother – a bright, lively and popular prince – had been killed on active service with the RAF. When the coffin with flowers and Prince George's cap on it passed down the aisle of Windsor Chapel, Noël Coward (who was also there as an old friend) 'gave up all pretence and stood with the tears splashing down my face. I was relieved and heartened', he noted, 'to see that both Dickie and the King were doing the same thing.'[9] But not Edwina. She did not cry at funerals, or on any other occasion for that matter.

The only domestic life Edwina allowed herself was with her girls. When conditions became safer in England Patricia and Pamela had returned from America. At nineteen Patricia had joined the WRNS and later left to join her father among the thousands at his headquarters at Kandy, Ceylon (now Sri Lanka). Pamela was dispatched to school, and Edwina saw much more of her, occasionally taking her to the theatre or cinema in London, and staying with her for a weekend at Broadlands.

10
Mistress of Welfare

At no time since her marriage had Edwina remained in Britain for so long without a break. She was too busy to suffer from the confinement, which she would have found intolerable before the war. Now, in June 1944, along with hundreds of thousands of others, she was able to embark for foreign shores. The liberation of France and Europe had begun; and Edwina, long groomed for the part for which she was to become best known to so many people, left for the Normandy beachhead to give comfort to the sick and wounded. Among those in the big American B17 bomber provided by the Supreme Commander, General Eisenhower, were her opposite number at the Red Cross, General Sir Bertram Sergison-Brooke, who had joined the Army before Edwina was born, and (very much younger) Lieutenant-Colonel Joe Weld, who worked as General Staff Officer 1 for Mountbatten's command in London and had been deputed to look after her. With an escort of fighters, although the danger at this time was not great, the Boeing crossed the Channel, and Edwina picked out the shores of France for the first time since 1939.

At the beachhead airfield where they landed an enormous HQ staff car, with motorcycle military police escort, awaited them. Edwina had met Eisenhower a number of times in London and liked and admired him tremendously. She almost always felt at ease with Americans. She greeted with equal warmth his driver-companion, maid-of-all-work Kay Summersby, who acted as hostess at the seaside villa which was HQ at that time. After lunch, the Supreme Commander got down to business with Edwina and Sergison-Brooke, exchanging information and formulating plans. The Brigade and Red Cross programme was chiefly concerned with the study of the conditions in French and Allied hospitals in the areas already liberated, and making recommendations on future policy - both civilian and military - as the Allies advanced into Europe. They were asked if they could report back in nine days.

For Edwina, this was the real war. It was a relief to get away from her desk, meetings and administrative problems in London and see at first hand the meaning behind the military liberation of Europe. The work was fascinating and utterly exhausting. She had car, driver, secretary and Joe Weld by her side; she had security clearance and the authority of 'Ike' himself, as shown on her windscreen stickers. Everywhere she was waved through by military police, and the best possible arrangements were made for her to sleep at night. But the self-imposed tempo was taxing. No one could help her through minefields, or unblock a line of stalled tanks.

Edwina's destination was always the next field hospital, or the next French hospital in Normandy. Casualties, both civilian and military, were nothing like so serious as had been predicted. But they were bad enough, especially among civilians around Caen where Allied bombing had been so heavy. Lieutenant-Colonel Weld (now Sir Joseph Weld, Lord-Lieutenant of Dorset) has told how Edwina would prepare and brace herself for the next visit and inspection: 'A few quick "repairs" to her make-up were followed by a brisk combing of her hair, patting it neatly into place and planting her hat attractively on top. Then out came a clothes brush to flick off stray powder and loose hairs from her collar, lapels and shoulders.'[1]

Then the performance began: the greeting, the small-talk with those in charge reduced to a minimum (sometimes abruptly), the facts and figures on patients, conditions, medical supplies, nurses and doctors, with a note taken of needs. Edwina inspected everything, taking account of adverse circumstances but not allowing anything to escape her eye. 'Sometimes the people in charge would try concealment, or try to hoodwink Lady Louis,' one witness reports. 'But they always regretted it and never tried again. She listened to reason but not to excuses. And she was as tireless in her inspections as she was quick and effective in providing for genuine needs.'

A FANY (First Aid Nursing Yeomanry) officer who saw Edwina on her rounds on several occasions recalled:

> Except that it was not acting – it was real – her visits were like a performance by a great actress. She had long since learnt her part perfectly and knew the cast and the cues and the entrances and all that. But every time it was like the first night. She put her all into every appearance – and was perfection. And I suppose that's what makes a great actress. It certainly made a great head of a great nursing organization.

Walking round the wards she was transformed from a superb inspector into a solicitous and attentive nurse-cum-visitor. She stopped at every bed or cot, and showed as much concern for those recovering in wheelchairs as for those recently back from the operating theatre, sick, bewildered and in pain. She had two special qualities, one of them unique. First, as an experienced practical nurse, she understood the nature of their injuries and their condition, and would sometimes change a dressing or a bandage or perhaps ease the patient into a more comfortable posture. Second, she gave every appearance of being in no hurry at all; moreover, to every patient to whom she spoke she gave the impression that he, or she, was the only person who mattered and was her sole and exclusive concern.

After this relatively brief tour, there were others, both to northern Europe and to Italy. The overall pattern was invariable, every visit a charge on Edwina's physical and mental resources, and every visit demanding her total attention, whether in a damaged civilian hospital in a bombed and shelled town, or a forward casualty clearing station under canvas, where the mud and blood were all too evident and the wounded still in shock.

On several occasions, especially in northern Europe, she was at risk and had to be warned back from enemy shelling or uncleared roads. Wherever it was possible, she flew to save time. She was given the use of a twin-engined Avro Anson, in which she experienced her closest shave. In October 1944, not long after the American 82nd Division had captured Nijmegen, Edwina wanted to get to the Dutch town, which was still only a short distance from the German line. The Anson's New Zealand pilot, flying very low, lost his bearings. Suddenly

> an anti-aircraft battery opened fire on them: actually they were about a mile off course and over the Germans. At only four hundred feet they were practically a sitting target. One engine was shot out, and the person sitting beside Lady Louis was hit in the face as flak zipped through the body of the plane. The pilot just managed to hedge-hop back over our lines, and the remainder of the journey had to be completed by jeep.[2]

Edwina had flown since her marriage, in early open cockpit planes, in wires-and-canvas biplanes, Tiger Moths, Puss Moths, Fokker trimotors, seaplanes and flying boats, and in the massive Imperial Airways Heracles. A much decorated lieutenant-colonel (now a retired brigadier) recalls flying with her from Sourayabaya to Batavia in a monsoon some time after the incident over Nijmegen. Their Dakota was forced down to 100 feet to remain clear of cloud, and below, flitting past in a dim green rain-washed blur, was apparently interminable jungle. Her soldier companion, who says he was decidedly scared, looked across at Edwina beside him.

She was quite unperturbed. 'The only person in the plane not frightened was Edwina.'

The weather was for her the worst hazard. Forgetful of the family flying catastrophe of 1937, she was prepared to fly under almost any conditions. But in the 1940s, with none of the sophisticated navigational and flying aids taken for granted today, the weather did quite often beat Edwina, frustrating her efforts to keep to her self-imposed packed timetable.

Edwina's first trip to Paris since 1939, however, was not made by air. It was only with the greatest difficulty that she got there at all. The city had only just fallen, not all the streets were safe, and identification and passes were scrutinized with suspicion. One of her friends in the Brigade recalls:

> It was a strange and terribly changed world for Edwina. And Edwina was terribly changed from the woman who knew it so well and for so many years had sought the bright lights and distractions. There weren't many bright lights and no distractions worth speaking of. There wasn't even enough food and drink, and although she put up at the Ritz it was not like the old times there – no lights and no hot water, and I believe she only managed to get some tinned meat.

But Edwina also loved to tell about visiting her old friend, the manager of Boucheron, where she had been a much valued customer before the war. She had ordered a pair of gold earrings when she had last been there. She did not expect that they could have survived the years of German occupation – surely, she thought, they would long ago have been looted. But when the manager heard that she was in the shop he came out with a gratified and delighted expression on his face, bearing in his hand a satin-lined box. Inside were the earrings and a card with her name on it. 'You don't imagine we would let the Germans have Madame's property!' In Paris, under these conditions, gold earrings seemed an anachronistic reminder of a distant age.

Shortly after Edwina's return from Holland in October 1944 she received a signal from Mountbatten at his HQ in Kandy. In effect it was 'Please come out here and continue the good work.' In the objective reckoning of both Eisenhower and his fellow 'Supremo' in South-East Asia, there was no one better equipped than Edwina for the supervision of recovery in the wake of a great military campaign. She had the breadth of vision, the administrative authority and skill, and the human touch – the attention to detail – that was unsurpassable. In Europe, between the summer and late autumn of 1944, her magic influence fell on liberated prisoners-of-war, dispossessed refugees, and wounded civilians and servicemen alike. She was the supreme mistress of welfare, and there was not a department of the giant machine serving mankind, after the suffering occasioned by tyranny and the military measures to eradicate it, that had not felt her strong grip of correction or congratulation. Now, as the campaigns in South-East Asia began to push back the armies of another tyranny, vast new opportunities for her special talents and energies were opened to her.

Edwina left on her last great wartime crusade on 9 January 1945, taking with her only her loyal and forever overworked secretary, Nancie Lees. They arrived in Karachi on 9 January 1945, Edwina feeling very poorly from the last-minute drugs she had been obliged to take as a precaution against malaria, typhoid and cholera. It did not alter by a minute the local timetable she had ordered to be drawn up for her. Mountbatten had dispatched Major Bryan Hunter from his staff as her escort for the entire tour. He made an admirable choice. He had been briefed comprehensively, and from the moment he met Edwina 'he was on her wavelength', as one observer noted. 'He was cheerful and enthusiastic – maybe he would have been less so if he had known what he was in for.'

Hunter took the two women by escorted car straight to Government House, where Edwina met Sir Hugh Dow, Governor of Sind, and his wife Ann. Dow had been in the Indian Civil Service since 1909 and was able to provide Edwina with a lot of information on conditions in India after more than five years of war as well as in his own province. Dickie had told her in his letters of the growing resistance to British rule, among Hindus and Moslems alike, and the threat of rebellion. Only the exigencies of war were preventing an explosion against the rule of the Raj, and if tens of thousands of Indians were fighting alongside the Allies in Burma, there were also many thousands fighting alongside the Japanese under the leadership of the violent former Congress leader, Subhas Chandra Bose.

One of the Brigade staff in Karachi recalls:

> Tired and ill as she must have felt, Lady Louis went into action on the afternoon of her day of arrival. I didn't see her until the evening but I was told she had already toured one of our thousand-bed base hospitals, where she had made clear what she was there for. And very sensible, too. She knew that the message would work through the medical grapevine quick as a monsoon gale. I was told that they had polished up one ward within an inch of its life and had informed Lady Louis that she could save her legs after her long flight because all the wards were the same. She was also asked rather pointedly *not* to shake hands with sepoys – 'Oh, that will never do!' Well you can imagine the response to that!

In the next few days she had swept through two rest camps, a Merchant Navy hostel, a convalescent home and another large hospital, with Nancie Lees always at her elbow, notebook in hand: 'We must ask Matron whether there is a shortage of dressings or nurses to change them. ... Corporal Johnson is worried that he hasn't heard from his wife since she left London because of the rockets. We must ask the local Brigade in Croydon if they can discover where she's gone.' A few more words with Corporal Johnson, who feels better already and much relieved, a smile and a hand-shake, and unhurriedly to the next bed. It was a routine she had perfected down to the last detail.

Nothing escaped Edwina's eye - even the oil leak in the plane Mountbatten had sent to fly her to Delhi. She spotted it after they were airborne, pointed it out to the pilot, who immediately reversed course and landed again. Then there was a long delay, much deplored by Edwina, before she took off in another aircraft. Dickie was at the airport to greet her, resplendent in admiral's uniform - three years earlier he had the four narrow rings on his sleeve of a captain RN. Now there was a thick ring and three narrow rings, the fastest promotion in naval history. From a flotilla of destroyers, he had now a vast army, a fleet and a powerful air force under his command.

Delhi held a special place in their hearts. Lutyens's masterpiece on Raisina Hill - the Viceroy's Court, the Great Palace, the Council Chamber, Government House and the spectacular Central Vista - which had only been under construction when they had become engaged there almost twenty-three years before, was now long since completed. They drove straight to the Viceroy's palace. Archibald Wavell, Field-Marshal and Viceroy, and his wife, greeted Edwina warmly, and over dinner there was a lot of talk about the old days before Edwina inevitably turned the direction of the conversation to her work.

Both Dickie and Edwina had separately made arrangements to take an afternoon off to make a pilgrimage to Old Delhi and the Prince of Wales's bungalow where they had become engaged. In the event, there was not even time for that. There was just too much to do before Edwina flew off to Bombay and Dickie back to his HQ in Kandy.

At Bombay His Excellency the Governor was John Colville (later Lord Clydesmuir), and Edwina's reception, treatment and work were typical of the whole exhausting tour. She was received as if she were a senior member of the Royal Family, if not the Queen herself, with ADCs and staff attached to her for the duration of her stay, a formal reception, banquet and meetings with the hierarchy. Instructions had been issued ahead to keep the formalities to a minimum, but Edwina knew that they were inevitable and, in many ways, useful.

A typical day on just one leg of her long tour of India, Burma and China went as follows:

It is 27 January 1945. Edwina is without her secretary or escort. Bryan Hunter has been bitten by a Portuguese man of war while swimming off Malabar Point; Nancie Lees is in bed from heat exhaustion. Her ADC for the day is Lieutenant A.W.M. Dickie, who was brought up in Enniskillen and knows Classiebawn and Mullaghmore. That is a good start, and they immediately get on well together. Edwina takes an early morning swim before a tour of some of the hospitals and clinics in the city.

It is 'hot as hell', but her interest in all and everything she sees never flags. By the end of the morning she has met as many as a hundred Red Cross and St John Ambulance Brigade workers. In the mid-afternoon on the lawns of Government House, she appears before a vast number of them, including those to whom she was introduced in the morning. Beside her is Sir Cameron Badenoch, Auditor-General of India and Chief Commissioner of the St John Ambulance Brigade in India.

Edwina climbs onto a grassy bank in order to see her audience more clearly. Less than four years ago she knew nothing of public speaking. She speaks now, brilliantly, for forty minutes. Her ADC recalls:

> She had no notes, and what I remember in particular was that she mentioned person after person she had met that morning, and when doing so indicated that particular one in the seated crowd below her. The effect on her listeners was quite extraordinary. How she could have taken in all she obviously had during that long hot morning was something that few could have equalled. 'And we must thank Mrs ...' (and then would come some lengthy Indian or Parsee name) ... 'for ...' and down she would beam at the good lady. You can imagine the effect!
>
> After a very hard day she appeared looking radiantly beautiful for the formal dinner. By about 11.30 p.m. Their Excellencies retired and the dinner guests departed.

Edwina's ADCs were the only people left, and she showed no signs of retiring. Now she was ready to relax and enjoy herself. 'After a time she enquired if there was any night spot that we could go to. She was genuinely very disappointed when we said that, to our knowledge, there was nowhere of the type we presumed she had in mind.'

There were no night spots in Calcutta either – nor in Jaipur or anywhere else. Instead there were shortages – often distressing ones: electric light bulbs, operating theatre equipment, magazines, small comforts and important necessities – like beds and nurses. The shortage of nurses was everywhere bad, in some hospitals crippling. There was little Edwina could do to cure immediately these handicaps. But the cables to Britain were peremptory and urgent. Meanwhile she persuaded a gentlemen's club in Calcutta to sacrifice half its ceiling fans, and conjured up the wire to get them rotating above the beds of sweating patients. An RAF commandant suddenly found that it was, after all, possible for the airfield's flight path to be changed in order to prevent his machines from flying low over the nearby hospital.

When complaints about troop trains – no room, no water, no lavatories – came to her ears, she did what she had been instructed in 1922 was impossible: she travelled third class overnight in a hot, packed troop train. 'I went with her from Dimapur to Gauhati,' Hunter recalls, 'and I have never forgotten it. We boarded a train at a quarter to ten that night . . . four wooden seats harder than park benches and two luggage racks above.' There were ten soldiers in there already. None of them recognized her.

> Determined to rough it, Edwina steadfastly refused to bring any cushions. The journey was in complete darkness. . . . Edwina made friends with the soldiers, listened to them moaning about leave arrangements which meant they spent more time travelling in awful trains than leave in shocking camps.
>
> After the soldiers had got their troubles off their chests they politely fell asleep, leaving the Supreme Commander's wife nothing better to do than follow suit. Without disturbing anybody she climbed up on to one of the luggage racks, and there she spent the rest of that pitch-black journey.[3]

Next her odyssey took her to Burma, and close to the front line. The Japanese were retreating, stripping everything as they did so, including the hospitals, where patients were left untended – just dumped on the floor, without beds, bedclothes or supplies of any kind. She met and talked to casualties on stretchers, still battle-shocked. She met corps commanders and divisional commanders – Generals Frank Messervy, Francis Festing and others, including a divisional general who, it has been recounted, broke off his conversation with, 'Would you mind waiting a bit? I've got a couple of battles going on near here and I'd like to see how we're doing.'

Her reception at American hospitals was invariably enthusiastic.

> How they loved her! She would come into a ward, greeted by whistles and catcalls, and she would sit down on the end of beds and crack jokes and have everyone laughing. It was a marvellous sight – talk about rapport. Of course I had always heard that she might have been an American but for that accent. She signed autograph books and plaster casts.

But there was also very little opportunity to exercise her reforming enthusiasm in American hospitals. They were, she discovered to her relief but not to her surprise, invariably clean, fully equipped, with pretty and efficient nurses in adequate numbers, bright curtains, chairs, recreation equipment and fans against the heat.

Mountbatten had been suffering from numerous frustrations in his efforts to evict the Japanese army from Burma. Just as one of his plans to speed the end was taking shape, he was deprived of the essentials to carry it out. Now, in the last weeks of 1944, it was becoming evident that Chiang Kai-shek was in dire trouble and needed reinforcements urgently from the Burma theatre if his capital and his regime were not to fall. Believing that the Chinese demand for further support was unreasonable, Mountbatten had decided to fly to Chungking and confront the Generalissimo personally.

When Edwina learned of this mission she determined to go along too. She regarded her crusade as a world-wide one. There were no frontiers, no barriers, in her preoccupation with the sick, wounded and homeless. Her concern for refugee Chinese peasants and soldiers in hospitals was as deep as for wounded Indian troops fighting on the Arakan front or half-starved Dutch refugees liberated but without a roof over their heads in Europe. There were no distinctions of race, colour or geography. But her determination to accompany her husband was sharpened by the certainty that she could give him essential support and not just take tea with Madame Chiang Kai-shek.

At every rung of the ladder, Edwina had been there to advise, support and encourage him literally to 'rise above it' to the next rung. Her contribution to his advancement was subtle, discreet, profoundly important and almost totally unrecognized by anyone but her closest friends and relations. One of them has said:

> The idea that Edwina did anything towards Dickie's successful career came as a surprise to most people. They vaguely feel that she was some sort of a handicap in his early days when she was really being rather naughty, and that she made a nice decoration on the throne in Delhi when she was Vicereine. But I believe it is doubtful if he would have made it without her.

To expect any credit for what she did was not within Edwina's nature. To claim any credit would have defeated at once what had been, since her marriage, one of the first aspirations and motivations of her life. Intensely competitive, intensely loyal, intensely dutiful as her character and upbringing had made her, she had determined that Dickie should fulfil all his great ambitions as a further extension of her own. Although she had never passionately loved him, nor anyone else so far in her life, and there were always rows when they were alone together, she was very admiring of him. In everything he took on, she wanted him to win, and, because Edwina always got her way, made sure that he won. Even during the most miserable years her loyalty to this cause never wavered. She might despise the monarchical system, but she acknowledged its strength in promoting her husband's advancement and was therefore prepared to accept the system as it was even while, such was her self-confidence and need to speak her mind, she was not prepared to conceal her contempt for it.

Edwina's support of Mountbatten had begun within weeks of their marriage when she persuaded the Prince of Wales to ensure that Dickie was not 'axed' from the Navy. At any rebuff she rallied Dickie, recognizing from early on how deeply insecure he was. When the Royal Yacht Squadron blackballed him, she pooh-poohed the Royal Yacht Squadron – 'a lot of nobodys', or 'how common!', two of her favourite expressions. When his life had been made miserable in the wardroom during early sea appointments, she told him that jealousy often took people with small minds in that way. She ingratiated herself with no one, least of all those in power, but she made certain in her devious, clever way that those in and out of the Royal Navy who could be of benefit to Dickie were made aware of his qualities. But, it must be added, if he had been less exceptional as an officer and a sailor than he was, nothing that Edwina could do would have benefited him.

And so it came about that the combination of Edwina and Dickie was a world-beater from the start. Nothing could have prevented Louis Mountbatten from leaping up the promotion ladder, over the heads of contemporaries, some of whom, by the very nature of things, were piqued. Nor was Mountbatten's star restricted in its constellation to the Royal Navy. The broad nature of their social life, made possible by her wealth and his rank, served to bring their qualities to the notice of the great men of affairs. Their striking appearance and colourful style did the rest. Even when Edwina disappeared for weeks, sometimes months, on end with a woman friend – or friends – or when they seemed close to permanent separation, the Mountbattens were seen as indivisible. They were Dickie and Edwina, and their joint star was forever on the ascendant. Politicians like Duff Cooper and Anthony Eden recognized it. So did many others.

Mountbatten's wartime career could have gone no farther than Chief of Combined Operations without American concurrence and support. But in America by 1943 word of the strength and quality of the Mountbattens had spread far beyond the East Coast social establishment and 'show biz'. The President had followed their wartime career, and it was not only Churchill's strong advocacy that led to Roosevelt's recognition of his value and his support of Churchill's nomination of Mountbatten as Commander-in-Chief of the new South-East Asia Command against the claims of numerous American commanders. It was not long before the American Chiefs of Staff, too, joined Roosevelt in their admiration for him, even 'Vinegar Joe', General Joseph Stilwell.

It was, above all, Churchill who recognized that a great deal of Mountbatten's value stemmed from Edwina. Churchill had any number of reservations about Mountbatten the man, but his qualities as a leader were never in doubt. He had known Edwina, through his close friend Cassel, long before Mountbatten had met her, had watched her mind and character develop, and had sent her a moving tribute to her grandfather when he died. No one admired her more, and no one recognized more keenly her contribution to her husband's career. Martin Gilbert has been quoted on the strength of Edwina's emotional appeal to Churchill, and as his official biographer no one is in a better position to confirm it. Churchill, like so many others, saw the Mountbattens as a *pair*. It is fruitless to speculate on the shape of Mountbatten's career and the extent of his achievement if he had been married to anyone else. All that can be claimed indisputably is that no one could have made a greater contribution to her husband's career than Edwina. It was a truly remarkable piece of good fortune for America and Britain, for the hundreds of thousands whose sufferings were relieved by Edwina's ministrations and for the Allied cause in the Second World War, that this union had been formed in 1922. Let it also be noted in Anglo-American terms that it was a remarkable American couple, the Vanderbilts, who brought them together for the first time.

The party of generals and their staffs, and Mountbatten and Edwina, landed at Chungking on the afternoon of 6 March 1945. The Generalissimo's Foreign Secretary was there to meet them on the tarmac, a band was playing a somewhat odd rendering of 'God Save the King'. Everything was done to impress the Mountbattens, including a vast banquet at Chiang Kai-shek's presidential residence, the hall decorated with SEAC (South East Asia Command) emblems, a banner stretched above reading 'In Honour of Lord and Lady Louis Mountbatten'. There were thirty-four courses on the menu. The Chinese war against Japan was going badly, Chiang Kai-shek was beset by internal divisions and threatened by the communist forces which would overwhelm his corrupt and discredited regime three years later. It was of profound political importance that Mountbatten should carry away an impression of success and buoyant optimism, and as important that Edwina's report to the Red Cross should be as favourable.

Never before had Edwina observed such painstaking efforts to present a polished front and conceal any shortcomings in the city's hospitals. But, as has been written, 'She was up to all the dodges. Side-stepping the officially prepared route, she went looking for the real patients, and found them on the floor in a basha hut.'[4] In the few days when she was in the Chinese capital she inspected ambulance units, schools, blood banks and delousing stations as well as all the hospitals, with Nancie Lees, as usual but at unusually high speed, taking down in shorthand Edwina's observations. In spite of all the local efforts, these observations were not all favourable. There were speeches, presentations and parades in her honour. The Generalissimo presented her with a Ming vase, a roll of white silk, a lyre and a signed photograph. Mountbatten left early, then she was off again on the first stage back: a break at Kunming, and a transfer from plane to motor car for the long journey over the Burma Road, which she had wanted to see again after her 1939 drive.

Edwina rejoined Mountbatten on 20 March at his HQ at Kandy. Much has been recounted and written of his SEAC headquarters in the beautiful botanical gardens in the heart of Ceylon, and his own offices in the white palace built for Queen Victoria, but never occupied by her. Julian Amery has said:

> His HQ combined the luxury of a palace with the clockwork efficiency of the Royal Navy: The atmosphere, too, was enlivened by the company in the intervals of business, of young officers and pretty girls. Carton [de Wiart, the fire-eating, one-eyed VC General], who was rather austere in such matters, scoffed at it as 'a court' and nicknamed Mountbatten 'the Archduke Charles'.[5]

Among these 'young officers and pretty girls' was John Ulick Knatchbull, seventh Baron Brabourne, who was Mountbatten's ADC, and Patricia, who looked very fetching in her well-tailored officer WRNS uniform. But, in spite of the peerlessly beautiful setting and the material comforts, it was not a relaxed family gathering. Mountbatten was still fretting about supplies and reinforcements and the state of the Burma campaign. In Europe the Rhine had at last been crossed and the end was in sight. In South-East Asia a long-drawn-out series of battles still lay ahead, or so it seemed from SEAC headquarters at Kandy.

Edwina was at work in London during those epochal months of April to August 1945 when the Third Reich finally crumbled, the dictators

Mussolini and Hitler died, and peace came to Europe. Edwina cheered VE-Day, cheered the victory of the socialists at the British general election on 26 July, and mourned the death of Franklin Roosevelt, a friend whose ideals she had always so warmly applauded. Dickie was due home in the middle of July. He had cabled her that he was to see de Gaulle in Paris and then fly to London. Instead, he was diverted to Berlin and the Potsdam Conference, and did not arrive until later.

Mountbatten's visit was a brief one, and even by his standards swift and eventful. There was no question of a visit, even of a few hours, to Broadlands. But late on their first evening together he told her, 'I have great and important news. Only the King and one or two of the highest in command know it. The Americans have invented a new bomb, an atomic bomb. Its power is devastating. Japan will capitulate, probably in less than a month.' Edwina was probably the only woman in the world who knew the greatest military secret in the world. It is a measure of Mountbatten's trust in her discretion that he did not hesitate to pass on this news which he was prohibited from telling even his own staff. 'I had no secrets from Edwina,' he would comment brusquely when the subject of confidentiality came up.

On 6 August 1945, the Hiroshima bomb was dropped, signalling at once the violent death of 100,000 Japanese civilians and the beginning of a new era for mankind. A few days after the Japanese surrender, Edwina received an 'immediate' message from Mountbatten which was to mark a new chapter in her own life, the start of the greatest work of salvation she was ever to undertake.

Mountbatten's *cri de coeur* was about the Japanese prisoner-of-war camps, packed with hundreds of thousands of Allied soldiers, most of whom had been incarcerated for more than three and a half years under conditions varying from bad to terrible. It was believed that already many had died from malnutrition, disease or violent treatment. This life-saving exercise was a massive one employing thousands of people of all the Services and a supply operation as complicated and vast as for Mountbatten's last great offensive, 'Operation Zipper'. Edwina's part in it was to act as independent and free-ranging vanguard. Armed only with a Dakota aircraft supplied by her husband, and a small staff, her powers appeared at first strictly limited within the context of the whole rescue and recovery operation concerned with what was believed to be no fewer than 250 camps. But her unique strength lay in her unlimited authority to which Mountbatten added his own. Add to this, again, her fearlessness, her organizational powers, her experience and steely determination to succeed to the best of her endeavour, and there was a life-saving formula indeed!

The risks involved in 'Operation Edwina' were very real. Sporadic fighting was still taking place in remote parts of the theatre; it was likely that word of the surrender had not yet percolated to some Japanese commanders; and there were roaming packs of armed bandits, 'freedom fighters' of all political and nationalistic hues, many of them now as hell-bent on throwing off the yoke of renewed Dutch, French and British colonial rule as they had been in throwing out the Japanese. In addition, the monsoon was still raging in some places, making flying, upon which she solely depended for mobility, additionally hazardous.

In her party, which set off first for Rangoon, were two senior members of the Brigade, Marjorie Miller, a County Nursing Officer, one of Mountbatten's ADCs, Major Abhey Singh, and Major-General Treffrey Thompson, Chief Adviser on Medical Services for SEAC. Rangoon had become a clearing centre for sick and wounded liberated prisoners of war, who were airlifted in and transported for urgent attention to the sick-bay before continuing their journey – those who were judged fit enough to survive it. It was Edwina's first sight of men who had survived the cruel rigours of Japanese prisoner-of-war camps. Nearly all of them were stretcher cases. 'Lady Louis went to them immediately. Shrunken and emaciated, the men lay like corpses, with only a feeble movement of an arm or leg to indicate there was still a sign of life. Many of them she could see had only just been brought in in time.'

Edwina made a series of thorough inspections, dispatched a report, and took her party on to Bangkok. Here, too, in the midst of all manner of difficulties, the machinery of recovery was already operating; Edwina's work was largely of an advisory nature and visiting the camps to practise her magic formula of giving cheer to those who had suffered for so long. At one camp, Nakom Nayok, she found her cousin, Aunty-Grannie's grandson, Harold Cassel (today a distinguished circuit judge), who had been reported missing three and a half years earlier and presumed long since dead by his family. Like his fellow prisoners, he showed signs of his ordeal, including the change in colour of his hair to snow-white.

To those who had been incarcerated for years, civilians and servicemen alike, Edwina appeared as a saint, no less, in her trim uniform, short-sleeve khaki shirt, two rows of ribbons, insignia of rank on her epaulettes, cap and dark glasses, which she always took off when talking. To those who had suffered anxiety for so long about the fate of wives, husbands or children, she would say, 'I'll find out for you as soon as I can. I have set up a Red Cross Information Centre. Just give me your name.' A Mrs Smith, interned with one of her children since the fall of Singapore, had last seen her other two children in the water after their ship attempting to escape had been sunk. Edwina eventually traced them down in Sumatra. 'She cut through red tape and insisted that they flew back with her to Singapore and their mother. She brought them straight to the hospital,' Mr C. G. Taylor recalls, 'and with my wife took them back to their mother on the ward – a very emotional moment.'

To those whose impatience and suffering had become almost beyond bearing, she would say quietly but with firm authority, 'Don't worry – I'll get things moving.' And she did.

From some of those who were attempting to get the rescue machinery working against a mountain of difficulties, she received a more restrained welcome. Did they not already have enough to do without having the Supreme Commander's wife poking her nose into everything? Lieutenant-Colonel Paul Crook's reaction to the arrival of Edwina at Singapore was understandable and typical of many officers at this early stage of operations.

Crook had arrived in Singapore with a small team on 5 September 1945 to supervise the recovery of prisoners of war. Food was desperately short and the newly arrived troops were on half rations. Crook, now a much-decorated retired brigadier, recalls:

> I had a signal from Kandy saying Lady Mountbatten was arriving to look after POWs. To me she was the famous playgirl of the twenties and thirties, and some people said she's only coming out here to pursue an affair. So I thought this was the last straw. The day after the surrender she came to see me in the morning, and immediately I succumbed to her charm. 'I know you are very very busy,' she said. 'I just want someone to take me around. You mustn't come yourself.' So I gave her the situation. 'I have a staff conference in the evenings,' I told her, and she at once said, 'I'll be there.' And so she was, at 6 p.m., having been round the Singapore camps. She sat quietly, and then she said, 'I have seen so-and-so and such-and-such – what can be done?'
>
> Later, I heard her dictate to her secretary, 'Send a signal to Dickie to have these ready.' And she listed them. 'I'll send a plane tomorrow for them.' And it worked. What we needed were soap and lavatory paper, drugs, knives and forks, writing paper, and so on. And we got them.
>
> She went off from Singapore all round the areas occupied by the Japs – often going to places where no one else was allowed to go, in many cases still dangerous. And wherever she went she would ask, 'Now, what do you want – tell me what you want,' and she would get it. The bravery of it all was quite remarkable. She would send me signals from Sumatra saying she was sending

so many ex-prisoners back, and it was up to me to find accommodation. I put many of them in Raffles Hotel, to the outrage of Army Command who tried to stop it until Mountbatten supported me.

Lieutenant-Colonel Crook thought at the time that she was paying the price for her unremitting work. 'She looked her age,' he recalls today. 'Very lined, almost withered.'

Sometimes Edwina was discovered in the unlikeliest places and she became something of a legend in those weeks when units were going in for the first time to newly liberated areas. David Holloway, a flight-sergeant navigator on Liberators, was one of many hundreds of aircrew who had turned from destruction to life-saving, and embarked on long flights to drop leaflets – 'Stay in your camp until help arrives' – and food and medical supplies to remote camps before anyone could get to them on the ground. He flew the nine-hour flight from Ceylon to Medan in Sumatra to make a drop at a camp close to the town, and circling above the airfield recognized the characteristic configuration of a Dakota aircraft on it. '"That's not supposed to be there!" we said. But we dropped our load and turned for the long flight home, landing in the dark. When we reported the presence of a Dakota at Medan we were told, "Oh yes, that'll be Lady Mountbatten."'

After the Singapore unit under Crook's command showed a score of 30,000 recovered prisoners, Mountbatten arrived to congratulate them all. Then Edwina arrived back from a distant camp packed with diseased and emaciated ex-prisoners of war. The Mountbattens threw a great party. It was their first peacetime party, the first for six years. It may have been a far cry from the Embassy Club or Brook House in the old days and the talk was unbroken by the sound of a single champagne cork. But it was a 'Dickie and Edwina' party all the same, an augury of peace and better times ahead. 'I thought it was lovely!' remarked one reveller.

Peace had come, and what did it now hold for this remarkable couple whose joint contribution towards winning the war on the one hand, and relieving the suffering entailed in the destruction of tyranny on the other, was unsurpassed?

11
'First and Only Love'

One of Edwina's socialist friends in London before the war was Vengalil Krishnan Krishna Menon, a Middle Temple lawyer-cum-politician who described himself as a teacher, journalist and publicist. His first function as a publicist was the cause of Indian freedom, his second the spreading of the cause of socialism, and in this capacity he was a borough councillor for St Pancras from 1934 and a one-time parliamentary candidate. He was the first editor of Pelican Books and co-originator of the paperback book concept which he had mooted to Allen Lane as early as May 1932 and which became Penguin Books. Edwina enjoyed his quick mind, his intellectualism, his ardent socialism and anti-imperialism. It was through Krishna Menon that Edwina had learned more about his disciple, Jawaharlal Nehru, and – in 1936 – she read Nehru's autobiography published by The Bodley Head, for whom Krishna Menon was editor of the Twentieth Century Library. Nehru, the Old Harrovian, ex-Trinity College, Cambridge, Inner Temple barrister, would be the first Prime Minister of a free India, according to Krishna Menon. He had joined the Gandhi non-violent, non-co-operation movement as long ago as 1920, and nine years later succeeded his father as President of the Indian National Congress. He was also known to be a man of immense charm and erudition. He had lost his wife in 1936.

Edwina's long and arduous months in India in 1945 raised even higher her curiosity to meet this man who had spent so much of his life fighting for the freedom of his country – and in prison, to which he had been confined in 1942. Her heart had been in his cause ever since she had first visited India in 1922, and Dickie had been refused permission to see him when, as later, he had been confined.

Mountbatten had been denied permission to see Nehru for a second time in January 1944 when Nehru was in Ahmednagar Fort. Mountbatten was as keen as Edwina to meet him now, but not only for reasons of

Joint War Organization Flag Day, 43 Belgrave Square, June 1941: 'Xandra, Angela, Edwina and Peggy' (otherwise, l to r, Mrs Alexander Fawcua, the Countess of Limerick, Lady Louis Mountbatten and Mrs Richard Jessel)

In the early days of the war with the Countess of Limerick

Above: Edwina the orator, something she had thought she could never be

Right: February 1943, with Dickie outside Buckingham Palace with her CBE medal

Left: Family scene at Broadlands, 1943: Dickie, Chief of Combined Operations, Edwina, Superintendent of St John Ambulance, and Pamela, with Mizzen and Jib

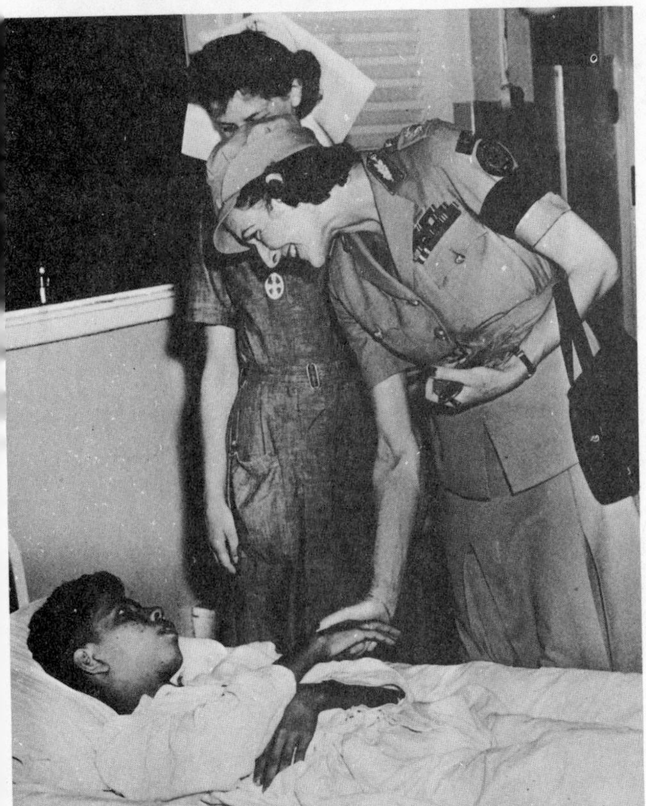

With Australian ex-POWS, May 1946. Edwina had first met many of them in Siam and Singapore when she was organizing their relief and repatriation

The healing touch: talking to a wounded soldier in Singapore

Edwina becomes familiar with the ubiquitous jeep (this is an amphibious one). She is inspecting casualty clearing stations, 1945

The dynasty endures. Edwina's elder daughter Patricia (the present Countess Mountbatten of Burma) marries Lord Brabourne, 26 October 1946. Left to right: back row, Duchess of Kent, Earl Mountbatten, Lord Brabourne, George VI, Edwina, best man; middle row: Dowager Lady Brabourne, Dowager Marchioness of Milford Haven (Dickie's mother Victoria), the bride, the Queen, Dowager Marchioness of Sligo; front row: Lady Pamela Mountbatten, Princess Alexandra of Kent, Princess Margaret Rose, Princess Elizabeth

Palam airport, Delhi, 26 March 1947. The old and the new, with the Mountbattens relieving the Wavells as Viceroy and Vicereine

The summit of Mountbatten fortunes and promotion: as Viceroy and Vicereine of India, 1947

Vicereine's reception, 2 April 1947. Left to right: Mrs Pandit, her brother Jawaharlal Nehru, Mountbatten and Edwina

Back from India for consultations, 19 May 1947

Left: India 1947. Left to right: Nehru, Edwina's portrait, Mountbatten

Below: With Mahatma Gandhi, 4 June 1947, ten weeks before independence

Indian independence. Mountbatten becomes Governor-General of the new dominion and, with Edwina, accepts the tributes of the joyful crowds, 21 August 1947

Comforting refugees in Lahore, 1949

curiosity. He felt a great affinity with India, which he believed he had saved from the Japanese yoke. He also felt a deep sense of responsibility for the country. Like Edwina, he knew that it was only a matter of time before power was transferred from Britain to the people of India, and he already recognized that he might well become involved in the process in one capacity or another. Some people think that his eyes were set on the Viceroyalty at the end of the war in the Far East. 'All this business about being surprised when he was offered the job of giving away India as Viceroy – and then at first refusing it – is all my eye,' one of his staff officers at the time remarked. 'Dickie was steering towards the Delhi job in 1945, maybe while the war was still on. It was all part of The Great Plan.'

Others have claimed that Sir Stafford Cripps, a member of the Cabinet Mission to India, wanted Mountbatten as the last Viceroy and put the idea to the Prime Minister on his return to London. Or was it Attlee himself who engineered the Nehru meeting in Singapore between Nehru and Mountbatten as an overture to the replacement of Archibald Wavell by Mountbatten as Viceroy?

Nehru himself stated to his biographer, Marie Seton, that Agatha Harrison, the Singapore Quaker who was Gandhi's representative in London, and Krishna Menon, also in London, set up the Singapore meeting and reception 'in cahoots with the British authorities'.

The facts are indisputable. Mountbatten was in Delhi in February 1946 at the time when Nehru, now released, expressed a wish to visit the Indian communities and Indian troops in Malaya and Burma. Wavell discussed the matter with Mountbatten, still Supreme Commander, who warmly approved. Wavell then sent an official telegram to the Governor of Burma, Colonel Sir Reginald Dorman-Smith, who declined to allow the visit. He was at once overruled by Mountbatten, who deputed two officers, Mohammed Ali Choudhury, future Prime Minister of Pakistan, and Major Sawhney, to make the arrangements in order to avoid any clashes. The situation in Singapore was at that time highly volatile. There were numbers of Bose's INA (Indian National Army) troops loose on the streets. They had fought with the Japanese against the Indian and Allied armies, and their leaders were still being sought by the British military administration. There was no doubt that Nehru would receive a tumultuous reception from his own people, and the military administration arranged to line the route from the airport to the reception at Government House with military police and troops.

Mountbatten, with Edwina, arrived in Singapore precisely twenty-four hours before Nehru's visit, and learned that the British, as a slap in Nehru's face, had refused to supply him with any transport. Mountbatten at once corrected this discourtesy by sending a car himself, and added to Nehru's welcome by issuing tickets to any Indians who wished to meet their hero at the airport, and offering them free truck transport. Thousands did so.

Nehru's plane landed just after noon on 18 March 1946, and he was received by a great cheer as he appeared at the door. Mountbatten's representative met him at the bottom of the steps and whisked him away in a car to Government House for tea, cheered all the way into the centre of the city. There Mountbatten met him and, an hour later, escorted him into his own open limousine. Marie Seton wrote:

> Side by side, with aplomb, the future Viceroy of India and Prime Minister were driven out of the tall wrought-iron gates into the street packed with Indians craning their necks to see Panditji. A cameraman caught the expression of surprise at the unexpected sight of Indian and British soldiers saluting side by side. As Mountbatten later told one of his staff, he was gratified and not a little amused to find himself included in the cheering.

Nehru was due now to travel to his hotel, but Mountbatten had another plan. 'My wife is very anxious to meet you. She is inspecting the welfare services in Singapore and is at the YMCA (Young Men's Christian Association) with a number of her workers,' he said. Nehru gladly agreed to the change of plan. He was as keen to meet the brilliant wife of the Supreme Commander who had already done so much for his fellow countrymen as she was to see him.

The change of route was soon observed and he had time only to enter the wooden single-storey building with Mountbatten before crowds of Indians poured in through the other doors and the ground floor windows.

Nehru's daughter Indira, now Prime Minister of India, relates today, with a nostalgic smile, 'Lady Mountbatten was flat on the floor when my father and she met in Singapore. When my father went in everyone rushed and they just knocked her down. So the first thing they had to do, Lord Mountbatten and my father, was to rescue her and put her back on her feet.'

Later, and under more tranquil conditions, Nehru and the Mountbattens were able to talk and laugh together about their first meeting and to range over the vast subject of Indian freedom which must now follow the defeat of Japan, and the need for urgency in the transfer of power before a dangerous vacuum was created with all its threats of inter-racial strife as well as anti-imperial violence. Nehru was astonished and gratified by the courtesy and charm with which both Mountbattens received him, and impressed by the broad and liberal views they expressed without inhibition on the need for ending all colonial rule in South-East Asia - British, French and Dutch - as well as British rule in India.

As one mutual friend, who saw them together many times, defines Mountbatten-Nehru relations, 'I can't think of any three people who had such a natural and uninhibited affinity with each other.' There is no friendship in history to parallel the highly significant and important friendship between the Mountbattens and the Indian leader, nor the speed with which it warmed during the few days they were all three in Singapore. It bore immediate fruit. Nehru was due to place a wreath on the recently completed memorial to the INA war dead, a ceremony with threatening and even dangerous overtones so recently after the end of hostilities. 'I persuaded him that this would not be a very good thing to do at present,' Mountbatten said later. But like so many of Mountbatten's achievements this one was brought about as much as a result of Edwina's charm and sensibility as by Mountbatten's pragmatism.

The fine-looking man whom Edwina first met while lying on the floor of a hut in the middle of Singapore was soon to become the most important person in her life, and to remain so for fourteen years. Nehru became, quite simply, Edwina's first and only great love. Many who witnessed this love have written or spoken of it, always emphasizing its depth and the number of levels over which it ranged. They were both remarkable people with highly developed intellects, and both were in need of each other. Nehru, a man of sensitivity and passion who had experienced much loneliness since the death of his wife, was in his prime and at the outset of the most important period of his life. He longed for a wise confidante and lover who would also keep his mind on edge and amuse him. Edwina's entry into his life was like a miracle, swift, bountiful and total, meeting all his needs.

Nehru's sister Nan, Mrs Ranjit Pandit, emphasizes today Edwina's importance to him

> at a very difficult time when he had no wife and was doing a very important job. He responded to her intelligent companionship and her warm personality. They were always able to talk intelligently to one another. Nehru liked beautiful women, and she was a big influence on his life because she brought warmth and friendship based on a sharing of values and intellectual pursuits.

His daughter Indira also emphasized that they were great friends. 'With the sort of life my father led, it was a great relaxation for him to have someone quite different. They could discuss things intellectually - and he was very fond of her.'

A woman who was close to them both for many years 'observed at once the closeness of their relationship' when she first arrived in Delhi. She says:

> It was one of the sweetest relationships I have ever seen. Her love for him was one of total empathy. She was mother and sister to him; he was brother and father to her. Their companionship was so lovely. It was a case of total devotion and worship, a fusion of minds. She was very courteous to him in public. In private they could be like a brother and sister sparring, then giggling with sidelong glances.

Many people believe that Nehru could not have withstood the strain and stresses of those early years of his premiership without the strength and stimulus Edwina provided. No one will deny that it was one of the great love affairs of history. There are countless precedents for extra-marital relations between men in power and intelligent women from whom they seek understanding, sympathetic support and a conspiracy of confidentiality. A recent example is the affair between Herbert Asquith, Prime Minister in the First World War, and Venetia Stanley, whose letters have recently been published. The letters between Edwina and Nehru may never be published but were warmly cherished by Mountbatten after Edwina's death and always referred to as 'the love letters'. He once lent them to his elder daughter and soon fretted for their return. Mountbatten told Marie Seton, 'It's my intention that they will ultimately be published. Letters from him to me', he added, 'were always typed. But letters to Edwina were always hand-written.'

Considering the nature of the relationship between these two highly emotional and sensitive people, it is impossible to believe that it did not extend to the physical level. This is of small importance compared with the fact that the great majority of people in India at the time believed that it did, and only a small number of those who knew them both believe that it did not. 'Though I stayed in the room where Edwina stayed,' recalls Marie Seton, 'and had the same bearer as she had, I really don't know about the physical side of their affair – I'd think probably yes.' Certainly Mountbatten himself knew that they were lovers. He was proud of the fact, unlike Edwina's sister who deplored the relationship and hated Nehru for the rest of his life as a result. Mary hated the wastefulness of the affair, believing that Edwina deserved a more worthy paramour. When she speaks today of Nehru's 'great hypnotic powers' she speaks from experience, only she did not succumb to them. 'Edwina had no will where he was concerned,' she says. 'Just like water.'

As Mountbatten's official duties separated him from Edwina at Delhi in

1922, so the official demands of work separated Nehru from Edwina in Singapore in 1946. The taste was brief and sweet, and no more. Edwina was to accompany Dickie on a tour of Australia and New Zealand at the invitation of the dominions' premiers, Edwina as Superintendent-in-Chief of the joint Red Cross and St John War Organizations. It was all part of the celebrations marking the return of peace and honouring both Mountbattens for their work, and was to culminate in an open carriage drive through the City of London and the receipt of the Freedom of the City on 10 July 1946. For the long Australasia tour the Mountbattens in their York aircraft, fitted out like a miniature maharajah's palace, were accompanied by a Dakota called 'Mercury', nothing more than a flying radio station which was reputed to be able to handle as much traffic as a warship's radio cabin, giving instant communication with the rest of the world. Mountbatten's staff, as always, was numerous and high ranking and of mixed quality. 'When they all lined up for pictures,' remarked one journalist, 'it was like a Gilbert and Sullivan parade of gilt and gongs.'

One of their friends recalls:

> 1946 was a funny year for Dickie and Edwina. Of course they got all those honours - Dickie a viscountcy though he expected an earldom - and the Sword of Honour and the Freedom of the City of London and all that. And of course it was a lovely summer, the first without any war for more than six years, and they were both on top of the world, longing to get Broadlands back as it used to be. But the fact was that it was all a bit of an anti-climax after all that they had been doing. In India and the Far East they were both the *absolute* centre of everything but though they got lots of cheers and everyone thought they were wonderful in England there were other people - like Monty and Attlee, and the King and Queen for that matter. Dickie got reduced in rank down to rear-admiral and Edwina wasn't saving people all day and night as she had been. I think, secretly, they were feeling a little low. But Patricia's wedding cheered everyone up.

The friendship in Ceylon between Patricia Mountbatten and Lord Brabourne had prospered, and they were married in Romsey Abbey on 26 October 1946. It was as if the upper echelons of British Society had stood still for almost a decade, and nothing had happened to disturb the satisfying processes and procedures of the class-and-wealth world as it had always been. As at the Mountbattens' own wedding, the guests numbered more than a thousand and the arrangements were as elaborate as they were extravagant. A train for many of the guests ran from London with a luncheon served on it which did not reflect the national shortage of food and delicacies. Limousines arrived by the score as if the days of petrol rationing had never occurred or were long since past. The King and Queen came, and Princess Elizabeth, Princess Margaret Rose, Pamela and Princess Alexandra of Kent acted as bridesmaids.

Excepting the presence of motor cars, the procession from the Abbey to Broadlands might have been a replica of the wedding of the bride's grandmother, with the present King's grandfather there, almost half a century earlier. A hint of the future shape of the monarchy was revealed when the heir to the throne, for the first time publicly, was photographed with Prince Philip, who had come over to the wedding from his naval base at Corsham in Wiltshire. Nor were the Brabourne and Mountbatten tenants forgotten: in the old tradition they were entertained at a hall in Romsey, with the King and Queen and the families doing their bit. The Brabourne union proved a fruitful one, seven children being born in the following eighteen years.

On the evening of 18 December 1946, Edwina learned from her husband that he had been asked to take up the appointment as Viceroy of India and to preside over the transfer of power from Britain to the Indian people. Although no official or unofficial hint had been dropped that he would be shouldering this task, and (contrary to later false tales of conspiracy and secret meetings with Nehru) no preparatory groundwork had been arranged, the appointment came as no surprise to Mountbatten. No one possessed more finely tuned antennae or a more highly developed prescience, especially as it affected himself. Nor should it have been such an unexpected appointment to anyone with a keen knowledge of the situation in India: the urgent need to bring about this transfer as rapidly as possible, the failure of recent initiatives, the stalemate in negotiations, and the absence of any clear-cut plans from London for the present Viceroy, Field-Marshal Lord Wavell, told its own story of an imminent end to his tenure of office.

Close friends and relations of Dickie and Edwina later believed that they had both considered the possibility of having this task thrust upon them but, characteristically, had not discussed it together. To most other people, including their children and Prince Philip, Mary, Dickie's mother, Victoria, and Noël Coward, it came as a total surprise, and for the last two at least a very unpleasant surprise because they thought that Dickie was 'being set up as the fall-guy'. But the King had been told and had warmly approved of the appointment. So did Edwina when Dickie told her. Although she had intended to continue with her charity work at the same high level as before, she had also fallen in love with India, and the romance of being Vicereine – virtually Queen – to almost 500 million people appealed strongly to her. Besides, whatever show of reluctance to take on the job Dickie deemed it diplomatic to affect, she knew as well as he did that it must advance his career and status even further, and secure the bonds to the Royal Family even tighter. As the King himself had responded to Mountbatten's expression of fear of damage to the Royal Family if he failed, 'Ah, but look how good if you succeed.'

And of course he would succeed. He was certain to succeed. Woodrow Wyatt had been personal assistant to Stafford Cripps on the recent Cabinet mission to India, and says today, 'Because Mountbatten was intelligent and had held high command and knew his way around, and was spectacular, he was the right man for the job and was bound to succeed.' And he adds, 'But he didn't have to initiate anything. He just carried out the policy laid down in London, and he did it very well. But he didn't give India its freedom.'

Mountbatten's complaint in 1941 was that he had been deprived of command of the *Illustrious* in order to become head of Combined Operations and then Supreme Commander in South-East Asia; now his complaint was that his naval advancement would be held up by being deprived of command of the 1st Cruiser Squadron in the Mediterranean, an appointment which he had been due to take up in April 1947. But he knew really that his naval career would be in no way damaged by this supremely important political-social appointment; and in any case he had been promised by Attlee that he would recover his naval command when he had completed his task in India.

Before the Mountbattens' departure there were numerous meetings and preparations on subjects as wide-ranging as the line to take with Mohammed Ali Jinnah, the Moslem leader who was certain to be obstructive, whether to take Pamela away from school in order to accompany them (she did), protocol details and what to wear. Mountbatten had several meetings in Whitehall with Wyatt, who was young, bright, well-informed, a socialist and recently returned, the ideal adviser by Mountbatten's reckoning. Wyatt recalls:

> He wanted to know what he should wear when he arrived. Someone had told him plain clothes, and he obviously found this a grave disappointment. 'Do you think so?' he asked me. I said, 'Certainly not. They'll expect you to be wearing full dress uniform with all your medals. You'll be greeted by a parliamentary delegation, bands and all that.' He seemed very relieved at that.

It was symbolic and fitting that one of the Royal Family's cars should drive the Mountbattens to Northolt airport for their departure. With them were Prince Philip, naturalized two days earlier, and Patricia and John Brabourne, who had all come to see them off. It was 20 March 1947, and it was a gusty, drizzly, miserable morning as they made their way up the steps to the four-engined York aircraft – Edwina first, then Mountbatten, Pamela, Captain Ronald Brockman RN, Mountbatten's naval secretary since 1943, Lieutenant-Commander Peter Howes, his ADC, Muriel Watson and Elizabeth Ward, Edwina's personal assistant and private secretary, Mountbatten's valet Charles and Edwina's maid. The big aircraft took off and turned south over London, against strong winds on course for Malta, where they were to spend the night. 'Don't worry,' were Edwina's last words to one member of her family. 'I'm not worrying. This is going to be a marvellous experience – and Dickie says we'll be back as soon as we can – and that means not long.'

How right Edwina was! Nothing can be gained by relating once more the sequence of events leading to the formal transfer of power on 15 August 1947, months before the deadline Mountbatten had been given. Mountbatten himself when discussing this period of his life with the author said, 'The story drawn from my own papers over six years and with my help has been written by Hodson in *The Great Divide*. There is really little more to be told, with that and the Collins-Lapierre version' – *Freedom at Midnight* (1975) based in part on thirty hours of tape recordings with Mountbatten and 600 pages of notes. Edwina's part in the extraordinary saga and its aftermath, however, is less known. The story begins, appropriately, at Palam airport, Delhi, in the early afternoon of 22 March 1947, when for the second time Edwina greeted Nehru and shook his hand as they stood on the carpeted tarmac at the bottom of the steps of the aircraft. She was dressed in a brown two-piece suit and tight-fitting hat, the skirt just below her knees, and, according to Mountbatten, 'looking absolutely terrific, absolutely knock-down charm, marvellous figure. ...' She was forty-five years old and, although she had been unwell shortly before leaving London, she looked younger and far less tired than at their last meeting a year ago. Nehru was dressed in his white Gandhi topi and elegant Sherwani coat. He would be fifty-eight in November. There was time for only a few words, and Edwina dutifully spent as long talking to and smiling at Liaquat Ali Khan, the General Secretary of the All India Moslem League, and other officials, and then turned, smiling for photographs.

The Mountbatten party arrived in an open landau in the courtyard of the Durbar Hall of Viceroy's House at 3.45 p.m., escorted by the Governor-General's escort and outriders. At the top of the red-carpeted wide steps the outgoing Viceroy and Vicereine waited to greet them: Wavell a stocky, all-square, grey-haired essentially military figure in Field-Marshal's uniform; his wife 'looking exactly like my wife's maid', as Mountbatten uncharitably described this excellent woman, 'very sort of mundane'. Edwina curtsied and Mountbatten bowed his head for the first and last time, and then the two men with the great gulf of age, style, character and experience between them, and their equally contrasting wives, turned and talked amiably for the cameramen. The next morning the Mountbattens travelled with them to the airport and saw them off, and returned to face the great task that lay ahead. India was in a state of turmoil and on the brink of inter-racial, inter-religious and inter-political anarchy. Now that the old common enemy, the imperial power of Britain, was known to be pulling out, Sikhs, Moslems and Hindus had turned upon one another; communal riots were already raging in many parts – especially in Bihar and Bengal – and Gandhi the man of peace was carrying out his 'repentance tours' through the worst areas.

The burning question of the hour was whether Britain would be able to hand over to a united India or an India divided in two – Moslem and Hindu. People with real knowledge of the situation recognized the inevitability of eventual partition. Jinnah was clearly going to be intractable – as he had always been – on the question of a united India. Woodrow Wyatt, who was liked and trusted by Jinnah, says:

> Partition was certain right from the beginning. Everyone knew that. The rest was all play-acting. Jinnah knew that however hard they tried, the Hindu element would predominate, everything in Congress would be expressed in the Hindu manner. Jinnah wasn't going to be entangled in a web of arguments. He just said what he had to say.

On the other hand, Indira Gandhi says today, 'A lot of people felt it could be avoided, and they blamed the Congress for agreeing to it. We accepted it but we felt it was a very big price to pay.' Mountbatten confided to Edwina that he agreed with Whitehall that Britain would never be able to hand over a united India: the racial hostility and suspicion were too great. Riots and strife he knew were inevitable, but within a few days of his arrival in Delhi he was confirmed in his impression that the sooner the two religions could be parted permanently behind their own frontiers the less would be the bloodshed. For the present, though, it was essential to give the impression, to India, to Britain and the world at large, that every effort was being bent towards creating a *united* free India.

Edwina's primary roles were twofold, the first political, the second humanitarian. The part played by women in the running of the country, before the advent of Indira Ghandi who has revealed it clearly to the rest of the world, was at that time considered negligible by most people outside the sub-continent. Edwina knew better; and her first task was to get the wives of the men of influence and power onto 'our side' and into a favourable frame of mind towards the intentions and work of transferring power smoothly, which was the sole *raison d'être* of this last Viceroyalty.

Edwina's second task was to reduce as far as was in her power the sufferings of the people in the riot-torn areas, organize relief, visit the victims, supervise evacuation, inspect hospitals – all the work she had done in Europe in 1944, and in South-East Asia in 1945 over again. She began meeting the wives, sisters and daughters of the Indian leaders immediately after the magnificent and extravagantly spectacular swearing-in ceremony on the day after the Wavells left. Of this ceremony in the Durbar Hall of Viceroy's House Edwina remarked lightly, 'I have never felt so like a queen', and Mountbatten said, 'I had been made the most powerful man on earth, responsible for the life and death of a quarter of the earth's population.'

'You could rely on Edwina starting with a bullseye,' one newsman remarked of the first meeting with Gandhi which the Mountbattens conducted together on 31 March. Every newsman and every photographer was on hand to gather what they could from this vitally important confrontation between these two contrasting figures, with the unexpected addition of Edwina. Half way through the two-hour talk, in which the Mountbattens had done no more than encourage the Mahatma to indulge in reminiscence, they strolled out into the Moghul Garden for a breath of (very hot) air and to expose themselves to the eager photographers. As they turned to go in again through the door, Gandhi was seen to place his hand trustingly on Edwina's right shoulder. It was a gesture signalling the end of conflict between Briton and Indian; and signified, too, the importance of the part Edwina was already playing. The moment was caught by an American photographer, Max Desfors, and within a few days the whole world had seen it and drawn its own encouraging conclusion.

Almost to a man (and woman) the British community in India had viewed with the gravest suspicion and doubt the appointment and arrival of the Mountbattens. This was understandable: not only was Lord Wavell a deeply loved and respected figure, but by the very nature of Mountbatten's brief – to deliver up India to the Indian people – they were unlikely to be welcomed with any great enthusiasm. It did not help that a great many members of the Indian Civil Service still regarded Mountbatten as a jumped-up ex-playboy and Edwina as a spoilt Jewish playgirl of doubtful morals, in spite of what they had done during the war. But in addition – and this came as a surprise – the great majority of the women of India's hierarchy 'were passionately anti-British and highly suspicious of the intentions of the representatives of Britain', Madeline Masson has written. 'All of them were intelligent, cultivated and closely associated with the work of the leaders of India. They had watched the arrival of the Mountbattens with deep misgivings and now, silently, they awaited developments.'

One of the first women Edwina was determined to charm and befriend was Mrs Asef Ali, who was notoriously anti-British. She was also a far-left socialist. When Edwina invited her to come to see her, she was rebuffed. But next time Gandhi came to talk to Mountbatten he had a woman in tow. 'I heard she wouldn't come,' remarked the Mahatma puckishly, indicating Mrs Ali, 'so I brought her with me.' In a short time, and in a welter of dialectic socialist exchange, they became firm friends. Another early convert was Gandhi's secretary for many years, who also loomed importantly in the political firmament, Rajkumari Amrit Kaur. Even Jinnah's very difficult sister Fatima (almost as difficult as he was) succumbed in the end. 'My wife looked after her marvellously, and got her to unbend a bit,' Mountbatten said later. Others who succumbed to Edwina's charisma and became life-long friends were Nehru's sister Mrs Pandit, Vallabhbhai Patel's daughter, Maniben, and the ageing, influential Sarojini Naidu, who, to Edwina's surprised delight, turned out to have been at school with her mother.

And so Edwina worked her way through all the important women, converting them from hostility to friendship. 'She was quite marvellous,' recalled one of her staff. 'They simply fell under her charm and pledged eternal love. She was almost better with women than men, and that's saying a lot.' 'They felt that she was one of them,' is Indira Gandhi's comment today.

By late April 1947 it became necessary for Mountbatten 'to take the temperature of his two most troubled provinces', the Punjab and the North-West Frontier. They flew first to Peshawar, taking Pamela, who had just celebrated her eighteenth birthday, with them. The size of the problem could be gauged by the crowd at the airport, summoned by Jinnah's Moslem League to demonstrate their feelings and now herded into a restricted area by the anxious local police. The worried Governor at first hustled the Mountbatten party away from the danger, and then when the crowd threatened to get out of hand, suggested to Mountbatten that if he showed himself it might quieten them.

Edwina insisted on accompanying him. Concealed from the crowd, whose increasing roars of frustration and fury shook the air, the Mountbattens then climbed a railway embankment and stood above them, helplessly vulnerable to hostile action. The effect of their appearance was astonishing, almost as if they had suddenly been converted into disciples of Allah. Mountbatten was wearing his camouflage wartime bush jacket, its green by chance matching the Pakistan national colour - Mountbatten luck again! Edwina raised her arm and began to wave. The crowd of 100,000 fell into silence, then broke out with ever increasing cries of 'Mountbatten Zindabad!' 'Mountbatten Zindabad!'

Later, at the town of Kahuta in the Punjab, they were able to see what could happen when crowds like this got completely out of hand. A Moslem horde had swept through the town, burning, killing, raping the women before killing them. There was no one left alive, not a building standing. The sight was for Mountbatten confirmation of the urgent need to reach a settlement before massacres like this could be ascribed to British dilatoriness, and for Edwina a reminder of the nature of the work that lay ahead as the torch of religious fervour began to set fire to great areas of this land.

Broken only by a brief visit to London with Mountbatten for consultations in the middle of May, and a break of a few days in Simla to recover from the heat, Edwina's work now began in earnest. The temperatures of up to 114 degrees in the shade raised inter-racial passions in the Punjab even further, and made Edwina's task of bringing what relief she could to the injured and homeless even more taxing. Migraine seized her as it always did in extreme heat and stress, and she found it necessary to wring out her sweat-soaked hair two or three times a day. Against a background of growing political accord in Delhi as the Mountbatten Plan for the transfer of power to a divided India approached, Edwina continued unremittingly with her relief work, sometimes close to despair as the riot victims increased in numbers to thousands a day and supplies became unprocurable. The shortage of nurses was even more serious. There were fewer in the whole of India than in London. An Indian Nursing Council Bill had been presented back in 1943 to help secure a steady stream of nurses, but had been held up by the exigencies of war. Edwina, working through political channels, ensured its adoption before the transfer of power to the Indian and Pakistani people.

Back in Delhi, her other self-imposed tasks were equally taxing during the hot season. She might go and visit Gandhi, squat on the floor of his room talking and watching him spinning, return to her office to dictate reports and letters, arrange banquets and receptions - for Field-Marshal Montgomery, visiting American dignitaries, Mountbatten's forty-seventh birthday, American Independence Day with the American Ambassador as guest of honour, their own Silver Wedding. This entertaining was similar to the duties of previous Vicereines, but the glittering yet seemingly carefree style in which it was conducted was very different from that of the past. The tours of devastated areas, the comforting of homeless, grief-stricken and often injured Indians who might have witnessed the burning alive of their children – all this, which filled the greater part of her packed timetable, was far removed from the work of Vicereines of the past and the lifestyle of the British Raj in the great imperial days.

American pressmen observed what Edwina was doing during these last raw and anguished days of imperial India. 'What can one say of this amazing Englishwoman who goes among the poor and the sick and the suffering like some latter-day Mary Magdalene?' asked one observer. And Norman Cliff, another reporter, wrote emotionally and from the heart: 'To the disabled and heartbroken there came not a grand lady standing at a distance, but a mother and nurse who squatted in the midst of the dirty and diseased, took their soiled and trembling hands in hers and spoke quiet words of womanly comfort.'[1]

The scene conjured up by this tribute is far removed from the figure in a full-length gold lamé dress, the very essence of grace, dignity and grandeur at the ceremonies celebrating the birth of free India. Mountbatten, with his love of anniversaries, had chosen 15 August, the second anniversary of the Japanese surrender, forgetting the Indian preoccupation with astrology. The date was an inauspicious one. When he confided this discovery to Nehru, Nehru said, 'Never mind. If you agree that we can have a midnight meeting and just before midnight strikes, we'll transfer power, that'll be the more auspicious.' They were both men who were capable of converting instantly a minor error to their advantage: Freedom at Midnight had the right ring to it.

So the arrangements for 15 August, Independence Day, were adhered to, and the ceremonies began, in temperatures already fast-rising, at 8.30 in the morning. The Mountbattens, no longer Viceroy and Vicereine but promoted Earl and Countess Mountbatten of Burma, first Governor-General of India and his wife, took their place on the golden thrones in Durbar Hall beneath illuminated red velvet canopies. An Indian Chief Justice administered the oath of office and an Indian Secretary of the Home

Department officiated at the swearing-in of the Ministers of the new Dominion. The playing of 'God Save the King' was followed by the 'Jana Gana Mana', the bronze doors of the hall were opened.

It was a long, exhausting, hot day of rides in an open landau, mobbed by cheering crowds, and more ceremonies, in the Council House and in the open, culminating in the unfurling of the national flag near the war memorial in Princes Park. Indira Gandhi recalls the scene today:

> It was, perhaps, typically Indian. The most minute details had been gone into by Lord Mountbatten himself and his staff, the military and civilian police. We were given a programme with minute timing, like 4 o'clock such and such, 4.02 so and so, 4.05 gentlemen will take off their hats – this sort of programme. And my husband and others all had invitations. My husband announced at breakfast that, 'Well, I'm afraid I've left my card behind in the Parliament office.' So my father said, 'This is a very strict occasion and you cannot get in without a card, but on the other hand you cannot miss it.' Parliament was closed and everything locked up, so finally my father said, 'You must get into my car and we'll see what we can do.'
>
> Now, when we arrived there, there were huge crowds [estimated at 600,000]. All the villagers from around Delhi had occupied the whole space. Where the Governor-General was to sit, the Prime Minister and all those areas were blocked, and finally Lord Mountbatten could not hoist the flag at all – he had to hoist it from a large distance with tied strings. The crush was terrible. At one moment a mother standing near to us could find no other place for her baby that looked safe except Lady Mountbatten's arms. She smiled and held it tight.

No one photographed that moment but there could be no more appropriate picture of Edwina's contribution to the peace and liberty of India than this. Mrs Gandhi sums up the occasion simply: 'It was really the people's day.'

According to Mountbatten's report, the flag-raising and the salute

> was done amid scenes of the most fantastic rejoicing, and as the flag broke a brilliant rainbow appeared in the sky, which was taken by the whole crowd as a good omen.
>
> Meanwhile danger of a large-scale accident was becoming so great that we decided that the only thing to do was to try and move the coach on through the crowd and draw the crowd with us. For this reason I invited Nehru to stay in the coach, which he did, sitting like a schoolboy on the front hood above the seats.[2]

As the thunder of the celebrating crowds died all over India, it was replaced by the terrible sounds of murderous rioting, rising now to new scales of horror with the hoisting of the national flags of Pakistan and India. Was all this the price of the over-hasty transfer of power, before proper arrangements could be made for re-housing the homeless refugees from minority regions? Or would it have been worse if the transfer had been longer delayed? No one will ever know the answer. But for Edwina it meant a further intensification of her work. This will never be forgotten by the Indian people; and it is certainly not forgotten by their Prime Minister today, who recalls 'how much she really endeared herself to the ordinary Indian public', citing one incident among many:

> After partition we had the most terrible riots with many dead. And when the news, highly exaggerated, spread here there was retaliation against quite innocent people. And this was going on for some time, and then suddenly we got the news that a whole train had arrived, full of dead bodies. The news went first to the Home Minister, and he phoned various people. But as soon as Lady Mountbatten heard, she just took off her high-heeled shoes and came to our house. We had a small dinner party with the Health Minister present. And Edwina said, 'I am just going to the station.' And of course there was no security, no arrangements. She just went.

And Mrs Gandhi's friend, Marie Seton, writes:

> With Delhi itself become a refugee camp, Edwina Mountbatten achieved the phenomenal feat of uniting fifteen organizations under the banner of the United Council of Relief and Welfare. Her husband's ADCs became chary of going out with her, because she would stop in the midst of sniping to pick up bodies and take them to the local infirmaries. Her gigantic effort explains Nehru's reference to 'her healing touch'.

The love between Edwina and Jawaharlal Nehru was born out of their joint concern for the sufferings of India before and after the transfer of power. Its depth and strength have been witnessed by many who saw them together, and needs no further emphasis. Delhi, its broad Lutyens avenues, its beautiful gardens, the cool marble corridors and low-windowed rooms of Nehru's house, the state rooms and drawing-rooms and bedrooms - slow-turning ceiling fans, silent-swinging punkahs - of the residence: this was the setting of their growing friendship, with a few precious days in the cool at Viceregal Lodge, Simla, and its Retreat at Mashoba. But it was the shared grief at the violence and death about them, tearing at their hearts, that sealed and made indissoluble their love. The fact that they saw one another for such short periods and only from time to time, and the nature of Edwina's work being both disagreeable and exhausting, only added to the depth and passion of their relationship. For days on end, Edwina would leave the capital on missions of mercy for Nehru's India, and return grey with weariness from the heat and work. She may have been aged another ten years by the experience, but each time she returned, her spirit and dedication seemed renewed rather than exhausted. To those who greeted her, and above all to Nehru, it was an extraordinary experience.

The toll of death and misery continued all through that first autumn of liberation for India and Pakistan as the religious minorities, still stranded on the wrong side of frontiers drawn up in Delhi, struggled to find a safe home or simply murdered, or were murdered by, their neighbours. Always at the centre of the rescue work, but assisted now by a growing army of workers of the United Council for Relief and Welfare, St John Ambulance squads, the National Christian Church, YWCA (Young Women's Christian Association) and other bodies, Edwina struggled against the tide of misery. Kashmir, a centre of fierce political dispute, and east Punjab, were the worst affected, and Edwina was constantly flying out to the camps set up for the refugees.

Far away, almost on the other side of the world, an event of a very different nature was soon to take place. The affairs of the British monarchy seemed remote from the sufferings of the Indian people who, weeks earlier, had been under the rule of the King-Emperor, George VI. But now this King's daughter was to be married in November to Mountbatten's nephew. The event was of momentous importance to Dickie Mountbatten, a great deal less important to Edwina, although she was fond of bride and groom. The match between Prince Philip and Princess Elizabeth was the culmination of years of thought and endeavour for Mountbatten, binding the Mountbatten dynasty unbreakably to the House of Windsor. When asked to what extent he had contributed to this match, Mountbatten would smile conspiratorially and say, 'Once you've planted a seed you don't keep digging it up to see how the roots are progressing.' As the appointment to the office of First Sea Lord was his ultimate professional ambition, so this marriage between the two families was the culmination of his domestic ambitions.

The date of 20 November for this royal wedding had long been settled, and it had been a consideration when Mountbatten had advanced the date for the transfer of power from June 1948 to August 1947. In April it was reasonable to assume that all political difficulties would have been tidied up and peaceful, contented Moslems, Hindus and Sikhs would be installed inside their frontiers by November. Instead, the internecine warfare, especially in Kashmir, was as bad as ever. Edwina had no intention of leaving her work for this ceremony in London. Mountbatten said he would go anyway; it was his duty, it would be a gross breach of ... Argument between the two raged for several days. Mountbatten resorted to asking the advice of members of his staff, knowing what the answer must be. They told him that it would only add to the sense of crisis in the public mind, in India and at home, if he did not go. Edwina recognized that it would certainly add to public anxiety, and curiosity, if Dickie went and she remained behind. In the end she gave way, with many misgivings.

They left Delhi on 9 November and arrived in London two days later, Edwina feeling ill and miserable. They took a suite at the Dorchester Hotel and Edwina got away from London as soon as she could to see her first grandchild, who had been born on 8 October, and to visit Broadlands and prepare it for the royal honeymoon.

From the chill of an English November, they were back in Delhi a week after the wedding, and Edwina threw herself into her work again. It ended only with Mountbatten's term of office as Governor-General, on 22 June 1948.

'What drove Edwina on – and on and on and on in India?' many of her friends and members of her family have asked. Her husband was enormously proud of her work, as he was proud of any family achievement, but of all her family he was probably least able to give an explanation. The late Bish Pandy, Nehru's most recent biographer, agreed that her Jewish blood had much to do with it, that she related to the Indian people in their sufferings, as downtrodden slaves of the imperial tradition and then as victims of plague, pestilence and Moslem cruelty, as the Jews had been persecuted through history.

Marie Seton, another biographer and close friend of Nehru and his family, and biographer and friend of Paul Robeson and his family as well, while offering the highest tributes to Edwina and her work, propounds another theory as the reason for Edwina's near-frenzied concern for the sufferings of India. She writes:

> To my mind, but for the dynamic, flexible cement supplied by Edwina, I can't imagine how a blood-bath *vis-à-vis all* India and Britain could have been avoided, much less a republic within the Commonwealth achieved. It was an incredible transformation.
>
> I've always thought *privately* that Edwina's truly remarkable role in India, her behaviour there which I luckily observed on more than one occasion, was

her form of 'penance' for the Robeson *People* case. In my mind she had paid her debt in this case by her *loyalty* to India and Nehru.

Tributes to Edwina and her work in India in 1947–8 are legion. A man who witnessed her work as closely as anyone was Lord Ismay, Mountbatten's Chief of Staff both as Viceroy and Governor-General. He wrote:

> She made us all proud of British womanhood. She was utterly dedicated, completely indefatigable and uniquely experienced. Undaunted by fatigue, danger, disease or stench, or the most gruesome scenes, her errands of mercy took her to hospitals and refugee camps all day and every day, and a good deal of the night. She had the missionary zeal of a Florence Nightingale, and the dedicated courage of a Joan of Arc.[3]

And what of Nehru and his family? His daughter, and successor as Prime Minister, today takes a broad view of Edwina's accomplishments:

> The general conception of her was her deep concern that things should turn out right, helping her husband and especially her feeling for India and her people, and understanding of the problems. I think she gave Lord Mountbatten a feedback on what the Indians of various groups were thinking. He was largely in touch with officials and government and the army; she made direct contact with the people.

Indira Gandhi emphasized the importance of Edwina's close relationship with India's first Health Minister, Rajkumari Amrit Kaur. Edwina was also, Mrs Gandhi emphasized,

> a very open person, so that everyone felt that they could go and see her even if she was in such a high position. I think she was a very fine person. Initially, people thought that, being in a high position, she wouldn't do her job seriously, like the usual social, superficial kind of thing. But then they discovered that there was great depth to her. That came as a surprise to me.

Another present-day personal tribute comes from Nehru's sister, who says, 'I'm not one who has had many friends, but I felt very close to Edwina. The courage of the woman was admirable.' Mrs Pandit continued: 'And all the Princes loved her, too. She was welcome in all their houses. You still hear them talk nostalgically about her today. She was a very popular person with us all.'

The last words must be Nehru's own, spoken at the last banquet, on the last evening of the Mountbattens' last day in India. Turning to Edwina, he said:

> The gods or some good fairy gave you beauty and high intelligence, and grace and charm and vitality – great gifts – and she who possesses them is a great lady

wherever she goes. But unto those that have even more shall be given: and they gave you something that was even rarer than those gifts – the human touch, the love of humanity, the urge to serve those who suffer and who are in distress. And this amazing mixture of qualities results in a radiant personality and in the healer's touch.

Wherever you have gone you have brought solace, and you have brought hope and encouragement. Is it surprising, therefore, that the people of India should love you and look up to you as one of themselves, and should grieve that you are going? Hundreds of thousands have seen you personally in various camps and other places and hospitals, and hundreds of thousands will be sorrowful at the news that you have gone.

12
'Love and Serve'

The summer of 1948 was an unhappy time for Edwina. No amount of praise and thanks from the Indian people, no honours awarded to her for her work, could diminish the grief she felt for the continuing sufferings of that great sub-continent. The assassination on 20 January of Mahatma Gandhi, a man she deeply respected and loved, had been a terrible personal blow. The violent end of one old man, and the funeral pyre in which his frail body was consumed, seemed symptomatic of the violence and unhappiness of so many of the Indian people at that time.

To suggest that Edwina was much more affected than her husband by the Indian massacres is not to ascribe to Mountbatten a callous attitude. He detested the brutal treatment of minorities by Sikhs, Moslems and Hindus equally. But he was a man of war, emotionally equipped to deal with loss of life among those under his command, be it HMS *Kelly* or Mother India. He knew that there would be riots and bloodshed; he hoped for the minimum. When the figures ran into millions rather than thousands, they registered in his mind with regret but not as a minus calculation in the sum of his achievement as the last Viceroy and first Governor-General. Edwina's figures were different figures – they were of individual corpses, stiff and stenchful under the hot sun of the Punjab. No arithmetic was involved in her mind, no plus or minus in credit due for handing India back to the Indian people.

The departure from India also marked a temporary break in her relationship with Nehru. She could no longer see him every day as she had when she was in Delhi, and talk and laugh with him as if they had known one another since childhood. It was for her a cruel severance, its pain eased only by the knowledge that he would be in England later in the year, and that they would be writing frequently to one another.

The loss of her dog was pain of a different kind and of a different measure, but quite as personal a deprivation. Her Sealyham Mizzen was twelve years old, and she had taken him to India in the full knowledge that he would have to be quarantined for six months on her return. She reasoned that at his age he might well die in the extreme climate of India, but he gamely endured it, and the decision had to be made: should he be put down or face the six-months-long separation in kennels? Mizzen was put down during the stopover at Malta, dying in her arms.

She arrived back in London in a state of deep depression and suffering from the strain and overwork of the past sixteen months. From a full and purposeful life in India in a palace with 7,000 servants, she faced a relatively restricted life and the small house in Chester Street with half a dozen servants. She escaped to Broadlands as soon as she could, savouring the peace and quiet of the beautiful house and the River Test.

'Edwina's rest cure – if you could call it that – was very brief,' a friend recalls. 'She really didn't enjoy idleness, I suppose because she didn't really know what it was. She had to be on the move and *doing* something.' 'Idleness to Edwina was things not happening and uneventfulness to her was sheer hell,' remarked another friend. 'You could *see* the pain on her face – adding to all those lines.'

The momentum was regained without any difficulty after only a few days of pacing restlessly about Broadlands and riding over the estate. There was plenty to do at Broadlands itself after its wartime use as a hospital. Classiebawn must be visited; she would take the girls there in August – Patricia's little son Norton, nearly one, would love it. Then she and Dickie were due in Toronto soon to open the Canadian National Exhibition. And they must go to France, of course, to visit old friends, and Dickie was keen that they should call on David and Wallis Windsor at the Villa de la Cröe. In October they would be back in Malta, where Dickie was due to resume his naval career.

A week or two before Edwina was to take up again the role of naval wife, Nehru arrived from India for the Dominions Conference, and as soon as he could be torn away from official functions in London Edwina carried him off to Broadlands. He found it as lovely in the last weeks of a beautiful summer as she had described it to him. With Dickie and Pammy, the foursome were reunited and resumed the easy family relationship they had formed in those hectic and sometimes terrible weeks before and after the transfer of power. Their friends came and went, there was a dinner party (mostly family), games on the lawn and riding, and in the evenings Dickie and Edwina taught the Prime Minister of India how to play racing demon.

At the end of the Second World War, many men and women who had enjoyed heavy responsibilities returned to the same humdrum jobs they had left in 1939; and many professional officers of the Services who had climbed high up the promotion ladder in an acting capacity reverted to lower ranks. No one shed more ranks and elevated duties than Dickie and Edwina when he fell from acting admiral (and acting general and marshal of the RAF too) to rear-admiral commanding a cruiser squadron, and Edwina became an officer's wife on Malta again. It had been noticed in London that Edwina's exalted status in India for more than a year had led her to assume a regal demeanour in public that was very different from the old days. The consequence of acting as queen of a sub-continent, of enjoying a lifestyle more formally magnificent than that of the British monarch, had had its inevitable effect. Her closest friends noted no discernible change. On less intimate social occasions there was a marked difference. 'She carried herself differently,' observed one acquaintance, 'as if she bore the weight of a crown. And one tended to address her as "ma'am" instead of Edwina.' At a luncheon at Buckingham Palace in honour of the Netherlands royal family Elizabeth Longford recalls, 'Edwina was looking absolutely lovely - especially with all those rather plain Dutch present. People were curtsying to her. Gerry Wellington was appalled. "Curtsying to Edwina!" he kept muttering.' But to a lot of people it seemed a natural obligation. If Mountbatten claimed to be 'a semi-royal', Edwina had become 'a semi-queen'.

After all this, how would Edwina comport herself in Malta as a naval officer's wife again? Would she be able to carry it off? was the question being asked ashore, and in the wardrooms of HM ships of the Mediterranean Fleet. The answer was, well - yes and no.

This period on Malta was like a repeat of earlier appointments, separated by six years of the greatest war in history, with all its massive political, social and personal consequences. Any sense of *déjà vu* was destroyed by the evidence of the years of bombing Malta had suffered. The rubble had been cleared from the streets, but Valletta was still a sorely damaged city and bomb craters scarred the island. The Mountbattens' old house still stood but had been converted into flats, and Edwina had to go house-hunting again, like many other wives, though she had more money in her purse. They lived in a hotel with Pamela for a while, acquired the substantial but unpretentious Villa Guardamangia, and moved in when it was ready for them by Christmas 1948.

Regular naval officers and their wives who had been in Malta in the mid-1930s, when the Mountbattens had provided the most colourful and ever-varied social life on the island, noticed both the similarities and contrasts between the earlier days and this period from 1948 to 1954, with a break when Mountbatten became Fourth Sea Lord at the Admiralty. The parties were still on a modest scale and confined mainly to members of their own circle until Mountbatten became Commander-in-Chief, when he had to give many more formal dinners and receptions. But the general level of living was much less raffish than it had been, and - not surprisingly - more substantially and conservatively regal, however democratically they behaved in public. This was underlined by the arrival of Princess Elizabeth towards the end of 1949.

Prince Philip had been appointed first lieutenant of the destroyer HMS *Chequers* and, when ashore, he lived with the Mountbattens as a matter of course and as a member of the family. There was riding and polo, sailing and aqualung skin-diving - 'the happiest period of my naval life,' as Mountbatten claimed. It was all marvellously relaxed in the small world within the larger social-naval world in which they lived. Edwina's sister, when she came out later, found the atmosphere completely congenial and everyone enjoying themselves. 'Lovely - I don't know when I've been happier in my life,' she remembers today. 'We used to ride out into the harbour before breakfast every morning, and Dickie taught me to play polo. . . .'

When the heir to the throne arrived the domestic arrangements in the Villa Guardamangia had to be altered to give Princess Elizabeth and Prince Philip a private suite. Inevitably there was a touch more formality now, and firmer steps had to be taken to secure the royal party's privacy outside their temporary residence.

But these Mediterranean days of the late 1940s and early 1950s were also as disturbed by unwelcome attention from outside, and unhappy notes of dissent from some of those about them, as had been the days of the late 1920s and early 1930s. The handicap from which both Edwina and Dickie suffered was the stunted growth of their powers of perception to see themselves as others saw them. This is a common, almost invariable failing of those who enjoy great power and/or wealth for so long a period that they can no longer imagine what it must be like not to possess the privileges power and wealth offer. It is a first cousin to megalomania, and it affects people of high and low quality alike. Unfortunately it also brushes off on those about them, as can be observed in the unimaginative and sometimes stupid comments and advice given by private secretaries, equerries and press officers. The disease can be observed in its most virulent form in politicians. One of its first manifestations is, naturally, a strong dislike of criticism and a blind assumption that all the world must love and admire you. When it is suddenly brought home to you, against all expectations, that it does not, it comes as an unpleasant shock and can lead to strong over-reactions.

A further consequence of the privilege of power and wealth is the affectation among those who possess it that so important is their time that they have none to spare for what they regard as trivia, like reading, which may offer such advantages as the truth or the need to think objectively about their role and their behaviour. The resulting underdevelopment of the imaginative processes can be highly damaging to those who have it, and to others, as instanced by the behaviour of Buckingham Palace and Edwina Mountbatten in the *People* libel case in 1932, and on innumerable occasions since, most notoriously in the Princess Margaret–Peter Townsend nonsense.

Both Edwina and her husband, a pair endowed with exceptional intelligence, suffered from this blindness and were greatly damaged as a result. In Mountbatten's case the handicap was matched by a deep sense of insecurity stemming from his German origins and the treatment his family had suffered since their arrival in Britain. For Edwina, it marched hand in hand with her socialist egalitarianism.

The trouble with Edwina was that she despised the average and commonplace and, for all her exceptional intelligence, she lacked the imagination to consider the pain caused by her indifference. She wanted the exceptional and nothing else. On her honeymoon she wanted the White House or a poor Mexican village, not the genteel home of the Mayor of Smalltown, Colorado. She wanted the biggest Rolls-Royce or an old Austin pockmarked with shell splinters in the London Blitz. She wanted the extremes of sexual experience, not the steadiness of monogamy, the luxury of a first-class seat or the back of an old donkey over the Andes, the best suite in the *Majestic* or a cranky, overcrowded copra boat. This need for the exceptional was what determined her to marry the handsomest naval officer closest to the monarch, in spite of what she thought about monarchs. It was a mainly harmless characteristic and was one of her antidotes to the dreaded disease of boredom. But her distaste for the middle way – and the middle classes – led her to commit unkindnesses to some and led others to dislike her for it.

A rare case of mis-identification may be taken as an example, contributed by the wife of an officer of the Mediterranean Fleet of superior rank to Mountbatten. At a dance at the officers' club on Malta this woman, now an elderly widow, had reason to ask a favour of Edwina. She recalls:

> It was only a trifling matter, but it seemed important at the time and it could not have meant a great inconvenience to Lady Mountbatten. But all I got was a rather fleeting charming smile and an 'I'm awfully sorry, I'm afraid it's impossible.' But later when I was about to go home and had my husband with me she caught my eye and came across the room full of apologies. 'Oh yes, of course I can. It'll be no trouble at all.' My husband told me later that there was a junior lieutenant in his ship with the same name as ours and Lady Mountbatten had got it all wrong.

Asked if she was hurt by this treatment, this wife said, 'I think I was rather. But what struck me most was that it was such a *silly* thing to do.'

In spite of the fame and success which Dickie achieved during the war, and the marvels of life-saving achieved by Edwina, the Mountbattens remained objects of doubt and suspicion in many middle-class homes, among people who had never met them, and in the Royal Navy among a proportion of officers (not only of middle rank) and their wives. Prejudice it may have been, but it undoubtedly existed. And the reason was that the Mountbattens continued to conduct themselves in public in a style that was not always sympathetic to the public pulse.

Mountbatten's rank qualified him for the use of a small man-of-war as his personal dispatch vessel, or 'private yacht' or 'Dickie's yacht' as his critics termed it. HMS *Surprise* was a new 1,600-ton armed vessel which increasingly sacrificed her fighting capacity for the greater comforts of her commander and his guests, quite legitimately, it must be added. In an era when post-war austerities still governed the standard of life of most people, the Mountbattens took their guests on cruises which did not necessarily enhance the fighting efficiency of the Mediterranean Fleet. When the family, in numbers, were invited on board for the first summer cruise of the Fleet in June 1952, one newspaper commented on the surprise caused by this apparent contravention of an Admiralty order that 'neither the wife of any officer nor of any man, nor any other woman, is to be allowed to reside on board . . . except with the express permission of the Admiralty'. Had the Admiralty's permission been granted? No one seemed prepared to answer that question.

In September of the same year, the *Surprise* departed on a thirty-one-day cruise. This included the ports of the French Riviera, when Henri and Yola Letellier came on board and afterwards entertained the Mountbattens to lunch at La Réserve at Beaulieu, followed by dinner with the Prefect of the Department. In October the Earl of Dalkeith, the family again and Malcolm Sargent, 'hon. musical adviser to the Fleet', joined 'Dickie's yacht'.

The publicity attracted by the movements of the *Surprise* was no more favourable than that attracted by the Mountbatten yacht *Shrimp* twenty years earlier. Edwina and Dickie remained sublimely ignorant of it, or brushed it aside as ridiculous gossip. But the publicity was in fact noted both in the Fleet and among the public at large, and it was damaging to them.

It is said that one piece of bad publicity leads to another. A retired captain RN recalls bringing back Edwina and Pamela to the *Surprise* from a shore visit to Prince Ibn Saud of Saudi Arabia in 1950. 'They were very preoccupied over the presents they had been given and seemed more concerned with their value than the spirit in which they had been given,' he remembers. 'They talked all the way about having them valued at Asprey's when they got back to London. "I've got this – look, ooh! you've got that!"' This sort of conversation within earshot of a number of officers, petty officers and ratings, all living on their relatively meagre pay, was not calculated to improve Edwina's standing.

Like a lot of rich people, both Mountbattens' attitude towards money was uneven and faintly unseemly. Like her father and grandfather, Edwina was always 'very tight'. Mountbatten made much of his parents' penury, and so did his sisters. People with more commonplace incomes might think otherwise. On the death of Queen Victoria, for example, Mountbatten's mother received an 'increase' of £2,000 a year, or about £30,000 in today's money; she still walked everywhere in London, or took a bus, never a hansom cab or taxi if she could help it. During his long life a great many people (including this writer) observed, to their surprise and sometimes their loss, the difficulty of extracting from Mountbatten money which he owed. On the other hand he would, for example, telephone for fifteen minutes long-distance at peak time in order to persuade some wretched tradesman to give him a ten per cent discount on some trifling purchase. Edwina was equally demanding about discounts and had a superb memory for them. She loved the minute economy while giving only a passing glance at the price tag on some totally unnecessary extravagance.

Edwina's attitude towards money became public knowledge in 1949 in connection with what became known as 'the Mountbatten Estate Bill'. On 10 March her solicitors issued a statement:

> A personal Bill is shortly to be introduced in the House of Lords, the object of which is to give the Countess Mountbatten of Burma greater personal control over her inheritance under the will of her grandfather. Under his will she was left the life interest in a capital sum which provided her with a large income, but the bequest was subject to restrictions which prevent her from dealing in any way with the capital and even borrowing upon future income. . . .

There had been an Act in 1935 which had rendered void restrictions upon anticipation by married women, but this had not been retrospective. Since then, the statement continued, there had occurred a great reduction in Lady Mountbatten's income caused by higher taxation and 'an ever-increasing range of public duties which have involved her in unavoidable and heavy personal expenditure'.

Having been known for many years as the richest woman in the land, and having always been unashamed of her wealth, this statement led to caustic comment and attacks in the press. Certainly surtax was now 19s 6d in the pound under a socialist government but that affected all who were fortunate enough to earn or receive large sums of money, and under the Attlee Government the nation was suffering one of its most severe bouts of egalitarianism, in legislation and in spirit.

'It is a bad principle when the law is pointedly altered in one case,' ran a typical newspaper comment. 'And the suspicion will remain that this exceptional treatment commends itself to Mr Attlee and his colleagues because the advanced views of the beneficiaries also commend themselves.'

Lord Simon opposed the Bill as 'a most flagrant piece of retrospective legislation. It cancels the terms of every single married settlement made to the beginning of 1936, and there have been hundreds of thousands of them.' Lord Swinton 'boggled' at 'the complete reversal of what a testator had laid down'. However, the Bill went through its three readings in the House of Lords. Fears of opposition in the Commons were realized, and after some hard-hitting comment in favour and against (much of it on a personal level), it was withdrawn, one proponent claiming to an incredulous House that Edwina's income had been reduced to £4,500 net. 'I don't believe for one minute that her private income was £4,500 then,' says Woodrow Wyatt today. 'But the whole thing by the Tory backbenchers was a pretty dirty trick. She briefed me on the business and the Bill beforehand.'

It is a sorry reflection on the lack of imaginative judgement of both Mountbattens (and their advisers) that this personal Bill, benefiting Edwina alone among the tens of thousands of women suffering identically, if on a smaller scale, was allowed to go forward at all. If it had been a general Bill, had been termed a restraint upon anticipation Bill instead of becoming known as 'the Mountbatten Estate Bill', it would have passed through both Houses at once – as indeed it did in its amended form in November 1949 with a majority of 180 to forty-seven.

'Edwina was now again a wealthy woman,' as one of her friends wrote, perhaps with tongue in cheek. Mountbatten's fellow naval officer,

Lieutenant-Commander Gurney Braithwaite, stated glumly, 'Now everybody will have to pay more in one way or another in order that relief may be given to these ladies.' At the time when the future Queen arrived in Malta for her long stay, her host and hostess were getting a poor press at home. 'The whole affair was badly handled from the start,' one of their friends commented. 'And I'm afraid Dickie and Edwina paid a heavy price for it.' They gave no public impression of minding, but it hurt Mountbatten badly, and he knew that the implacable, unforgiving enmity of Lord Beaverbrook was one of the forces behind all this public criticism.

Beaverbrook's hatred of Mountbatten was as powerful as ever, and it brushed off on Edwina, too. It extended even to his objecting to one of his newspapers serializing Noël Coward's latest volume of autobiography because it included a few words of praise of Mountbatten. A few months after the Mountbatten inheritance Bill unpleasantness, Mountbatten heard that Coward had had a *rapprochement* with Beaverbrook, and he and Edwina sought out 'the Master' when they were in London. Coward wrote in his diary:

> [Max Beaverbrook] is still a bitter attacker of Dickie, and I sensed in the atmosphere a certain whiff of self-justification. It was all somehow uneasy, as though I were being subtly briefed for any future talks I might have with Max, and equally subtly there was a feeling of appeal. I must say I felt astounded and rather cross. I do resent having my intelligence underrated.[1]

Edwina could now dig into her capital as freely as she wished, and by way of celebration bought from Lady Dorothy Charteris a substantial house in Wilton Crescent in January 1950. She had quite outgrown the Chester Street house, she told her friends, who reasoned that, after the Brook House penthouse (from which she had extracted the Rex Whistler murals), anything would feel confined. Now they were at least back to nine bedrooms and five bathrooms for their London *pied-à-terre*.

During their periods in London they revived their pre-war entertaining, though on a less exuberant scale. Friends tended to refer to 'a small select party at the Mountbattens including Prince Philip and Sophie Tucker' rather than 'the huge routs' of the 1930s. Undoubtedly there was less fun than there had been, and more earnestness, as Edwina took on more and more charitable responsibilities and Mountbatten continued his long fight to get to the top of the Navy, against tough opposition, including Churchill's. They lost some of their friends on the way. 'Not many people refuse invitations to Dickie and Edwina – that's true,' one of their friends said. 'But I don't think anyone has as much fun as they used to.' 'They have both changed beyond recognition,' wrote Noël Coward more extremely. 'No more humour and an overweening pomposity. It is a shame but there is obviously nothing to be done. "*Tout lasse, tout passe, tout casse.*" Life goes on and little bits of us get lost.'[2]

Relations with both sides of the family, and of course with the Royal Family, remained as cordial and as tight as ever. Both the Queen and Prince Philip were extremely fond and admiring of Edwina, and she loved them in return – more than the Queen's uncle, father or grandfather, though she always retained the fondest memories of the Queen's great-grandfather with all his cigar smoke and coughing and beard and fat belly criss-crossed with gold chains. Edwina did not, however, much care for Dickie's new campaign, as important in his eyes as reaching the First Sea Lord's office. This was his attempt to seal the royal bonds even tighter by getting the Queen to change her name to Mountbatten-Windsor; he also had plans (highly confidential at this early stage, and of course quite unknown to the young children) to arrange a match between their grandson Norton and the Queen's young daughter Princess Anne.

When Mountbatten succeeded in his first endeavour just before Edwina died, his victory got the sort of reception she had feared. 'Some will have reservations,' was the staid *Daily Telegraph*'s opinion. The *Daily Herald* regarded it 'as a victory for Prince Philip and his uncle', although Prince Philip had no strong feelings about the matter; while the *Daily Mirror* stated firmly that 'the Queen's decision will *not* be applauded by the British public', and asked, 'Is the decision prudent? If it is prudent is it necessary? If it is necessary, is it well timed?' As to Mountbatten's matchmaking, Edwina supported this so long as, at the appropriate time, the very young couple showed that they really loved one another. With all her confused notions about the Royal Family and the monarchical principle, she would have greatly enjoyed seeing her grandson married to the Queen's daughter, with all the colour and pageantry the nuptials would present.

Edwina now arranged her life in order that she could visit India and see Nehru frequently. She had kept alive her association with charities in India, and her overseas inspections on behalf of the St John Ambulance, the Red Cross and the Save the Children Fund all brought her to Delhi, sometimes several times a year. These long charity tours from Malta in the immediate post-war years were in curious contrast with the excursions she had made with Nada and Marjorie Brecknock to Polynesia, Africa and North and South America in those earlier Malta years. The restlessness was as powerful as ever, the purpose very different. Duty certainly called, loud and clear, but there was always the reward of staying in Delhi, usually on the way out and again on the way back. Nehru and his family provided her with the intellectual stimulus, the witty conversation and total relaxation which she needed periodically on these tours.

We can catch glimpses of her in the early 1950s staying in the Nehru household, usually in February or March, and sometimes after the monsoon, in October, which is a particularly beautiful month in Delhi, perhaps with Rajkumari Amrit Kaur, or Indira and her husband Feroze and their two boys, the more amusing of Nehru's ministers, and often visiting Britons and Americans. 'I would love India to be the centre of music between East and West,' Nehru had let it be known. Yehudi Menuhin had offered to come and play to raise money for the recent Madras Famine Fund. 'Nehru replied that he would like us to stay with him,' Diana Menuhin recalls, 'and 1952 and its repeat in 1954 not only raised 76,000 dollars but began a close and continuing friendship between the Nehrus and us.' Marie Seton was there later, lecturing on film appreciation, and stayed for many years before writing her biography of Nehru.

Jacob Epstein arrived in Delhi in 1952 to do a bust of Nehru. Another friend of both Nehru and Edwina writes:

> It was, strangely enough, not one of his best works. Edwina enjoyed being present at all the sittings and at those moments when inevitably Nehru was called away, irritated the eccentric old sculptor by asking him whether he did not find Nehru the most beautiful and remarkable looking man he had ever translated into sculpture. Epstein could not bear being, as it were, persuaded, or questioned. He liked to work in silence, only himself uttering ejaculations of various kinds, and I think he deliberately reduced the power and beauty simply because he was being asked to recognize it.

Another friend recalls Edwina arriving in her white St John uniform while the Nehru household was having tea on the grass terrace in the garden.

> It was terribly hot and Edwina had arrived from Hong Kong only half an hour earlier after a really gruelling flight. She looked as cool and neat as if she was just leaving Wilton Crescent in the morning for a day at the office, smiling sweetly at us all and greeting everyone by name of course although I had only met her once before, and that had been three years earlier. Then she was off to change and came back in a light cotton frock looking more marvellous than ever. I remember glancing at Nehru and seeing the admiration in his eyes and I thought 'Yes, I can understand all right.' It had not been a dull tea party before but now she lifted everyone up with her charm and vivacity.

One day, after a hard time at the office, Nehru suddenly turned to Edwina, Yehudi and Diana Menuhin and Indira and said, 'Let's go for a swim!' They went to 'a funny old British Raj pool, decently protected by high wooden fencing,' surrounded by lush green trees. They had a delicious flounder and then Edwina lay on her back, raised 'her lovely lissom legs high above her head on the surrounding lawn and, grinning, said in her inimitable sweet frank way, "Not bad for fifty, is it?"'

The close Mountbatten-Nehru relationship, which had added to Moslem suspicions and the difficulty of negotiating with Jinnah in 1947, continued into the uneasy peace between India and Pakistan after the transfer of power. In January 1951 Edwina accompanied Nehru to disputed Kashmir, and this was observed with fury in Islamabad. 'The fact that the last Viceroy's wife went to Kashmir with Nehru will be taken to mean that Lord Mountbatten favours India's claim and backs Nehru in his defiance of the United Nations' resolution,' commented one London newspaper.

Mountbatten's deep-seated dislike of Jinnah has been confirmed recently by the revelations in *Mountbatten and the Partition of India* by Larry Collins and Dominique Lapierre. Edwina shared his distaste and suspicion, and while she worked with equal vigour to ease the sufferings of Sikhs, Hindus and Moslems alike in the bloody riots of 1947–8, she laid the blame for the massacres firmly at the feet of Jinnah and the Moslems.

With his lifelong ambition realized by his appointment as First Sea Lord in April 1955, Mountbatten planned a number of overseas visits with Edwina 'to show the flag'. These were to include, in March 1956, New Zealand, Australia, India, Ceylon and Pakistan. It soon became clear that they would be *personae non gratae* in Pakistan. A group of Pakistanis appealed for the cancellation of the proposed visit. 'No guest can be more unwelcome and unwanted,' they declared. 'The wounds inflicted by Lord Mountbatten as the last Viceroy of India are still festering.' The *Civil and Military Gazette* wrote, 'Lord Mountbatten will be unwelcome in Pakistan.' In London the *Daily Express* seized the opportunity to make one more vigorous anti-Mountbatten attack. 'All this goes to show the folly of appointing as First Sea Lord a figure of political controversy. It should be mere routine for the head of the Navy to inspect overseas stations. But Lord Mountbatten's background turns it into an occasion of embarrassment and ill-will.'

With Pakistan and India intermittently at war in the 1950s, the continuing close relations between Nehru and the Mountbattens were observed with dismay and suspicion by the Pakistan authorities. In 1956, after the cancellation of the Pakistan tour, Nehru arrived in London for consultations and called on Edwina at Wilton Crescent with his Christmas present. Later, he stayed at Broadlands as he always did when in England, this time with his sister Mrs Pandit in company. It was a crowded, noisy and entirely happy Christmas Day.

Throughout the 1950s Edwina managed to find time to visit her friends in America, and during the Eisenhower years always called on him at the White House. One of her last visits was in October and November 1957 when Mountbatten was on official business conferring with the American Chief of Naval Operations and the Chairman of the Joint Chiefs of Staff. Edwina met a lot of people officially, including supporters of the Save the Children Federation, and many more purely socially. When she met Averell Harriman, the Governor of the State of New York, Edwina told reporters afterwards that she had first met him back in 1924 'when we were giddy young people'.

Some measure of the responsibilities Edwina had taken upon herself in the mid-1950s can be gained by a glance at a part of her *Who's Who* entry at that time:

> Superintendent-in-Chief St John Ambulance Brigade, Governor Westminster Hospital Council, Governor Girl Guides Association, WVS Advisory and General Purposes Committee, President Dumb Friends League, President Save the Children Fund, Vice-President Royal College of Nursing, patron, president and chairman of many other organizations. . . .

An examination of Edwina's timetable during the last years of her life shows an increase in the tempo of her professional activities in spite of worsening health. No one – least of all her family – could prevail upon her to let up. She visited West and East Africa, Burma and Malaysia, Hong Kong and Ceylon, the West Indies and India. Scarcely was she home – filing reports, making speeches, visiting her grandchildren, supervising more work at Broadlands, staying at Sandringham, Balmoral or Windsor with the Queen and Prince Philip, attending meetings in London – than she was off again.

One of her friends in Delhi tells of her arrival after another testing trip to the Far East, 'her face lined like a *very fine* cobweb'. 'Oh! please,' she begged, 'don't wear yourself out on yet another of your endless tours. Each one etches yet another line on your lovely face.'

A few weeks after her New York visit she was in Trinidad. Miss Judy

Admiring her second grandson in Princess Elizabeth's arms at the christening in 1950. First grandson, Norton (now Lord Romsey), holds his father's hand

With Nehru and Health Minister Rajkumari Amrit Kaur at the Asian games, March 1951

Top: Flanked by Nehru and Yehudi Menuhin; Marcel Gazelle, Menuhin's accompanist, and Diana Menuhin on left, Calcutta, 1952

Right: On duty in London, 1952

Above: Off duty at Broadlands, aged fifty, 1952

Above left: Comforting a bereaved and frightened woman after the Greek earthquake, 1953

Above: Coronation robes, 1953

Left: The film premiere of *Dunkirk*, 1953

"Only been Viceroy of India and First Sea Lord! Why, he's 54 and still to get up to British Railways Chief, Prime Minister, and Director-General of Television."

Left: Cummings cartoon, 1954

Above: Malta, 1954, with the Queen, Prince Charles and Princess Anne

Below: With children awaiting treatment, Kuala Lumpur, March 1954

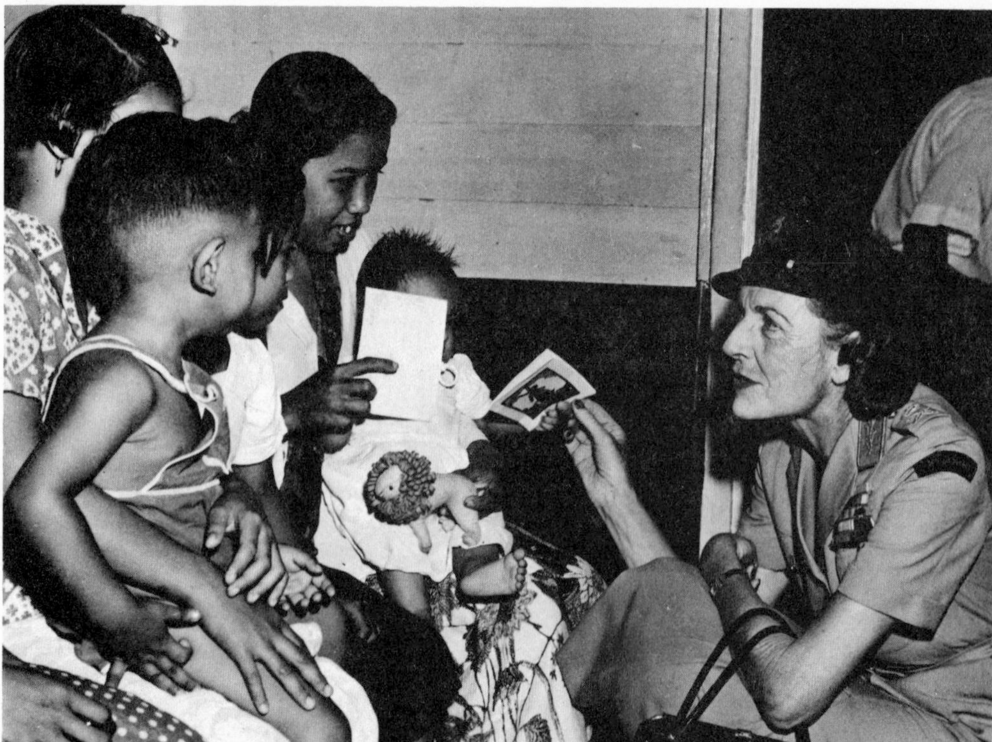

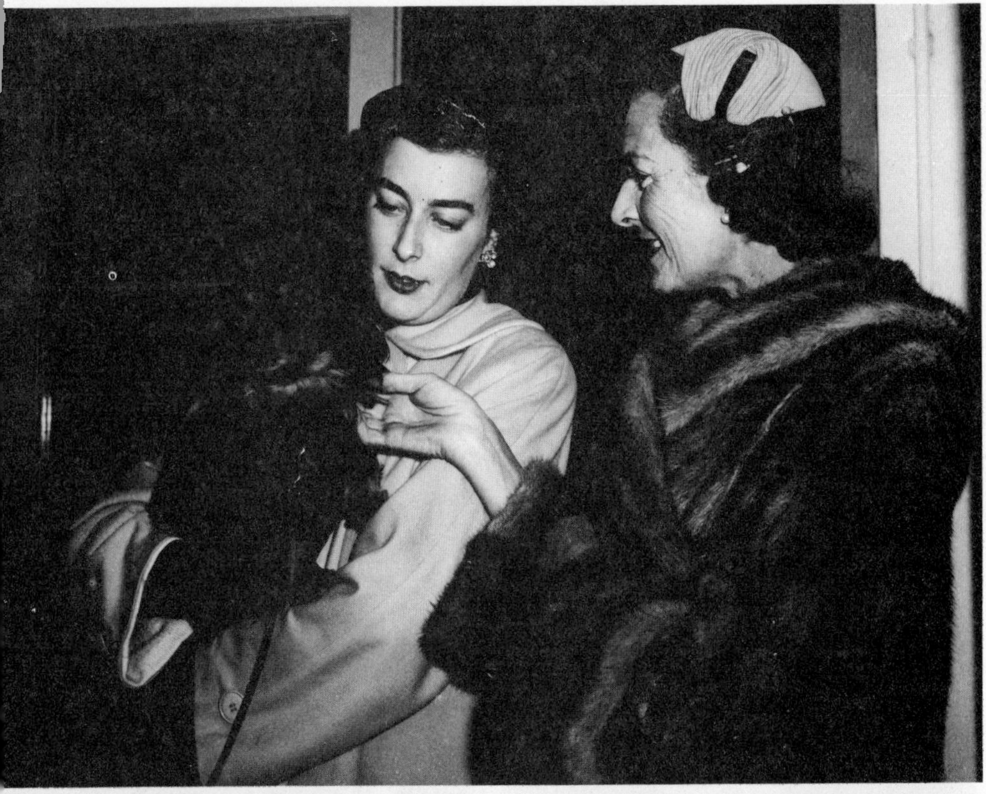

Top: Shared affection. With Pamela, December 1954

Left: At an Indian High Commission reception given by Mrs Pandit: Nehru is sixty-five and Edwina fifty-three

Above: A rare quiet moment at Broadlands, 1955

Above: A Burmese Embassy reception a year before her death

Left: Another war film premiere, *Cockleshell Heroes*, November 1955

Top: With Mrs Pandit in London, July 1955

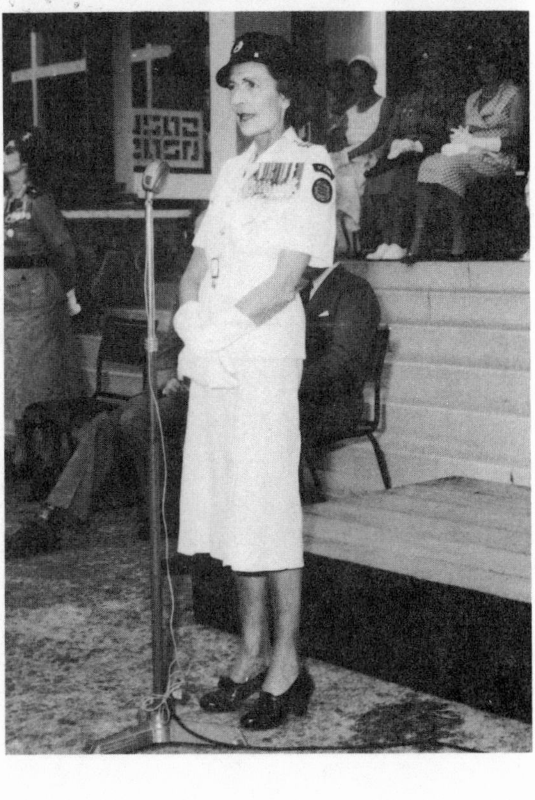

Above and right: Jesselton, February 1960: greeted by Noel Turner, Acting Governor of North Borneo; and giving her last address the day before she died

Top: Pamela marries David Hicks, 14 January 1960. Edwina is between the Duke of Edinburgh and Lord Brabourne

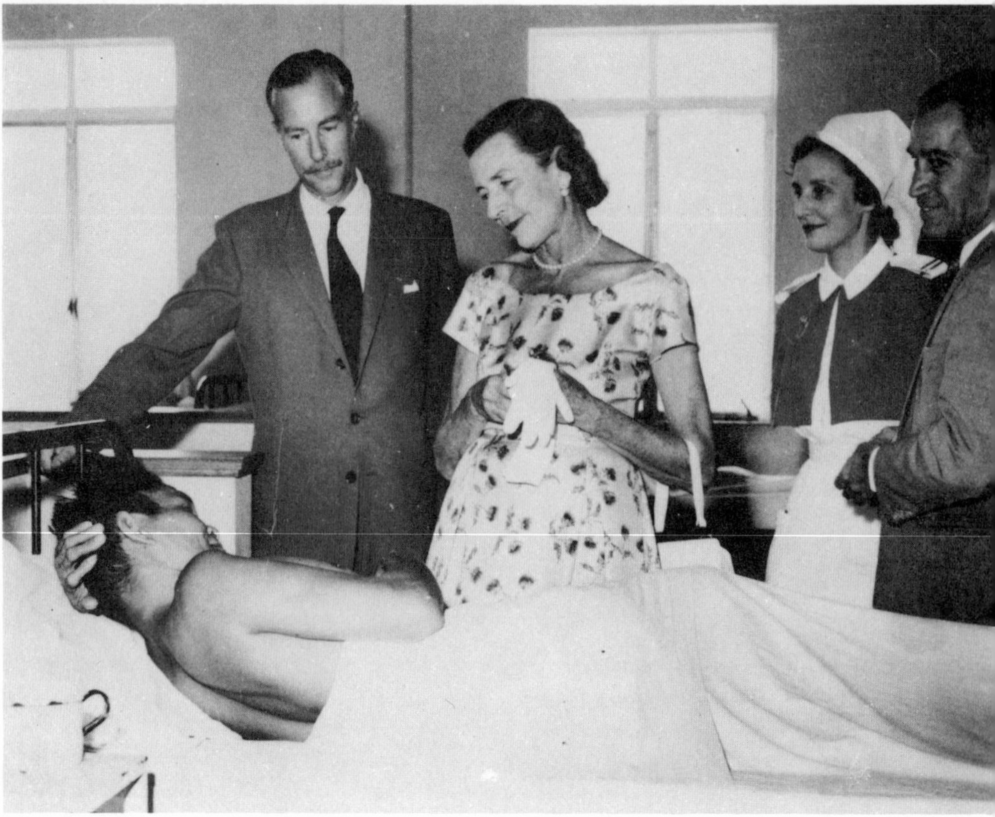

Total concern, Jesselton, 1960. The next day Edwina's coffin is carried out for the flight home

Hutchinson, lady-in-waiting and private secretary to the wife of the Governor-General of the West Indian Federation, Lady Hailes, described Edwina arriving 'direct from London in burning heat on 20 January 1958' and at once going into action inspecting St John units etc. Miss Hutchinson recalls:

> We expected someone terribly grand. I was amazed at her consideration under the most exacting conditions of heat and work. I felt that everything she did and said came from the heart. She would come back in the evening, change into any dress that came to hand, put on a feathery hat and set off to social functions. I was astonished by her non-stop work from 8 a.m. onwards.

After she had left Miss Hutchinson wrote home, 'We've been hectic with Lady Mountbatten's visit. She has been the gayest, kindest and most considerate visitor one could have. The energy! In this heat I can't understand how she does it. Her speeches were brilliant, she was kind and thoughtful to everyone, and she gave us all great encouragement.'

It seems impossible to understand how Edwina kept up this tempo year after year. Her actual working procedures are on record and go some way towards explaining her efficiency, always supported by her ever-loyal staff and her ever-diligent private secretary, Elizabeth Collins. Nearer to home - almost on her doorstep in fact - a typical inspection of the St John Ambulance Brigade in Wiltshire is described by the local Commissioner:

> She flew down from London after lunch, and inspected the Swindon Divisions in the afternoon. As was her usual habit she shook hands with most of the personnel and spoke to about one in three. Immediately after she attended a tea party for officers and their families and invited guests, and again as was her habit, had no tea, but spoke to everyone. After that she went to the Mayor's parlour for a drink. She then went to the hospital to present awards to the nurses and gave a short address.
>
> She returned to Broadlands for the night, and next morning was at Chippenham at 10.30 to inspect the Divisions in the north-west of the county. This was followed by a coffee session to meet invited guests, and then on to Salisbury for a lunch with senior county officers, at which she was joined by the Lord-Lieutenant, the Duke of Somerset. In the afternoon she inspected the Divisions from the south of the county, followed by a tea party for invited guests. About a month previously at her request I had sent a list of those invited to this party with details of their connections or interest in St John. As soon as I introduced anyone, Lady Mountbatten spoke as though I had just given her their history, no looking at notes, no hints, and never a mistake. And this was the third performance in thirty-six hours.

For a woman of Edwina's temperament and impatience it is as remarkable that this repeated routine, for months and years on end, did not bore her to death as it is that the physical demands did not undermine her health. But the cost to her health did have to be paid in the end. By 1956 angina was beginning to trouble her, and as it became worse she found it impossible to conceal it from her family and closest friends. Finally, early in 1957 she saw a heart specialist who, after promising total confidentiality, even to Mountbatten, confirmed that her cardiac condition was not satisfactory, and that it would grow worse if she kept up the present tempo of her life. He gave her three years if she did not ease the pace. It was not possible for her to do so. She ignored all the pleas of Dickie and her daughters, who saw that she was not well. Even the Queen's pleas fell on deaf ears; she continued exactly as before.

In 1958 she suffered a small stroke and was taken to hospital. It was put about that she was having dental treatment, which caused the 'stiffness' in her right cheek but mercifully did not seriously impede her speech. For several weeks she did not appear in public. When she did so on 27 October to meet Mountbatten disembarking from the *Queen Elizabeth* at Southampton she was seen to be wearing dark glasses, a lilac tweed suit with a diamond on the lapel, 'her right cheek still drawn'.

The year 1959, the last complete year in Edwina's life, was also one of her busiest, with a series of tours as strenuous as any she had undertaken in the past. In the previous summer she had caught a very virulent form of chickenpox from one of her grandchildren which laid her low for some weeks. She never completely regained her strength. In January 1959 she went to Delhi 'for a complete rest', returning at the end of March still feeling tired. However, she did not cancel her visit to Canada in August, returning on 2 September, and departing again for New York on 4 October.

In London on 16 November she delivered the tribute at a dinner to celebrate Nehru's seventieth birthday two days earlier. The Royal Family descended on Broadlands on 20 December in the run-up to Christmas; and no matter if you did call the Queen Lilibet and had many times bathed the Duke of Edinburgh when he was a small boy, everything had to be just right, from choosing a suitable film for showing in the special little theatre upstairs, to ensuring that there was a spread of grit on the wooden bridge over the Test when the Queen took her morning ride.

Then there was Pammy's wedding to David Hicks which, in spite of the disparity in wealth and rank, had perforce to be accorded all the trappings of royal-Romsey Ashley-Mountbatten nuptials. The preparations had begun in the early autumn of 1959, the date of 13 January chosen because it was convenient for all the Royal Family. But it was highly inconvenient as far as the weather was concerned, January that year being a particularly cold month. There were two special trains for the guests, the royal train from Sandringham (where the Queen was awaiting the birth of her third child) managing to get through the snow. The local schoolchildren were given a half day off and spent hours in the specially built stands in Romsey waiting to cheer the procession. But a procession was out of the question, so they froze for nothing. Another cold child was Prince Charles, who wore a short-trousered grey suit but, due to some oversight, no overcoat. Princess Anne, aged nine, was one of the five chill bridesmaids; and Canon W.E. Norris, who officiated, looked blue with cold.

'My dear – the cold!' exclaims one of the guests today. 'It was unbelievable. The moment the Abbey doors opened a blizzard from Siberia came roaring in and we at the back were all turned into snowmen!' The journey to Broadlands was like the Monte Carlo rally with limousines slithering on the icy roads. And then, just as the Royal Family entered Broadlands all the lights went out, and as by now there was virtually no daylight, this led to a great deal of hilarity and confusion. The bride's father resourcefully appeared with a five-branch candelabra which he held above the happy couple, wax dripping over Pammy's priceless lace, as they received the guests.

'Of all the grand receptions there had been at Broadlands with kings and queens and people, this one must have been the biggest riot, and the most fun. The Queen Mum especially enjoyed it – I've never seen her laugh so much,' another guest recalls. The lights went on again, the cake was cut, and everybody said how well and happy and lovely Edwina looked.

But Edwina was not at all well and Mountbatten and the Brabournes did their utmost to persuade her to cancel her imminent trip. When these pleas failed, they were equally unsuccessful in persuading her to reduce her programme: 'Just go as far as Delhi and cut out the Far East and Malaysia. . . .' A contemporary of Mountbatten's, who had served in the Mediterranean with him and was a close friend of them both, begged her not to go. 'She was looking awful.' But Edwina shook her head. 'You know it's impossible,' she replied. 'I've simply got to go – I *have* to.'

Two days after seeing the Queen and bidding her good-bye, Edwina was at Heathrow wearing a heavy white coat with astrakhan collar and a little feather hat, off to India for the last time, smiling sweetly at the photographers and reporters, not one of whom knew what Mountbatten knew – 'she was a dying woman and we didn't think we would see her alive again'.

Cyprus, Karachi, Delhi. The happy few days in India with her beloved friend, whose touch and looks, whose wit and incisive mind, meant everything to her. But feeling ill all the time, sleeping worse than ever, chest pains. Refusing to acknowledge to herself how awful she felt, and of course not a word to Nehru. Nehru taking her to the airport. The last farewell.

The ordeal of keeping going without a sign of flagging, through the self-imposed packed itinerary and daily timetable. The sweltering heat of Singapore. How was she to survive? No one guessed how fine the balance was between life and death for her. The morning take-off, the vibration and heat of the Viscount. The landing at Kuching. All through the midday heat, circling the airfield, final approach, touch-down, the cabin door opening like an oven's after a long bake. Jesselton at last. But no peace and privacy yet. The party on the tarmac to greet her.

Those last days were a blur of exhaustion and pain. But she played her part 'just like an old trouper who cannot stop', as someone who had failed to dissuade her from making this trip had told her reprovingly. And the last ghastly evening when she knew that she was cracking up, hardly able to focus on the faces about her, an arm holding her as she was led away, up the half-flight of stairs, away to the peace of her room. No more than a subdued murmur from the guests as if at her funeral – premature mourning, but only just premature. . . .

For Mrs and Mrs Noel Turner in Jesselton, the full implications of the catastrophe of Edwina's death were delayed by the amount that had to be done throughout 21 February after they and Miss Checkley quietly closed the door of the room in which Edwina had died. Before any official announcement could be made, a telegram had to be sent to London so that Mountbatten and the rest of the family could be told first. But there was nothing that could be done to prevent a crowd unaware of her death gathering at the airport to bid Edwina God-speed on the next stage of her journey to Hong Kong via Singapore. Everybody rallied round marvellously. Miss Checkley and the hospital matron, Miss J.H. Burnham, performed the last offices, and Mrs Turner and Miss Checkley tidied up the bedroom and packed her clothes. Characteristically, Edwina had scattered her jewellery, worth tens of thousands of pounds, carelessly about the room, and Evelyn Turner and Penelope Gray, the wife of the Acting

Chief Secretary made an inventory of it and packed it carefully. (They received neither thanks nor even acknowledgement of safe receipt.)

Then a coffin had to be ordered and made rapidly, while in the room the Right Reverend James Chung Ling Wong, the Assistant Bishop, conducted a moving little service in the presence of the Turners, Miss Checkley, the Director of Medical Services, the hospital matron and Mrs. Gray.

Turner put through an urgent call to General Sir Richard Hull, the Commander-in-Chief in Singapore, asking for a plane to be sent as soon as possible. Edwina's body was then driven in an ambulance to Government House where there was powerful air-conditioning. At 12.30 Turner permitted a brief public announcement to be made and all flags were lowered to half-mast.

At 6.15 that evening the Assistant Bishop again said a few words over the coffin, which was now draped with the St John flag. There were already ten wreaths, including three from the Governor of Hong Kong. Four boxes of orchids which had been sent from Singapore for the Jesselton Flower Show were opened, and now embellished a more solemn occasion. Then the plane from Singapore was seen to approach; it circled and landed.

'We made our way to the airport,' wrote Turner later, 'where the Brigade and Association provided bearers, and the coffin passed through two lines of members of the Brigade as it made its way to the aircraft.'

Edwina's body was carried from Singapore to London in a Qantas Boeing 707, arriving at Heathrow on the morning of 24 February. It was then taken direct to Broadlands and later to Romsey Abbey, where it lay in state until the next morning.

Mountbatten was awoken by a telephone call at 3 a.m. 'It was a poleaxe blow. I simply couldn't grasp it,' he recalled. But he, too, was for the present mercifully overwhelmed with activities and obligations, including the arrival of over 6,000 telegrams and letters. The Queen and Prince Philip were stunned. They knew that Edwina had not been well but they had no idea of the critical nature of her illness. Lord Brabourne, as soon as he heard, raced to London airport where his sister-in-law was due back from her honeymoon. He broke the news to the couple and drove them to Wilton Crescent.

But nowhere were the shockwaves more violent than in Delhi. The news was broken to Nehru shortly before he was due at the Indian Council for International Affairs where Arnold Toynbee was to speak on 'India within the framework of history'. Nehru decided, typically, to keep the engagement. Marie Seton, who had not yet learned the news, watched him arrive, 'his face expressionless and self-contained, and he took no notice of anyone'.

Marie Seton wrote:

> All the 563 seats in the theatre were occupied. Professor Kabir, then Minister of Scientific Research and Cultural Affairs, rose from his seat on the stage and made the announcement that Lady Mountbatten had been found dead in bed that morning. There came a gasp, followed by a wave of people rising to their feet to maintain silent homage. . . .

The next day Members of Parliament rose and stood in silence for two minutes before business started, and later the Nehru family attended a private service in her memory.

Of all the losses Nehru suffered in the last years of his life this was the one that affected him most and left him most bereft of companionship. A light had indeed gone out of his life and for a time he was quite inconsolable. He died, at the age of seventy-five, four years later.

Nehru's last act on behalf of the woman he loved was to order an Indian warship to accompany as escort the British frigate in which Edwina's body was transported for burial at sea. To be buried at sea was a surprise request of Edwina's which puzzled and worried Mountbatten at first, especially as she had never much cared for the sea and was a poor sailor. 'I believe she was thinking of the *Kelly*,' was one friend's comment. 'She felt she wanted to share the seabed with all those sailors she had known back in 1940.' The naval authorities rallied round at once. In the early afternoon of 25 February, the coffin was taken from Romsey Abbey after a short service of prayers and thanksgiving, and taken to Portsmouth Dockyard, where it was met by, among others, the Commander-in-Chief, Admiral Sir Manley Power, the First Sea Lord, Mountbatten's successor and old friend, Admiral Sir Charles Lambe, the Duke of Edinburgh and his mother, and the family.

The frigate *Wakeful* had been selected for this solemn ceremony. She steamed out to a point four miles south of the Nab Tower. It was a cold, grey day, with flecks of wind-driven rain and spray, the Indian *Trishul* in close company as if to ensure that due and proper honour was given to 'their ' Edwina. The coffin lay on a steel-grey bier on the man-of-war's quarterdeck. Dr Fisher, the Archbishop of Canterbury, who had broken his holiday at Minehead, conducted a brief and moving service. Everyone was freezing cold, scarves pulled tight, coats buttoned up against the wind, the men bareheaded. Royal Marine buglers sounded 'The Last Post' and 'The Reveille'. The coffin slipped into the sea and Mountbatten kissed his wreath and cast it into the water. Prince Philip's was next, on behalf of the Queen and himself; then came those of the two daughters, Princess Alice and other relations and mourners. More wreaths were cast from the deck of the *Trishul*, including Nehru's own, joining together with the others in the wake of the frigates, falling astern in a scattered, uneven line as the ships gathered speed and headed back to land.

Edwina had been specific in her will, not only about being buried at sea, but also, surprisingly, in wanting no flowers and asking instead for contributions to the St John Ambulance. All royal engagements were cancelled, and it is certain that Edwina would have been amused by the Royal Family's last minute non-attendance at the premiere of the film *Battle of the Sexes*.

Over the days and weeks that followed the tributes came pouring in. On the day following the funeral the Chairman of the Joint Committee of the Order of St John of Jerusalem and the British Red Cross Society, Lord Woolton, wrote in *The Times*:

> She did her work superbly well with a personal sympathy and sincerity which gave comfort and hope to many thousands of men and women.... She was not only indefatigable, she was formidable: the blood of the redoubtable Sir Ernest Cassel continued to flow in her veins, and when she saw what she conceived to be wrong, officialdom soon learned that action and speed were called for. What was her secret? Beyond amazing endurance I think it was devotion to the service.... She was aided by an enviable – and trained – memory; as she went round the hospitals she remembered names of the men she had met before – she recollected conversations about their wives and their mothers, and if official action were needed she knew all the ropes – and used them. Not only the patients, but the staff and the nurses have been warmed and encouraged by the radiance of her devotion to their work and their cause. She has left personal friends among the thousands of little known people – and what higher tribute can be paid to her – or one she herself would more highly prize?

Many other similar tributes graced the pages of magazines and newspapers all over the world. Memories of Edwina today are legion, some dating back to the lively 1920s and 1930s, more of them from the war years and the 1950s. In India wherever you go they all speak lovingly of her and of what she did for their country. In America her friends still mourn her. This biographer has received numerous tributes to her from people, humble and grand, who learned that a book about her was being written. One admirer from Belton, near Doncaster, who met her only once and many years ago, recalled Edwina as President at a rally in Leeds of the Returned Prisoners-of-War Association. Ralph Kitson, who had just been repatriated after five years in prisoner-of-war camps, treasures the memory of that occasion:

> I was presented to Lady Mountbatten, and she said, 'What are you going to do now?' I said, 'I'm going to get married next week.' She asked, 'Has your girl waited for you all those years?' and I said, 'Yes.' There was a moment's silence, then she got up and hugged me, kissed me on the lips and said, 'You deserve to be very happy.' And so I have been.

Edwina had four grandchildren when she died. Her daughter Patricia, once 'the world's richest baby' and now Countess Mountbatten of Burma (thanks to a special inheritance of title Bill), has had three more since, although one of her twin boys was killed with Mountbatten in 1979. Pamela and David Hicks have had three children, and their names tell all: Edwina, Ashley and, the youngest, India.

Of some of the others in Edwina's life, Charles Baring, aged eighty-four, still lives in the Isle of Wight. Barbara Cartland at eighty-two is as amusing and as fluent a writer of romantic novels as ever and was Mountbatten's closest woman friend during his last years; Jean Norton died in 1945 (as Lady Grantley); and Edwina's cousin, Marjorie Brecknock, lives in the family home of Wherwell Priory and Mountbatten's last London home, 2 Kinnerton Street, Belgravia.

From Edwina's Broadlands childhood, all the servants are now dead, but Robert and Henry Everett are well, Robert a retired surgeon, Henry a retired admiral. Mary says she still misses dreadfully her older sister who looked after her when they were virtually motherless, consoled her when she suffered at the hands of her stepmother (who died unloved and unmourned by Edwina on 30 June 1954) and shared so much with her during the 1920s and 1930s. Lively in mind, cheerful in spirit in spite of the many sadnesses she has suffered, Mary lives at the Hall on Sir Ernest Cassel's old shooting estate, Six Mile Bottom, near Newmarket, with numerous mementoes of Edwina.

An extract from a letter Mary wrote at the time of Edwina's death to Robert Everett, whom she had not seen since she was eighteen when she was living with Edwina and Dickie at Brook House, spans the years and recalls their childhood:

23.3.60

My dear Bobbie,

I was so very touched by your kind letter of sympathy about darling Edwina. She seemed so *well* and *happy* at Pamela's wedding that it made the blow doubly terrible were such a thing possible.

I remember all the Head Room days perfectly and my white rat is mourned to this day ...

Yours very sincerely,

Mary Delamere

'The enigma of Edwina', one of her friends said, 'was what made her keep going, driving herself to her death when she was still only a middle-aged woman. I don't think even her closest friends knew the answer – I certainly didn't. In a way it looked almost like suicide, but of course it wasn't that literally.' One of her greatest admirers, Mrs Pandit, says,

> I remember her well on her last trip. We spoke on the same platform, and she was very sick-looking and ill. I knew that her doctor had told her not to go, but she went just the same. She was very obstinate. But more than that, for Edwina a commitment was a commitment. She *cared*. She never took on a job she didn't care about, and when she did, nothing would stop her from completing it.

Mrs Gandhi, who had had an operation and was feeling ill herself when Edwina arrived for the last time in Delhi, says, 'She wasn't well at all. We were told, "Please see that she goes slow and doesn't do too much." But of course she took no notice. Pammy had written asking if we could persuade her to go quietly somewhere and have a rest.'

Part of the reason for Edwina's bustle, above the call of duty, lay in her highly developed competitive sense. It got her into the first tennis team at The Links when she could not see the ball very well and possessed little natural aptitude for the game. It got her everything she wanted in life – possessions, men, women, appointments at the top. She wanted Mountbatten in 1921 against very heavy competition, chased him to Delhi and got him. Then she found that Mountbatten was equally competitive; and soon they were mutually inflaming one another to ever-higher competitive peaks. It never stopped, never let up for a minute, neither the competition nor the friction it created, even though, half-paradoxically, they both wanted the other to reach the top and beat everyone else and be a source of reflected pride to the other.

In all this lay a strong ingredient of their success, individually and together. But it was highly damaging to themselves individually and to their relationship. Edwina even competed with herself, like an only child breaking its own records, and that as much as anything else was what kept her going – just that little bit more after you have reached the limit, like a four-minute miler.

Many people found this competitive element in the Mountbattens daunting. 'It was so strong that you felt you might get burnt,' someone remarked to one of the Mountbattens' closest friends. Mary found that she could stand clear on the bank of this roaring tide of competition. 'I knew that nothing I ever did would be as good as Dickie's, or Edwina's,' she says modestly, 'so there was none of that competitive feeling as far as I was concerned. Edwina felt she had to compete on her own feet, in her own way, with the marvellous things he was doing.' It was one of the reasons, she says, why 'I truly loved them both.'

Nehru understood Edwina's competitiveness, as he understood everything about her; and he, more than anyone, could recognize how much his friend Dickie owed to Edwina, not only for pressing his career forwards but for bracing him up in difficult times, and, with her instinct and sagacity, keeping him balanced. As one somewhat disrespectful naval friend said as long ago as 1941, 'The *Kelly* wouldn't have been hit and gone down if Edwina had been on the bridge with him. He always needed her.' And, four years later in Kandy, one of Mountbatten's staff was heard to remark scathingly, 'There wouldn't have been 7,000 of us in Command HQ if Edwina had been "Supremo". There would have been 700, and we'd have been in Singapore six months before Hiroshima instead of after.'

Nehru could also recognize the sickness and strain in Edwina in February 1960 in spite of all her efforts to conceal them. But he knew that she would die working, that rest or retirement were outside her consideration. Mountbatten, too, knew that she would go down, like the *Kelly* he would say, with all guns firing. Marie Seton, who saw much of Edwina during those last days in Delhi, later wrote, 'I felt that Mountbatten realized that Edwina and Jawaharlal were vital personalities who must die in harness.' Which indeed they did.

All these explanations of Edwina's over-paced activity are valid, but they do not complete the picture. The difficulty in drawing a true portrait of Edwina Mountbatten is that, like a good caricature, the simple features of the subject appear to tell all. But of course they do nothing of the sort. She was an immensely complicated woman who, chameleon-like, could change both in small ways, like going native one week and going to a ball in the biggest chauffeur-driven Rolls the next week, and also in her complete style of living, as in the metamorphosis from self-indulgent frivolity to dedicated crusading in 1938–9.

The last weeks and days of her life were typical of the crusading Edwina, typical of her character and working style. The programme was punctiliously completed for as long as she had strength and life left to her, in Cyprus, India, Malaya, Singapore, and on to North Borneo, missing nothing, remembering everything, the very quintessence of concern for every sick person to whom she spoke. There is a photograph of her, within a day of her death, in Jesselton hospital, her face expressing compassion, hope and total relationship with the patient to whom she is talking. 'I felt as if I was the only person in the world who mattered as far as she was concerned.' How often people had made such a remark after she had left! This sick man was one of the last.

A further difficulty in drawing a true likeness of Edwina is that she never exposed her feelings and seemed to confirm the impression of simplicity she made on many people with her downright, predictable views and comments – 'The monarchy is out of date – ridiculous!', 'Well, he'll have to learn to look after himself', 'Everyone should have an equal chance in life', and, rather sharply, 'Of course I'm well, I'm always well.' Nothing was to be gained by arguing with Edwina. Her beliefs were like granite rocks, impossible even to chip; but they might suddenly roll away out of sight, which was surprising and painful if you happened to be in their path.

There was a deep-lying kindness in Edwina as we have seen, but she could be utterly ruthless in getting what she wanted, without too much thought for anything or anyone who got in the way. That is why she was such a first-rate commander and reformer. The last weeks of her life pointed this up. Her motive for insisting on making this long and arduous trip – with, it must be added, the perennial and life-sustaining delight in seeing Nehru – was laudable in itself. As Mrs Pandit says, for her a commitment was a commitment. The deep anxiety it must cause her family and the Royal Family, with the Queen expecting a child, was nothing to her. The pain and worry her death might cause those who at the time were offering her hospitality was not considered. The job had to be done, and that was that, no matter that her heart specialist had given her three years – and proved correct to the month.

In fact Edwina's host and hostess in North Borneo were deeply sensitive people, quite as dutiful as Edwina, and experienced a great feeling of responsibility for this visit by someone as grand as Edwina. Jesselton was a far-distant outpost where the arrival of a guest of importance was a rare event. And Edwina was Royal Family as far as they were concerned. Her death was accordingly a grievous and damaging shock to her host and hostess. They both felt that, at best, they had become associated with failure. They could not accept that nothing could have saved Edwina; they could not know that she was indeed dying on her feet. It was only a mercy that she died in her bed and not in the middle of one of the taxing functions in that North Borneo heat.

Edwina found her peace at last in that bed in Jesselton. She never knew any peace in the fifty-eight years while she lived – neither peace nor contentment. She was not even searching for it. The machine which long ago had been set into too swift motion had worn out and that was that. The friend who had likened Edwina to 'a bluebottle that is driven nearly frantic in a room and suddenly finds the open window' in the demands of war had not fully understood Edwina's restlessness. The open window only led to another closed room.

It is impossible to discount the immense general benefit derived from Edwina's passion for speed. Its sum total in the saving of life, the granting of relief from pain and the gift of contentment to others is incalculable. But within Edwina this life-long urge for frantic activity led to the loss of contentment for herself, which led in turn to a distorted interpretation of priorities, as much among her friends as in her home where charity did not begin, her two children often receiving scant thought and attention for months on end.

In one way she did find the destiny of which she had talked to others besides the young Charles Baring. In the calculations of lives saved, the extraction of benefits to mankind from the ruins of violence, and on a more prosaic level (which she thoroughly enjoyed) the titles and honours and lines in *Who's Who* – in all this achievement, carried out with bountiful charm and grace, surely *there* is a destiny fulfilled?

She never believed that this was so. She believed that it was possible to fire a shell that never curves in its trajectory, that races on higher and higher – towards what? She did not know; and in that lies the real tragedy of Edwina Mountbatten – sometimes a selfish woman, sometimes unthinking and giving needless hurt, with an overdeveloped appetite for extreme experiences and for material possessions. But for all that she was a good and kind woman with a deep concern for the welfare of the unfortunate and underprivileged – a woman who lost her way when she was growing up and never really found it again. In her blood and her intelligence, in her childhood deprivations and unhappiness, and in her excessive wealth, lay the seeds of her massive achievements and the seeds of her self-destruction. She remains one of the most astonishing, spectacular and memorable women of this century, a worthy upholder of the Shaftesbury motto 'Love and Serve'.

Tributes

The Chief Commander of The Order of St John, Major-General P.R. Leuchars CBE, has written for this book this special tribute to Lady Mountbatten as 'a contribution on her work with St John':

THE ORDER OF ST. JOHN
In service of mankind

After the war and on her return from her tremendous exploits in the Far East, Lady Mountbatten turned her energy to the welfare of wounded servicemen still in hospital and to the plight of the unfortunate refugees in Central Europe. This work was, however, cut short by the appointment of Lord Mountbatten to the post of Viceroy of India and later Governor-General of the Dominion of India from 1947–8, followed by two years in Malta, then back to England and then again back to Malta from 1952–4. When she finally returned to England, her energy was undiminished and she was able to concentrate on the task she had set herself of raising the status of the nursing personnel in St John, which she achieved with great success. She was also largely instrumental in expanding the work of the Order throughout the Commonwealth and was indefatigable in making long and exhausting tours overseas. Alas, in spite of many warnings to take care of her health, she insisted on carrying out an unnecessarily strenuous programme on her last tour and sadly died in her sleep in North Borneo (now Sabah), having insisted on carrying out every engagement on her programme in spite of being obviously very ill. Her death was a stunning blow to the St John Ambulance Brigade but happily the work she initiated has prospered and her memory is still an inspiration to the members.

The Director General of Save the Children has also kindly provided this excerpt from an official tribute to Lady Mountbatten published by the Fund at the time of her death:

Save the Children

Through the death of Countess Mountbatten of Burma the Fund lost a President whose enthusiastic and infectious dedication to the cause of children in need was an inspiration to SCF workers and supporters throughout the world. And through her personal example of untiring service, the ideals of the Fund's founder, Eglantyne Jebb, to help children everywhere – irrespective of race, nation or creed – were given practical force.

Above all, wc shall remember Lady Mountbatten as a practical President. In 1953, when a disastrous earthquake devastated large areas of the Ionian islands of Greece, she was one of the first on the spot, and was able to advise the Fund on immediate relief measures. During the thousands of miles she travelled on behalf of the Fund in Europe, Asia and Africa, official routes and programmes were often overruled while she crawled into African huts, Arab tents and the poorest tin shacks in Korea, determined, as ever, to see things for herself.

Lady Mountbatten loved children, and the tragedy of children in need was one of her most urgent concerns. There can be no more lasting tribute to her memory than the many thousands of children throughout the world whose future is assured through her untiring efforts and achievements.

Chapter Notes

Chapter 2: The Roots of Wealth

1 *Dictionary of National Biography*
2 Ibid.
3 Brian Connell, *Manifest Destiny* (1953), p. 60
4 Vittoria Colonna, *Things Past* (1929), p. 136
5 Elizabeth Longford, *Victoria R.I.* (1964), pp. 185–6

Chapter 3: The Growth of Promise

1 Colonna, *Things Past*, p. 136
2 Ibid., p. 144
3 Madeline Masson, *Edwina: The Biography of the Countess Mountbatten of Burma* (1958), p. 58.

Chapter 4: An Indian Romance

1 Richard Hough, *Mountbatten: Hero of our Time* (1980), pp. 28–9
2 Frances Donaldson, *Edward VIII* (1974), p. 78
3 Prince of Wales to Victoria Milford Haven, 5 June 1921 (Duke of Windsor's Archives)
4 Ibid.
5 Dennis Holman, *Lady Louis: Life of the Countess Mountbatten of Burma* (1952), p. 36

Chapter 5: The Wedding of the Year

1 Masson, *Edwina*, p. 73
2 *The Times*, 19 July 1922

Chapter 6: To Sea with the Fleet

1 Connell, *Manifest Destiny*, p. 99
2 Hough, *Mountbatten*, p. 65
3 Holman, *Lady Louis*, p. 45
4 Alfred Duff Cooper, *Old Men Forget* (1953), p. 131
5 Donaldson, *Edward VIII*, p. 124
6 Noël Coward, *Present Indicative* (1937), p. 205
7 Ibid., p. 202
8 Ibid., p. 214
9 Hough, op. cit., p. 96
10 Diana Cooper, *Autobiography* (1979), p. 298
11 Ray Murphy, *The Last Viceroy* (1948), p. 55
12 Cole Leslie, *The Life of Noël Coward* (1977), p. 139

Chapter 7: The Restless Heart

1 Murphy, *The Last Viceroy*, p. 55
2 Masson, *Edwina*, p. 98
3 Marie Seton, *Paul Robeson* (1958), p. 84

Chapter 8: Relationships and Reappraisals

1 Donaldson, *Edward VIII*, p. 209
2 Hough, *Mountbatten*, p. 113
3 Duke of Windsor Archives
4 Duchess of Windsor, *The Heart has its Reasons* (1965), p. 185
5 Holman, *Lady Louis*, p. 160
6 Murphy, *The Last Viceroy*, p. 14

Chapter 9: Crusader at War

1 Masson, *Edwina*, p. 119
2 Holman, *Lady Louis*, p. 62
3 Sir Henry 'Chips' Channon, *Diaries* (1967), p. 323
4 Cole Leslie and Graham Payn, *Noël Coward and his Friends* (1979), p. 173
5 Graham Payn and Sheridan Morley (eds), *The Noël Coward Diaries* (1982), p. 7
6 Masson, op. cit., pp. 125–6
7 Channon, op. cit., p. 323
8 Payn and Morley, op. cit., p. 16

Chapter 10: Mistress of Welfare

1 Holman, *Lady Louis*, p. 72
2 Ibid., p. 72
3 Ibid., p. 80
4 Ibid., p. 84
5 Julian Amery, *Approach March* (1973), p. 412

Chapter 11: 'First and Only Love'

1 Connell, *Manifest Destiny*, p. 116
2 Appendix to Report of the Last Viceroy
3 *The Memoirs of Lord Ismay* (1969), p. 436

Chapter 12: 'Love and Serve'

1 Payn and Morley, *The Noël Coward Diaries*, p. 152
2 Ibid., p. 357

Acknowledgements

The author is grateful to the following for permission to quote copyright material in this book: The Viscount Norwich for extracts from *Old Men Forget* by Alfred Duff Cooper and *Autobiography* by Diana Cooper; Brian Connell Esq, the author of *Manifest Destiny*; Weidenfeld and Nicolson for extracts from *Victoria R.I.* by Elizabeth Longford, *Edward VIII* by Frances Donaldson, and *The Noël Coward Diaries* edited by Graham Payn and Sheridan Morley; The Hutchinson Publishing Group Ltd for extracts from *The Last Viceroy* by Ray Murphy and *Things Past* by Vittoria Colonna; John Farquharson Ltd for extracts from *Edwina: The Biography of the Countess Mountbatten of Burma* by Madeline Masson; The Hamlyn Group for extracts from *Lady Louis: Life of the Countess Mountbatten of Burma* by Denis Holman; Dr Jan Van Loewen Ltd for extracts from *Present Indicative* and *Hands Across the Sea* by Noël Coward; and A.D. Peters for extracts from *Decline and Fall* and *Vile Bodies* by Evelyn Waugh.

Index